COGNITIVE INTERVIEWING PRACTICE

SAGE was founded in 1965 by Sara Miller McCune to support the dissemination of usable knowledge by publishing innovative and high-quality research and teaching content. Today, we publish more than 750 journals, including those of more than 300 learned societies, more than 800 new books per year, and a growing range of library products including archives, data, case studies, reports, conference highlights, and video. SAGE remains majority-owned by our founder, and on her passing will become owned by a charitable trust that secures our continued independence.

Los Angeles | London | Washington DC | New Delhi | Singapore

COGNITIVE INTERVIEWING PRACTICE

EDITED BY
DEBBIE COLLINS

NatCen
Social Research that works for society

Los Angeles | London | New Delhi
Singapore | Washington DC

Los Angeles | London | New Delhi
Singapore | Washington DC

SAGE Publications Ltd
1 Oliver's Yard
55 City Road
London EC1Y 1SP

SAGE Publications Inc.
2455 Teller Road
Thousand Oaks, California 91320

SAGE Publications India Pvt Ltd
B 1/I 1 Mohan Cooperative Industrial Area
Mathura Road
New Delhi 110 044

SAGE Publications Asia-Pacific Pte Ltd
3 Church Street
#10-04 Samsung Hub
Singapore 049483

Editor: Katie Metzler
Assistant editor: Lily Mehrbod
Production editor: Tom Bedford
Copyeditor: Rosemary Campbell
Proofreader: Rose James
Indexer: Silvia Benvenuto
Marketing manager: Sally Ransom
Cover design: Shaun Mercier
Typeset by: C&M Digitals (P) Ltd, Chennai, India
Printed in Great Britain by Henry Ling Limited at
The Dorset Press, Dorchester, DT1 1HD

Library of Congress Control Number: 2014938086

British Library Cataloguing in Publication data

A catalogue record for this book is available from the British Library

ISBN 978-1-4462-5600-8
ISBN 978-1-4462-5601-5 (pbk)

At SAGE we take sustainability seriously. Most of our products are printed in the UK using FSC papers and boards. When we print overseas we ensure sustainable papers are used as measured by the Egmont grading system. We undertake an annual audit to monitor our sustainability.

CONTENTS

LIST OF FIGURES

NATCEN SOCIAL RESEARCH

NatCen Social Research is one of Britain's largest and leading independent social research organisations. It was established in 1969 and is registered as a non-profit, independent educational charity. NatCen Social Research has a staff of around 200, with offices in Edinburgh (ScotCen Social Research), London and Essex. It carries out quantitative and qualitative research across all major social policy areas. NatCen Social Research specialises in the development and application of rigorous social research methods with work commissioned by central government departments, public bodies, and funded by research councils and grant-giving foundations. Our staff share their expertise through NatCen Learning. NatCen Learning supports skills development and capacity-building across the research sector through a programme of short courses, consultancy and research support. We provide training and learning for external organisations and researches working in government, academia and other settings.

In 2006 NatCen established a specialist Questionnaire Development and Testing Hub. NatCen Social Research has for many years utilised qualitative research methods in the design of surveys and was one of the first survey organisations in the UK to embrace cognitive interviewing methods to evaluate questionnaires. The Hub brought together these two disciplines, creating a centre of expertise. The Hub works with a wide range of organisations to help them improve their communications and data collection tools with their stakeholders, members of the public and survey participants through the application of good design principles and rigorous testing and evaluation.

All the authors are current members of NatCen Social Research and are committed to improving the communication of information and the robust measurement of social phenomena through survey questionnaires.

LIST OF CONTRIBUTORS

Editor and contributor:

Debbie Collins is Head of Questionnaire Development and Testing at NatCen Social Research. An experienced survey researcher, Debbie has specialised over the past decade in survey methodology, questionnaire development and testing. Debbie founded NatCen's Questionnaire Development and Testing Hub with Michelle Gray in 2006, and has developed and tested survey questions and data collection tools for a wide range of clients. Debbie's research interests include novel uses of cognitive interviewing, effective combinations of pretesting methods, and the design of web and mixed mode questionnaires.

Contributors:

Margaret Blake is a senior research director at NatCen Social Research with experience in survey methodology, qualitative research and survey data collection. She worked for four years in the Questionnaire Development and Testing Hub, specialising in question design and cognitive interviewing. She now manages the data collection for the English Longitudinal Study of Ageing (ELSA). Margaret's research interests are survey questionnaire development, research among minority ethnic groups and social care.

Jo d'Ardenne is a Senior Researcher within NatCen's Questionnaire Development and Testing Hub. She specialises in research on measurement, questionnaire development and testing. She provides consultancy on questionnaire design issues for a range of public and third sector organisations. Jo's research interests include novel applications of cognitive interviewing, user-testing, asking sensitive questions and measuring patient experience.

Michelle Gray is a Research Director with 10 years wide-ranging experience in both qualitative and survey research methods. In 2006 Michelle helped to set up NatCen's Questionnaire Development and Testing (QDT) Hub where she now works. Michelle's research interests include: questionnaire development; use of pretesting methods to improve public information leaflets and research on equality issues.

PREFACE

The motivation for writing this book is a desire to share the learning and experience we have acquired together over the years, testing survey questions and other materials. We wanted to write a book that is primarily concerned with practice: how you undertake cognitive interviewing. This book reflects the practices that we have developed in our day-to-day work and which are reflected in the courses we run, through NatCen Learning, for a wide range of people who want to understand and use cognitive interviewing – be they students, practitioners or commissioners.

There are several excellent books concerned with cognitive interviewing already available. Gordon Willis' book *Cognitive Interviewing: A Tool for Improving Questionnaire Design* is concerned principally with the interviewing process and describes in some detail the probing technique. Other elements of the cognitive interviewing process – sampling and recruitment, data management, analysis and using findings to make recommendation are not discussed in any great detail (Willis, 2005). Miller et al.'s *Cognitive Interviewing Methodology* puts forward the case for cognitive interviewing as a tool to evaluate the validity of survey concepts and constructs, with cognitive interviewing seen as a tool that can be used to explore the way in which participants and researchers construct meaning (Miller et al., 2014). However, neither of these offers a step-by-step guide to the design, conduct, analysis and use of cognitive interviewing findings to 'repair' survey questions that are not working as intended. Nor do they focus on the practical, pragmatic decisions that often face the question tester who is working in an applied social policy/national statistics environment where time and money are in short supply.

The aims of this book are to provide you, the reader, with:

a) An overview of the cognitive interviewing method, its origins and the theory that underpins it
b) An appreciation of what the method can and cannot do, when to use it and how it can be combined with other pretesting methods

c) Guidance on how to design, conduct, analyse and report on cognitive interviews

d) Ideas and tips on how to use the method in particular circumstances, i.e. in testing questions for inclusion on mixed-mode or cross-national surveys, or when using the method to test other kinds of documents designed to convey and or collect information from people.

This book is divided into three parts: Part I is concerned with (a) and (b) above, providing you with an overview of the origins and theoretical underpinnings of cognitive interviewing (Chapter 1); and of other pretesting methods (Chapter 2).

Part II is concerned with (c) above, providing a step-by-step guide to the planning (Chapter 3), sampling and recruitment (Chapter 4), interview protocol development (Chapter 5), interviewing (Chapter 6), data management (Chapter 7), analysis (Chapter 8) and application of findings (Chapter 9).

Part III is concerned with (d) above: providing guidance and tips in the use of cognitive interviewing to test survey questions designed for different modes (telephone, mail, web) and for mixed-mode surveys (Chapter 10); in cross-national, cross-cultural and multilingual settings (Chapter 11); and for testing other kinds of survey materials (Chapter 12).

Throughout the book we use examples, the vast majority from our own work, to illustrate our points. Much of the work we do is commissioned by research funders, typically government departments and their agencies, though we also carry out research for public, voluntary and private sector organisations and research councils. We use cognitive interviewing and other pretesting methods as part of the questionnaire development process but also to evaluate existing survey questions. In much of our work the output is a set of recommendations on the future wording (and design) of the test questions. In this book we illustrate how you can move from findings to recommendations (Chapter 9) and the trade-offs that may need to be made: a step that is rarely discussed in the literature.

The majority of the survey questionnaires we design and/or test are surveys of individuals and this is reflected in this book. The use of cognitive interviews to test business survey questions requires some additional considerations and we provide an overview in Chapter 3. However, if you are interested in this area then we strongly recommend that, in addition to reading this book, you refer to texts that focus on business surveys, such as Snijkers et al. (2013).

This book is the distillation of the knowledge and experience of many people, however, and we would like to acknowledge former colleagues who have worked with us on projects cited in this book: Fiona Andrews, Meera Balarajan, Hayley Cripps, Kate Green, Sophie Green, Curtis Jessop, Avneet Johal, Robin Legard, Hayley Lepps, Matthew Hall, Alice McGee and Joanne

Pascale. We're particularly grateful to Kate Green and Sophie Green for their help with compiling this manuscript. We're also immensely grateful to our team of wonderful cognitive interviewers – Malik Waqar Ahmed, Sue Archer, Jenny Cooper, Karen Joyce, Oxana Metiuk, Ann Roberts, Graham Smith and Colin Tuck, and to former members, Julie Foster, Amanda Maltby and Geoff Morris, and to the hundreds of participants who have so freely given of their time to help us 'test' our questions.

We'd like to acknowledge our collaborators on cognitive interviewing projects: Amanda Wilmot at RTI International; Rory Fitzgerald, Sally Widdop and Lizzy Gatrell at the Centre for Comparative Social Surveys (CCSS), City University London; Pam Campanelli, The Survey Coach; and Noah Uhrig at the Institute for Social and Economic Research, University of Essex.

We also owe thanks to the members past and present of QUEST – the international working group on QUestionnaire Evaluation STandards – for their ideas, encouragement and support of our work and to Gordon Willis for his comments on this manuscript. We are grateful to Jane Ritchie, Jean Martin and Roger Thomas who shaped and encouraged our passion for good questionnaire design. And finally we are indebted to Pam Campanelli and Graham Farrant, who founded the cognitive interviewing tradition at NatCen back in the 1990s and were part of a small group of practitioners who pioneered the use of cognitive interviewing methods in questionnaire development in Great Britain.

References

Miller, K., Willson, S., Chepp, V. and Padilla, J.L. (eds) (2014) *Cognitive Interviewing Methodology*. Hoboken, NJ: Wiley.

Snijkers, G., Haraldsen, G., Jones, J. and Willimack, D. (2013). *Designing and Conducting Business Surveys* (Vol. 568). John Wiley & Sons.

Willis, G. (2005) *Cognitive Interviewing*. Thousand Oaks, CA; Sage.

PART I
BACKGROUND AND CONTEXT

ONE

COGNITIVE INTERVIEWING: ORIGIN, PURPOSE AND LIMITATIONS

DEBBIE COLLINS

1.1 Introduction

The aims of this chapter are to provide you with an overview of the cognitive interviewing method and to illustrate how it can be useful to you in the development of a survey questionnaire. Specifically we will:

- Summarise the theory behind the method
- Set out its origins
- Describe the method and the interviewing techniques it uses
- Examine its limitations.

Let's start by considering the purpose of a survey and the factors that can affect the data it produces.

> A "survey" is a systematic method for gathering information from (a sample of) entities for the purpose of constructing quantitative descriptors (statistics) of the attributes of the larger population of which the entities are members. (Groves et al., 2009, p.3)

We carry out surveys because we want to find out information about the population of interest, and we want that information to be statistical so that we can answer questions such as how many, how much, of what strength and size? We want this information because it is needed by policy-makers and decision-makers in government (national and local) and organisations such as health authorities, service providers and advocacy groups to inform decisions about issues that affect citizens, service users and so on. And we collect this information typically by asking people questions.

There are many factors that can influence the accuracy of the statistics collected by a survey. These include:

- Sample design and implementation – for example the completeness of the sampling frame and how well the responding sample covers the target population.
- Data collection – for example the mode of data collection, the characteristics of the interviewer, the environment in which the interview takes place or the questionnaire is completed, and the design of the questionnaire.
- Data processing – for example how the data are edited and coded.

These factors can introduce errors and biases to the data collected, which can impact on the accuracy of the statistics generated by the survey (see for example, Biemer and Lyberg, 2003; Groves et al., 2009; Oksenberg et al., 1991).

In this book we are concerned with errors that can arise during data collection when asking people questions. The survey method is underpinned by the premise that if we use standardised tools and standardised procedures in collecting our data, we will be able to observe real differences between participants. By 'standardised tools' we mean questionnaires that determine the exact form of the questions to be put to each participant. By 'standardised procedures' we mean training interviewers to only read the questions exactly as worded, to use neutral probes, and so on (Fowler and Mangione, 1990).

However, standardising the questions asked may not on its own ensure that we obtain valid, reliable, unbiased, sensitive data (Fowler, 1995). One obvious problem is that participants may not understand the questions being asked of them – or not in the way that the question-designer intended.

Given the challenges posed by the question design task, as designers we need feedback on how well we are succeeding. Ideally, feedback is required *before* the main survey is committed, so that attempts can be made to improve questions that do not seem to be performing as they should. Fortunately, methods exist for checking whether or not the questions can be answered, and whether the response task is being interpreted and carried out in the way intended before a questionnaire is finalised. One of those methods is cognitive interviewing.

1.2 Understanding the question and answer process

Cognitive psychology provides a useful model that can help us understand how participants answer survey questions. In its simplest form the model specifies four distinct processes that must be completed in order to answer a question. Participants must:

(a) comprehend the question;
(b) retrieve the necessary information (usually from long-term memory);
(c) make a judgement about the information needed to answer the question; and
(d) respond to the question. (Tourangeau, 1984)

In many real-life situations the question-and-answer process is probably not a simple linear progression but rather involves numerous iterations of and inter-actions between the different phases, as shown in Figure 1.1. For example, participants may make judgements at (C) about the level of detail needed to answer a survey question based on how difficult it is to retrieve the informa-tion required (B) and/or by the way in which answers are to be reported or the answer categories provided (D). This may then cause them to review (A). For example, is the question asking for the exact number of occasions I visited my doctor in the past six months, or is it asking for an indication of frequency – none, between 1 and 5, 6 or more? Having arrived at a provisional response at (D), I may then review it for social acceptability before actually reporting it. For example, will I appear out of the ordinary if I give the answer I am minded to give?

What has been said so far covers interviewer-administered questions. When the questionnaire is in a self-completion format, the question-and-answer process

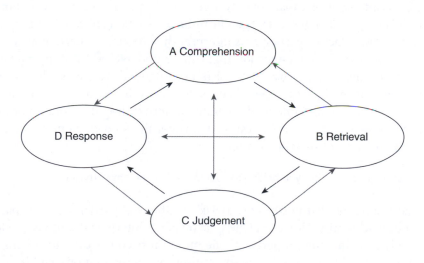

Figure 1.1 Elaborated question and answer model

Based on Tourangeau's 1984 Four Stage Question and Answer Model. Created by Debbie Collins.

contains two additional stages: firstly participants have to perceive the information being presented to them (i.e. they have to recognise that this is a questionnaire that they need to complete); and secondly they have to comprehend the layout of the questionnaire: the visual aspect. Then they have to go through stages (a) to (d) above, and finally comprehend the routing to the next question. For further information on the cognitive steps involved in the question-and-answer process for self-completion questionnaires, see Jenkins and Dillman (1997).

Let us now look at each of the four main stages in the question-and-answer process in a little more detail.

1.2.1 Comprehension

There are a number of comprehension issues that you need to consider when designing and testing a survey question.

- Does the participant fully understand how the question is structured (syntax) and the vocabulary used?
- Is the participant able to keep all of this in mind when formulating an answer to the question?
- Does the participant understand the question in the way the researcher intended?

This last point is important because if participants interpret the questions in a different way from the way you intended as the question designer, conclusions drawn based on these answers may be flawed. Worse still, if different participants interpret the question in different ways from each other, and from what the researcher intended, comparisons between participants' answers will not be valid. This is a problem because it can introduce systematic bias into survey estimates if certain types of participants interpret the question in particular ways.

Your goal is to design a question that can be understood by all participants, in the same way, and in a way the researcher intended. However, this is more difficult than it might first appear because the meaning of a question has two components – literal and intended. Literally understanding the words is not sufficient to be able to answer the question. Consider the following question and its use as an indicator of social inclusion

'How strongly do you feel you belong to your immediate neighbourhood?'

The question's intended meaning is to ask whether the participant feels part of his or her community. However, when participants interpret the phrase 'belong to' literally as being 'the property of', the question becomes difficult to answer. Focusing on the literal meaning is something that is seen among children and people whose first language is not that used by the questionnaire. A clearer wording of the question might be:

'How strongly do you feel you are part of your immediate neighbourhood?'

How participants interpret such a concept within a question will depend on the context in which the question is asked, with participants drawing on the assumptions that are unthinkingly used in conducting daily conversation. This is because we often draw upon our stock of background information and knowledge in interpreting text, which means we will often fill in gaps, add details and make inferences based on our background stock of knowledge and what the survey interview requires (Grice, 1991).

1.2.2 Retrieval of information

Having comprehended the question the participant then (usually) has to retrieve the relevant information – be it factual or attitudinal – from long-term memory. This depends on the way in which the memory is stored or 'encoded' by an individual participant. In the case of factual information – either current or historical – a number of factors may affect the retrieval process.

Firstly, if the retrieval context is different to the original encoding context the participant may not be able to recognise that the event took place or be able to recall the correct event (Tulving and Thomson, 1973). Secondly, the rarer or more distinctive an event is, the more likely participants are to remember it. Consequently similar, commonly occurring types of event such as routine journeys or interactions will be harder to distinguish and recall individually (Anderson, 1983). Moreover, over time participants are likely to have experienced more similar events, so that rare or more distinctive events will become scarcer. This means that accurate recall (memory) of many events will become more difficult because there are fewer distinctive events, see Example 1.1 (Gillund and Shiffrin, 1984; Johnson, 1983).

> **Example 1.1   Remembering commonly occurring events**
>
> Remembering details about what I did on my first day at work in my current job diminishes the longer I am in my current job because I have more memories of work days featuring similar activities from which to select my first day.

Finally, often details are lost in the encoding process and inferences and interpretations are added. This can result in individuals 'recalling' in all sincerity events that did not actually occur. Such inferences may be added in response to the retrieval context, for example inferring the severity of damage sustained by a vehicle in a car accident from how the accident was described by the questioner rather than recalling the film footage of the accident (Loftus and Palmer, 1974).

In summary, there are several processes involved in the retrieval of factual information, including: adopting a retrieval strategy; generating specific retrieval cues to trigger recall; retrieving individual memories; and filling in partial memories through inference (for example, 'what I must have done is…'). Certain characteristics of the question and the material retrieved from memory can affect the completeness of the retrieval phase.

Attitude questions collect subjective information about opinions, values, beliefs and norms. Tourangeau et al. (2000) argue that attitudes have a memory structure that contains existing evaluations, vague impressions, general values, and relevant feelings and beliefs. When participants think about an issue on any given occasion, they will draw upon a subset of these contents. Depending on the requirements of the question and what is recalled, an existing evaluation may be reported, updated, refined to cover the new situation or discarded and an entirely new view formed. They contend that the type of information drawn upon by participants when answering attitude questions depends both on its accessibility and how motivated participants are to produce a 'defensible position'.

When testing attitude questions it is therefore important to explore reasons for confusion around, or inability to answer, particular questions: are the problems participants are having to do with confusion about the wording of the question or is there evidence to suggest that participants simply do not have a view on the topic or do not hold a strong attitude about what was being asked about? Is the task too complex – is forming a view difficult because of the amount of material that needs to be considered (for example, because this is not an issue the participant has thought about before)? Does the mode of data collection help or hinder the formulation of an answer?

1.2.3 Judgement

In designing a survey question, you assume that participants can provide the information being requested. This assumption, however, may be flawed because:

- the information being sought is difficult to recall accurately (such as dates or frequencies);
- what can be recalled may be incomplete (such as recalling the details of a particular event); or,
- in the case of attitude or opinion questions, the question is asking the participant to express a view or opinion on something which they may not have thought about (for some time), or in that context.

Judgement can therefore be seen as the process by which participants formulate their answers to a survey question from the 'raw material' that they have retrieved from memory. This process involves participants considering, for example, whether they understand the question, whether the question applies to their situation, whether it is asking for information they have, how detailed this information needs to be, how accurate it needs to be, whether they need to modify their answer to meet the perceived needs of the question, and so on. These judgements may be made at any stage during the question-and-answer process, and can inform the comprehension, recall and response phases (see Example 1.2).

Example 1.2   Judgement

In being asked a question about how many times I have visited a doctor in the past six months, I may refine my comprehension of the terms 'visited' and 'doctor' in light of my first recall attempt. I may tighten or loosen my definitions depending on how easy it has been to retrieve the information required. I may consider that if I am having difficulty recalling the event then perhaps it happened infrequently. Alternatively I may be uncertain of the exact dates and thus make a judgement about whether I think the events I can remember happened within the reference period or not.

Judgemental short cuts

Cognitive 'short cuts' or heuristics are often used by participants when formulating answers to questions about the frequency of events or behaviour. This is because memory is not perfect and decisions often have to be taken about how to compensate for incomplete or inaccurate information. For example, research has shown that the number of items to be recalled is the most important factor in determining whether the participant will adopt a counting or estimating strategy in order to give an answer about frequency (Blair and Burton, 1987; Sudman and Schwarz, 1989). A number of different strategies for estimating answers to frequency questions have been identified and can be classified as follows:

- enumeration, or counting up, of specific events (for example counting up the number of sessions of exercise done in the last week);
- estimation based on recall of summary information about the rate of occurrence of the event;
- recall of an exact count or tally of events (for example remembering the exact number of pregnancies ever had); and,
- estimation based on a general impression (Tourangeau et al., 2000).

An alternative classification of how participants answer 'frequency' or 'amount' questions is based on the work of Tversky and Kahneman (1973, 1974). They consider how available the information is to the participant (ease of recall), how representative the information retrieved is of the 'normal' state of affairs, and the use of context to anchor-and-adjust the answer (see Example 1.3).

Example 1.3 Judgement short cuts

For example, in answering the question 'How many hours did you work last week?' participants could opt for an easily available answer such as their contracted hours. Alternatively participants may feel that their contractual hours are not representative of the true hours they work, and thus they may decide to average out the hours they worked over a number of weeks. Finally, participants may take their available or representative answer and adjust it in light of the survey context, the answer categories provided or the special circumstances of last week.

1.2.4 Response

The final task described by the question and answer model is the response stage. There are two components involved in responding to the question: formatting and editing the response (Tourangeau et al., 2000), and these two stages are described below.

Formatting the response

The response-formatting process is needed when a closed answer is required, with the predefined answers having already been designed by the researcher. The participant has to fit her or his answer into one of the categories provided. For example, the following pre-specified answers could be offered for the question 'How often do you exercise regularly?'

Everyday

Every other day

At least two or three times a week

At least once a week

Less often than once a week

Never

As the question designer, your choice of response alternatives may affect the way in which participants comprehend the question and the recall and judgement strategies they use. For example, the pre-specified answers provided for the question above about the frequency with which people exercise could influence the participant's answer by implying that it is common for people to exercise at least once a week. This is because only two of the six answer options provided refer to exercising less often than once a week, and one of those options is never exercising. This may suggest to participants that, whatever is meant by 'exercising', the majority of people do it quite often. Thus they may use this inference to anchor and adjust their own answer to the question. A further problem here, of course, is the lack of a clear definition of 'exercise'.

Editing the response

Participants may want to edit their answers before they communicate them because they may want to conform to notions of social desirability (Couper and Groves, 1992) and self-presentation (Goffman, 1959). These effects may be more profound in face-to-face interviews than telephone or self-completion data collection methods because social effects are more intense in a face-to-face situation (Green and Krosnick, 1999).

The impact of social desirability factors on response is often limited to questions perceived by participants as being sensitive and potentially threatening. What constitutes a sensitive or threatening question and therefore is considered socially desirable, will depend on the survey context – the mode of data collection, the characteristics of the interviewer and participant, who else is present when answers are given, apart from the interviewer, the content and purpose of the interview, and so on (Krueter et al., 2008; Lind et al., 2013).

1.3 Application of the question and answer model

Things can go wrong when participants are unable or unwilling to perform one or more of these tasks. Applying the question and answer model described in section 1.2 is useful in helping you to identify the aspect or aspects of the question that are problematic. Let's consider the following example, Example 1.4.

Example 1.4   Identifying cognitive problems with questions

How many pints of beer did you drink in the 7 days ending yesterday?

If a participant were to be asked the above question by an interviewer as part of a health survey, the following might be the thought processes that she goes through in formulating her answer.

OK, this question is asking about pints of beer I drank last week. Right, let me think. Last week. Did I go out last week? Yes, I went to the pub with some people from work last Thursday.

What did I drink? Shandy [beer mixed with lemonade], I didn't want to get drunk. I was drinking halves. No, that's not true; I bought a pint when I arrived, then two more halves I think.

Um, now the question asks about pints of beer, does that include shandy? No, I don't think so.

Then Saturday it was Sarah's birthday and she had a party. I had a few bottles of beer there, but I can't remember how many I actually drank. I

(Continued)

(Continued)

got fairly drunk. I kept putting one down to go and dance and would come back and find it had gone. I probably opened about ten but I don't think I drank that much. Let's say I drank five.

Now how much is in a bottle, less than a pint? I think it's a half-pint. Oh this is hard work! Then I had a few beers on Sunday, in the pub watching the football. I probably had about four pints, I usually do. Right so that's six-and-a-half pints. Oh and I went out Friday night and had a few beers then, four or five pints I think. So that makes ten-and-a-half pints.

Gosh that sounds a lot. I don't usually drink that much, do I? No, I think it's more like four or five pints. I don't want to sound like I'm an alchie. I'll say four.

Let's evaluate what went on here by applying the question and answer model. The model indicates that the first thing the participant has to do is to comprehend the question. Our participant does this. She thinks about the beer that she drank last week, outside the home. She thinks about occasions when she had been out over the past week and whether she drank beer. She did not appear to consider any beer she might have consumed inside her home. She imposed this definition; it was not part of the question wording. Furthermore, the term 'beer' caused her a problem, as she was not sure whether shandy (beer mixed with lemonade) should be included or not. She decided to exclude it.

The model suggests that having understood the question participants have to recall the information required to answer it. In this example the participant started to think back over the course of the last week about times she had been out. Her interpretation of the question, thinking about beer consumed outside the home, impacted on the way in which she recalled the information. She was only recalling events involving being out and drinking alcohol. Her recall was hindered at times by the fact that she could not accurately remember how many 'pints' of beer she had drunk on each occasion. This was partly related to the units in which she was drinking on a particular occasion not being the same as the units being requested in the question. For example, she was drinking bottled beer at the party, not pints. Also there was a difference between how many beers she bought or was given and how many she actually drank. For example, she estimated she drank half the beers she started at the party.

At times the participant was not able to recall exactly how many beers she drank and so she made a judgement about how to deal with this imperfection in her memory. In some cases she estimated (based on the number of times she went to the bar), in others she applied an easy 'rule of thumb' approximation ('*I usually have four pints when I go to the pub to watch the football*').

Having come up with an answer the participant decided that it was too high, feeling that others, perhaps the interviewer or the researcher, would form a negative view of her drinking. So she decided to 'edit' her response, to an amount she felt was more 'typical' and perhaps more socially acceptable. Another reason for such editing may be that the participant honestly (and sometimes correctly) believes that the researcher wants an answer that is 'typical' of her 'normal' behaviour. However, if the research aim is actually to obtain an estimate of *variation* in weekly consumption rates this type of editing will cause distortion of the estimates.

This example illustrates a number of problems and potential sources of error with the question.

- The definition of 'beer' is unclear; for example should shandy be included? This uncertainty could lead to under reporting, or over-reporting resulting from drinks being incorrectly classified.
- A tendency for participants to exclude beer they drink at home could lead to under-reporting.
- The problem of accurate recall, particularly where the participant drinks a lot (is too drunk for the information to be retained in long-term memory) or drinks frequently and has difficulty distinguishing one drinking occasion from another, could lead to under or over-reporting, as participants estimate or guess their beer intake.
- Calculation errors could occur where participants try to count up pints drunk over the course of the week. These could occur because participants make errors adding up the amounts or in converting the units drunk into the units required in the question – bottles or cans into pints for example.
- Unwillingness to admit to the true total arrived at, leading either to avoidance of giving a usable response (e.g. 'Can't remember'), or to adjustment of the total arrived at so as to present a more 'socially desirable' self-image. In this case that led to under-estimation of beer intake.

The question and answer model, derived from cognitive psychology, can provide you with a useful framework to understand how 'errors' or different interpretations of reality occur.

Cognitive question testing methods help you to do this to some extent by exploring the processes by which participants answer survey questions and checking for unwanted influences on the answers they provide. Such methods include cognitive interviewing, paraphrasing, self-reported ratings of confidence in the accuracy of responses given, card sorts, vignettes, and response latency – measuring how long it takes participants to come up with an answer. These are described in outline below (for further details on cognitive methods refer to Czaja, 1998; Forsyth and Lessler, 1991; Jobe and Mingay, 1991; Sudman et al., 1996).

1.4 Cognitive interviewing

1.4.1 Origins and description of the method

Cognitive interviewing has developed over the past 30 years or so out of the Cognitive Aspects of Survey Methodology (CASM) movement. This movement emerged from two meetings – one held in the United States in June 1983 (Jabine et al., 1984) and the other held in Germany in July 1984 (Hippler et al., 1987) – that pushed to the fore the importance of participant task analysis and measurement error. (For a more detailed history of the development of the CASM movement see Tanur (1999) and Aborn (1999)). The dual development of theories of survey response and cognitive interviewing methods has greatly added to our understanding of the sources of measurement error, and cognitive interviewing methods are a useful tool for exploring participants' thought processes as they attempt to answer survey questions.

The window on this usually hidden process provides us with an opportunity to assess whether participants are answering the question we think we are asking them in a consistent way. Some of the techniques have their origins in cognitive psychology. The 'think aloud' interviewing technique, where participants are asked to verbalise their thought processes as they attempt to answer a survey question, has its roots in the 'verbal protocol' tool used by Ericsson and Simon (1980) to explore decision-making. Probing (asking open questions to explore aspects of the question and answer process) and observation have their roots in the work of Belson (1981) and ethnography respectively. The use of card sorts and vignettes (see section 1.3.1) are also used in cognitive interviewing to explore conceptual boundaries and decision-making and have their origins in social psychology. Cognitive interviewing can therefore be seen as an umbrella term, covering a range of techniques, which have a common goal.

Cognitive interviewing focuses mainly on the questionnaire rather than on the survey process as a whole. It pays explicit attention to the mental processes participants use in answering survey questions, and thus allows hidden as well as overt problems to be identified. It involves direct interaction between you, the researcher (or a trained cognitive interviewer) and a small sample of people drawn from the population to which the main survey will be addressed (refer to Chapter 4 for more details on sample design). In the case of surveys where the data are collected by remote self-administration this is likely to be the only point at which you can observe directly how participants cope with the instrument that you have designed.

The two most commonly used cognitive interviewing techniques are:

- think-aloud interviewing; and
- probing to expose the participant's thought processes.

Both methods involve an interviewer asking the participant about how she went about answering the survey questions. In the first approach the participant is asked to 'think aloud' as she answers the question or completes the questionnaire. In the second the interviewer asks specific questions or *probes* about how the participant set about answering the questions being tested. The wording of probes may be semi-standardised, the aim being to elicit *but not alter or bias* an account of the participant's thought processes at the time he or she was answering the question being tested. The think-aloud technique is usually used to collect information on what the participant is thinking as she answers each survey question or completes a self-completion questionnaire (concurrently). Probing can be used either concurrently with the process of answering the question, or retrospectively after a set of questions has been answered (Beatty and Willis, 2007; Collins, 2003; Willis, 2005). More detail on how to develop a cognitive interviewing protocol is provided in Chapter 5.

1.4.2 Other cognitive techniques

Paraphrasing involves participants being asked to paraphrase the survey question, or rephrase it in their own words. This technique is principally concerned with identifying comprehension problems and may be incorporated into a cognitive interview using a standard probe such as: 'Could you tell me in your own words what the question is asking?' or 'How would you say that question to yourself?' Something to bear in mind is that participants can interpret these probes as asking them to reword the question and this can be difficult when the participant can't think of a better way of expressing the question at that moment. These types of probes work well, in our experience, when checking understanding of more complex information or tasks, such as what participants understood from a set of instructions or a long survey question that, for example, includes a definition of what to include and exclude.

Confidence ratings involve participants being asked to rate the degree of confidence they have in their answer to a survey question. As with paraphrasing, this technique can be incorporated into a cognitive interview using a probe such as: 'How confident are you in your answer – where 10 is very confident and 0 is not at all confident?' This type of probe can be useful when testing questions that require participants to perform a calculation, such as come up with the number of times in the past week they did any exercise, lasting 30 minutes or more, that made them feel hot or sweaty. It provides a way in to exploring the strategies participants use to come up with their answer. Participants may be confident of an answer because they have simplified the calculation or the definition they are using of what to count as exercise, but this may not be what the question required. The confidence rating alone is therefore not sufficient to assess whether the participant has answered the question as intended.

Observation of participant behaviour can help the researcher to understand cognitive processes and give insight into the ways in which participants use survey materials, such as self-completion questionnaires, show cards, calendars and diaries. It can be combined with cognitive interviewing methods or usability testing (refer to section 2.2.4). Observation can identify problems that participants are themselves not fully aware of, as well as acting as triggers for probing. For example, if a participant hesitates, looks puzzled or re-reads the question, the interviewer can ask, 'What are you thinking about?' (see section 5.6.1).

If you are testing a self-administered questionnaire then making notes or filming participants as they complete the form can provide information on, for example:

- where people start reading/ filling in the form;
- whether they look at the instructions or refer back to them at any stage;
- where they seem to take longer to answer a particular question.

Using a pro forma to record behaviours can be useful as it provides a structure, see section 5.6.1 for further discussion and an example.

Bear in mind that if the observation is overt then this may affect the behaviours being studied. It's also important to think through the ethical issues relating to your planned observation (see section 3.9).

Response latency involves measuring the time elapsed between the presentation of the question and the giving of a response. It is a specialised and focused form of observation (see for example, Bassili, 1996; Bassili and Scott, 1996) although paradata, in the form of individual question time stamps in computerised questionnaires, can be used. An unduly long latency may indicate comprehension difficulties or reluctance to answer; an unduly short latency may indicate use of some 'short cut' to providing an answer (Draisma and Dijkstra, 2004). On their own response latency data can be hard to interpret as other information is needed about the nature of the difficulty, especially since survey satisficing (where participants give insufficient attention to answering the questions (Krosnick, 1991)) could lead to short response times. When combined with other methods such as participant debriefing or cognitive interviewing, response latency analysis can provide valuable information.

Card sorts and **vignettes** involve presenting participants with a range of hypothetical situations, either on cards or as oral questions. They must be carefully worked out and prepared beforehand and are more explicitly hypothesis-driven than other elicitation methods.

Card sorts are used to explore how people group items together, and are useful in exploring and developing typologies and classifications (Spencer, 2009). In a 'free sort' participants group items that seem to them to naturally go together, for example activities that participants think of as being training or not training (see Campanelli and Channell, 1994). In a dimensional sort participants are asked to place items along a pre-specified dimension *or dimension* – see Example 1.5.

Vignettes are short descriptions of hypothetical situations or scenarios, and are useful in understanding how participants would answer questions about these situations and in showing whether the conceptual boundaries of the domain vary between participants (Arthur et al., 2013) – see Example 1.6.

Example 1.5 Meaning of 'value for money' in relation to the BBC licence fee

The purpose of this card sort exercise was to explore the types of factors people considered when deliberating the value for money of the licence fee, which pays for BBC television, radio and internet content. Participants were asked to group together items that were 'big' factors, 'smaller' factors and those that were not a factor in their deliberations. Twenty-four cards were given to participants, each containing a different statement, including:

Quality of programmes

Range of programmes

Affordability

Whether the BBC is well run

Trust in the BBC

The BBC's independence

The BBC being objective and impartial

The BBC's accountability

The BBC's transparency

The classification of statements by each participant was recorded. Following the card sort exercise participants were asked to talk through how they decided on their classification. The findings provided insight into what people thought about when asked in the BBC Trust's survey for their views on whether or not the BBC was delivering value for money.

Example 1.6 Household classification vignettes

In this example vignettes were used as part of a cognitive interview to establish the feasibility of collecting information from short-term migrants in the 2011 population census. The vignettes were used to explore the definition of 'short-term migrant' with this group (Balarajan and d'Ardenne, 2008).

(Continued)

(Continued)

Sample vignettes

Scenario A

Ricardo is staying with friends in the UK for three weeks to improve his English. Is Ricardo a visitor, a usual resident or a short-term migrant? How would you describe him?

Scenario B

Sara is in the UK for one month studying a language course at a university. Is she a visitor, a usual resident or a short-term migrant? How would you describe her?

Scenario C

Michael is in the UK for three months working as a Computing Assistant. Is Michael a visitor, a usual resident or a short-term migrant? How would you describe him? Which option or options would he tick on the Census form?

Scenario D

Nina is staying with her relatives for a three-month summer vacation. How would you describe her? Is Nina a visitor or usual resident on the Census?

Scenario E

Patrick is on an inter-company transfer to the UK. He has only been in the country one week when the Census is conducted. He has a job which has a four-week probation. If he is successful he would be able to work in the UK for a year. He would like to stay. How would you describe him? Do you think Patrick is a visitor or a usual resident on the Census form?

Scenario F

Jane has the right to come and live in the UK whenever she likes. Jane has come over for a conference in London for one week, and is then working at her head-office in London for a week afterwards. She will then be holidaying for two weeks with her friends in the UK. How would you describe her? Is she a visitor or a usual resident in the Census form?

The important thing to note with both card sorts and vignettes is that it is essential to develop good examples that map all the dimensions of the topic under investigation. Qualitative work, such as focus groups or depth interviews (see section 2.2.1), may be required to develop such examples.

Cognitive interviewing techniques can be combined in different ways and this gives the method flexibility and, some say, a lack of standardisation (Willis et al., 1999). However, at its heart cognitive interviewing is characterised by four features:

- it is a qualitative approach;
- it focuses on stimulus material – survey questions, information leaflets, etc.;
- it uses techniques that explore participants' thought processes; and
- it collects verbal reports.

These characteristics, however, can limit its usefulness.

1.5 Limitations of cognitive interviewing

Figure 1.2 summarises the criticisms levelled against cognitive interviewing in relation to each of the four features described above. In the rest of this section we discuss these criticisms in a little more detail.

Features	Criticisms
Method is **qualitative**, involving small, purposive samples and use of (some) unscripted probes.	It can't tell you the size or extent of problems identified. Data collection and analysis methods are not standardised and findings are therefore not seen as being replicable.
Focus is on survey questions (or other test materials): the words, syntax, layout.	It doesn't tell you about the length and flow of the whole questionnaire. If probing occurs after each question (Q) or set of Qs it may change the way in which participants (Ps) think about subsequent Qs.
Techniques identify 'hidden or covert problems' through exploration of Ps verbal accounts of their thought processes.	The method relies on P's ability to articulate thought processes: not everyone can do this (well). Not all thought is conscious and therefore capable of being articulated.
Interviewers collect **verbal reports** by encouraging Ps to 'think aloud' and/or ask questions or 'probes' to explore thought processes.	Cognitive interviewers may not ask the survey Q as worded/follow the interview protocol. Interviewers may not ask the same probes or in the same way. The choice of CI methods and the order in which they are used may bias the findings. The rapport built up in a cognitive interview between interviewer and participant may hide problems, such as non-response that may happen in the actual survey.

Figure 1.2   Features of the cognitive interviewing method and common criticisms

1.5.1 Qualitative method

Cognitive interviews are qualitative in nature, involving an in-depth interviewing approach and typically small, purposive samples. In these interviews we can explore the cognitive processes that go on while a participant is attempting to answer a survey question. The method helps us identify different types of problem that participants encounter and provides us with evidence about why these problems occur. However, cognitive interviewing cannot provide quantitative information on the extent of the problem or the size of its impact on survey estimates. For example, we might find that people misunderstand the concept being measured in the question, such as paid work, but we don't know what the prevalence of this misunderstanding is and therefore what impact it has on the survey's estimate. We can hypothesise (see Chapter 8) but samples are usually too small, and cases not selected with a known and equal chance to support such extrapolation. Furthermore, cognitive interviewing does not provide quantitative evidence on whether the revised version of the question proposed after cognitive testing is better than the original.

1.5.2 Focus

Cognitive interviewing is focused on individual survey questions and the cognitive processes involved in understanding and responding to them. It is not possible to assess questionnaire length from cognitive interviews because the survey questions are interspersed with the verbalisation and exploration of thought processes. Knowing how long the questionnaire will take to complete is important. Participants like to know how long it will take and, if the questions are to be asked by an interviewer, the length of the interview affects costs.

Cognitive interviewing is an intensive process. During a one-hour cognitive interview only 15–20 minutes of survey interview content may be tested (Fowler, 1995). This means that the questions being tested can rarely be tested in the context in which they will be asked in the main survey (in terms of topics covered and question ordering). The context in which questions are asked may impact on how participants answer or how willing they are to make the cognitive effort necessary to answer.

1.5.3 Techniques

Cognitive interviewing methods rely on participants' verbal reports of problems. Not all cognitive processes can be verbalised; processes involving discrete mental steps are more easily remembered, such as those required to recall the frequency of a behaviour (Tourangeau et al., 2000), whereas those 'intuitive' or subconscious processes (such as reporting on attitudes) can be harder, if not impossible, to verbalise.

Moreover, it is thought that cognitive interviewing favours people with a higher level of education, as they find it easier to articulate their thoughts, particularly when using think aloud (Fowler, 1995). If a questionnaire needs to be tested with a group who are less willing to participate in a cognitive interview, or who are not confident in expressing their views during a cognitive interview, important findings may be missed if cognitive interviewing is the only pretesting method used. Some of the probing techniques used in cognitive interviewing (paraphrasing for example) can be problematic in certain cultural settings (see section 11.5.1).

1.5.4 Interviewer

Cognitive interviews are typically structured so that participants first receive the standardised survey question (stimulus) and then their answer (response) is recorded. The capturing of the cognitive process may happen simultaneously using thinking aloud, or subsequently by probing the participant on aspects of the question and answer process. It is important that in testing interviewer-administered survey questions the test questions are read as worded and that thought is given to how the test material is introduced and what participants are asked to do. If the interviewer says that 'we are looking for problems' this may encourage participants to helpfully find them, even if they personally don't find the test questions problematic. In addition, providing additional prompts or information to the participant before eliciting their survey answer can contaminate the question and answer process and your test findings. For example, asking participants to 'read through the instructions before completing the questionnaire' may change the participant's behaviour and encourage them to read something that, left to their own devices, they would not have done.

Moreover, participants may alter what would be their 'usual' survey interview behaviour in a cognitive interview (see Wilson et al. (1995) for a summary of studies showing such an impact). Participants are asked to consider questions in more depth than in a survey interview (particularly a telephone interview) or than when completing a self-completion questionnaire. They have more time to consider the survey questions and, as a result, they may look for and sometimes find problems which might not actually have existed if the question was administered in the context of a survey interview. They may spend (more) time reading the questions or other materials than they would do if no interviewer was present and this may be a problem if you are testing materials where no interviewer will be present in the survey itself, see Chapter 10. They may be asked about their understanding of certain key terms used in the question. Even if they understood the terms as intended within the context of the question, when asked for a standalone definition they may struggle to provide one. Instead of providing a description of their understanding of the term which shaped their answer, a participant may well provide more of a 'textbook' definition of the term.

Conversely, some problems may be hidden in the context of a cognitive interview where an interviewer is on hand to assist. For example, routing problems in a self-completion questionnaire where participants skip or answer questions incorrectly may not occur because the interviewer intervenes. Cognitive interview participants may also be more motivated and so not display satisficing behaviour (Krosnick, 1991) during the interview (e.g. choosing the middle category or choosing the same answer to every question in a series) because of the presence of an interviewer and the more informal, conversational, nature of a cognitive interview compared with a survey interview.

It is well documented that the survey setting can have an impact on the quality of the data collected. For example it has been found that surveys conducted with children and young people in schools will yield different results compared to the same surveys conducted in a home environment (Brener et al., 2006; Griesler et al., 2008). These differences are most likely caused by different perceptions of privacy between the two environments. In particular, the proximity of parents or siblings could have an impact on whether young people choose to give accurate reports on undesirable behaviours (Tourangeau and Yan, 2007). Other factors can also impact on perceived privacy. For example, a study of young people in schools found different response patterns between paper and computerised self-completion questionnaires (Beebe et al., 1998). Students who completed the paper version of the questionnaire reported more sensitive behaviours (e.g. drug use and vandalism) than students completing the computerised questionnaire. The authors speculated that the different reporting levels could be related to privacy perceptions. Proximity to other students may have been a factor in sites where computers were placed close together and students may have been concerned about other people observing their answers on the screen.

The utility of cognitive interviewing to detect problems resulting from the survey setting is debateable. Cognitive interviews are normally conducted one-on-one in a private setting whereas survey questionnaires may or not be completed in these conditions. Therefore, inaccurate responses resulting from a perceived lack of privacy may not occur in a cognitive interviewing setting but could still occur in a survey setting. Participants may also be more willing to provide sensitive information in a cognitive interview than in a survey due to the different dynamic between interviewer and participant (d'Ardenne and Collins, 2013). Therefore, cognitive interviews may fail to detect some issues related to a participant's willingness to provide accurate answers due to the different contexts in which the information is collected. This fact needs to be considered carefully when you plan your testing and is discussed further in Chapter 3.

It's important to be aware of these limitations. Some can be overcome through interviewer training, a careful design of the cognitive interviewing guide, or probe sheet, and a rigorous and transparent approach to data collection, reduction and analysis. This book provides guidance in these areas. Other limitations, however, will remain and to tackle these, a multi-method approach to testing is required. Chapter 2 looks at other methods available to you in the development and testing of your survey questionnaires and how these can be combined to good effect.

1.6 Chapter summary

Cognitive psychology has helped us to understand the survey 'question and answer' process. Tourangeau's four-stage question and answer model (1984) is the most widely cited and provides a useful framework involving: comprehension, retrieval, judgement and response. The model has been elaborated to cover self-completion questions by Jenkins and Dillman (1997).

Cognitive interviewing covers a set of techniques that help us reveal these cognitive processes during the question and answer process to expose any potential problems with validity and measurement. The techniques include think aloud, probing, paraphrasing, confidence ratings, observation, response latency, card sorts and vignettes, though think aloud and probing are the most commonly used.

Cognitive interviewing has a number of limitations.

- It is a qualitative method, which cannot tell you the size or extent of problems identified and its implementation is not always standardised.
- It is focused on the question and answer process: it doesn't tell you about other issues such as length or flow of the questionnaire. Moreover, the cognitive interview can change the way in which participants go about attempting to answer the test questions.
- It identifies problems through exploration of participants' verbal accounts of their thought processes. However, this relies on participants' ability to articulate their thought processes and assumes that all thought is conscious and capable of being articulated, which it is not.
- The collection of participants' verbal reports is subject to error: interviewers may not read the test questions as worded; they may not ask the same probes and the rapport between the participant and interviewer may hide problems. In addition, your choice of cognitive interviewing methods and the order in which they are used may bias your findings.

In the rest of this book we set out how these criticisms can be ameliorated through careful design and implementation of cognitive interviewing. In Chapter 2 we discuss how cognitive interviewing can be combined with other pretesting methods to provide a more rounded assessment of the performance of your survey questions. Finally, it is worth noting that findings from cognitive interviews can be used to help interpret survey or experimental results (see for example, Padilla et al., 2013).

References

Aborn, M. (1999) 'CASM revisited', in M.G. Sirken, D.J Herrmann, S. Schechter, N. Schwarz, J.M Tanur and R. Tourangeau (eds), *Cognition and Survey Research*. New York: Wiley. pp. 21–38.

Anderson, J. (1983) *The Architecture of Cognition*. Cambridge, MA: Harvard University Press.

Arthur, S., Mitchell, M., Lewis, J. and McNaughton Nicholls, C. (2013) 'Designing fieldwork', in J. Ritchie, J. Lewis, C. McNaughton Nicholls and R. Ormston (eds), *Qualitative Research Practice*. London: Sage. pp. 147–76.

Balarajan, M. and d'Ardenne, J. (2008) *Inclusion of Short-Term Migrants in the 2011 Census*. Office for National Statistics. Available at: www.ons.gov.uk/ons/guide-method/census/2011/the-2011-census/2011-census-questionnaire-content/inclusion-of-short-term-migrants-in-the-2011-census.pdf

Bassili, J.N. (1996) 'The how and why of response latency measurement in telephone surveys', in N. Schwarz and S. Sudman (eds), *Answering Questions: Methodology for Determining Cognitive and Communicative Processes in Survey Research*. San Francisco, CA: Jossey-Bass. pp. 319–46.

Bassili, J.N. and Scott, B.S. (1996) 'Response latency as a signal to question problems in survey research', *Public Opinion Quarterly*, 60(3): 390–9.

Beatty, P. and Willis, G. (2007) 'Research synthesis: the practice of cognitive interviewing', *Public Opinion Quarterly*, 71: 287–311.

Beebe, T.J., Harrison, P.A., McRae, J.A., Anderson, R.E. and Fulkerson, J.A. (1998) 'An evaluation of computer-assisted self-interviews in a school setting', *Public Opinion Quarterly*, 62: 623–32.

Belson, W. (1981) *The Design and Understanding of Survey Questions*. Aldershot, England: Gower.

Biemer, P.P. and Lyberg, L.E. (2003) *Introduction to Survey Quality*. Hoboken, NJ: John Wiley & Sons.

Blair, E.A. and Burton, S. (1987) 'Cognitive processes used by survey respondents to answer behavioral frequency questions', *Journal of Consumer Research*, 14: 280–8.

Brener, N.D., Eaton, D.K., Kann, L., Grunbaum, J.A., Gross, L.A., Kyle, T.M. and Ross, J.G. (2006) 'The association of survey setting and mode with self-reported health risk behaviors among high school students', *Public Opinion Quarterly*, 70(3): 354–74.

Campanelli, P. and Channell, J. (1994) *Training: An Exploration of the Word and the Concept with an Analysis of the Implications for Survey Design*. London: Employment Department, Research Series No.30.

Collins D. (2003) 'Pretesting survey instruments: an overview of cognitive methods', *Quality of Life Research*, 12(3): 219–27.

Couper, M. and Groves, R. (1992) 'The role of the interviewer in survey participation', *Survey Methodology*, 18: 263–78.

Czaja, R. (1998) 'Questionnaire testing comes of age', *Marketing Bulletin*, 9: 52–66.

d'Ardenne, J. and Collins, D. (2013) 'Horses for courses: why different question testing methods uncover different findings and implications for selecting methods'. Paper presented at 5th European Survey Research Association conference, Ljubljana, Slovenia.

Draisma, S. and Dijkstra, W. (2004) 'Response latency and para linguistic expressions as indicators of response error', in S. Presser, J. Rothgeb, M. Couper, J.T. Lessler, E. Martin, J. Martin and E. Singer (eds), *Methods for Testing and Evaluating Survey Questionnaires*. Hoboken, NJ: Wiley and Sons. pp. 131–48.

Ericsson, K.A. and Simon, H.A. (1980) 'Verbal reports as data', *Psychological Review*, 87: 215–51.

Forsyth, B.H. and Lessler, J.T. (1991) 'Cognitive laboratory methods: a taxonomy', in P.P. Biemer, R.M. Groves, L.E. Lyberg, N.A. Mathiowetz and S. Sudman (eds), *Measurement Errors in Surveys*. New York: John Wiley & Sons. pp. 279–301.

Fowler, F.J. (1995) *Improving Survey Questions: Design and Evaluation* (Vol. 38). Thousand Oaks, CA: Sage.

Fowler Jr, F.J. and Mangione, T.W. (1990) *Standardized Survey Interviewing: Minimizing Interviewer-Related Error* (Vol. 18). Newbury Park, CA: Sage.

Gillund, G. and Shiffrin, R.M. (1984) 'A retrieval model for both recognition and recall', *Psychological Review*, 91: 1–67.

Goffman, E. (1959) *Presentation of Self in Everyday Life*. Garden City, NY: Anchor Books.

Green, M.C. and Krosnick, J.A. (1999) 'Comparing telephone and face-to-face interviewing in terms of data quality: the 1982 National Election Studies Method Comparison Project'. Available at: https://pprg.stanford.edu/wp-content/uploads/2001-Comparing-telephone-and-face-to-face-interviewing-in-terms-o.pdf

Grice, P. (1991) *Studies in the Way of Words*. Cambridge, MA: Harvard University Press.

Griesler, P.C., Kandel, D.B., Schaffran, C., Hu, M.C. and Davies, M. (2008) 'Adolescents' inconsistency in self-reported smoking: a comparison of reports in school and in household settings', *Public Opinion Quarterly*, 72(2): 260–90.

Groves, R., Fowler, F.J., Couper, M., Lepkowski, J., Singer, E. and Tourangeau, R. (2009) 'Inference and error in surveys', in *Survey Methodology* (2nd edition). Hoboken, NJ: John Wiley & Sons. pp. 35–67.

Hippler, H.J., Schwarz, N. and Sudman, S. (eds) (1987) *Social Information Processing and Survey Methodology*. New York: Springer-Verlag.

Jabine, T., Straf, M., Tanur, J. and Tourangeau, R. (eds) (1984) *Cognitive Aspects of Survey Methodology: Building a Bridge Between the Disciplines*. Washington, DC: National Academy Press.

Jenkins, CR. and Dillman, D.A. (1997) 'Towards a theory of self-administered questionnaire design', in L. Lyberg, P. Biemer, M. Collins, E. de Leeuw, C. Dippo,

N. Shwarz and D. Trewin (eds), *Survey Measurement and Process Quality*. New York: Wiley. pp. 165–96.

Jobe, J.B. and Mingay, D.J. (1991) 'Cognition and survey measurement: history and overview', *Applied Cognitive Psychology*, 5(3): 175–92.

Johnson, M.K. (1983) 'A multi-entry, modular memory system', in G.H. Bower (ed.), *The Psychology of Learning and Motivation* (Volume 17). Orlando, FL: Academic Press. pp. 81–123.

Kreuter, F., Presser, S. and Tourangeau, R. (2008) 'Social desirability bias in CATI, IVR, and web surveys: the effects of mode and question sensitivity', *Public Opinion Quarterly*, 72(5): 847–65. [Updated 2009 – version available online.]

Krosnick, J.A. (1991) 'Response strategies for coping with the cognitive demands of attitude measures in surveys', *Applied Cognitive Psychology*, 5: 213–36.

Lind, L.H., Schober, M.F., Conrad, F.G. and Reichert, H. (2013) 'Why do survey respondents disclose more when computers ask the questions?', *Public Opinion Quarterly*, 77(4): 888–935.

Loftus E. and Palmer J. (1974) 'Reconstruction of automobile destruction: an example of the interaction between language and memory', *Journal of Verbal Learning and Verbal Behaviour*, 13: 585–9.

Oksenberg, L., Cannell, C. and Kalton, G. (1991) 'New strategies for pretesting survey questions', *Journal of Official Statistics*, 7(3): 349–65.

Padilla, J.L, Benítez, I. and Castillo, M. (2013) 'Obtaining validity evidence by cognitive interviewing to interpret psychometric results', 9(3): 113–22 (doi: 10.1027/1614–2241/a000073).

Spencer, D. (2009) *Card Sorting: Designing Usable Categories*. New York: Rosenfeld.

Sudman, S. and Schwarz, N. (1989) 'Contributions of cognitive psychology to advertising research', *Journal of Advertising Research*, 29: 43–53.

Sudman, S., Bradburn, N.M. and Schwarz, N. (1996) *Thinking about Answers. The Application of Cognitive Processes to Survey Methodology*. San Francisco, CA: Jossey-Bass.

Tanur, J.M. (1999) 'Looking backwards and forwards at the CASM movement', in M.G. Sirken, D.J. Herrmann, S. Schechter, N. Schwarz, J.M. Tanur and R. Tourangeau (eds), *Cognition and Survey Research*. New York: Wiley. pp. 13–20.

Tourangeau, R. (1984) 'Cognitive science and survey methods: A cognitive perspective', in T. Jabine, M. Straf, J. Tanur and R. Tourangeau (eds), *Cognitive Aspects of Survey Design: Building a Bridge Between the Disciplines*. Washington, DC: National Academy Press. pp. 73–100.

Tourangeau, R. and Yan, T. (2007) 'Sensitive questions in surveys', *Psychological Bulletin*, 133(5): 859–83.

Tourangeau, R., Rips, L. and Rasinski, K. (2000) *Psychology of Survey Response*. Cambridge: Cambridge University Press.

Tulving, E. and Thomson, D.M. (1973) 'Encoding specificity and retrieval processes in episodic memory', *Psychological Review*, 80: 352–73.

Tversky, A. and Kahneman, D. (1973) 'Availability: a heuristic for judging frequency and probability', *Cognitive Psychology*, 5: 207–32.

Tversky, A. and Kahneman, D. (1974) 'Judgement under uncertainty: heuristics and biases', *Science*, 185: 1124–31.

Willis, G. (2005) *Cognitive Interviewing*. Thousand Oaks, CA: Sage.

Willis, G., DeMaio, T. and Harris-Kojetin (1999) 'Is the bandwagon headed to the methodological promised land? Evaluating the validity of cognitive interviewing techniques', in M. Sirken, D. Herrmann, S. Schechter, N. Schwarz, J. Tanur and R. Tourangeau (eds), *Cognition and Survey Research*. New York: Wiley. pp. 133–53.

Wilson, T.D., LaFleur, S.J.and Anderson, D.A. (1995) 'The validity and consequences of verbal reports about attitudes', in N.Schwarz and S. Sudman (eds), *Answering Questions: Methodology for Determining Cognitive and Communicative Processes in Survey Research*. San Francisco, CA: Jossey-Bass. pp. 91–114.

TWO

OTHER PRETESTING METHODS
MARGARET BLAKE

2.1 Introduction

In Chapter 1 we described in broad terms what cognitive interviewing is and its limitations. However, cognitive interviewing is just one of a number of pretesting methods that you can use to evaluate your questionnaire. The aim of this chapter is to provide you with information on some alternative pretesting methods, which will help you to decide which method or methods to use and how to combine them to test your questionnaire effectively.

Specifically we discuss:

- Depth interviews and focus groups
- Desk appraisal
- Expert review
- Usability testing
- Piloting and debriefing methods
- Behaviour coding
- Paradata
- Split ballot experiments.

This is by no means an exhaustive list but it covers the main methods in use. We summarise each method and indicate when in the development process it may be suitable to use it. Finally, we discuss the factors that should be considered when deciding on which pretesting method or methods to use and give examples of how we have combined different methods with cognitive interviewing to develop new survey questions.

2.2 Other methods for developing, testing and evaluating questionnaires

In this section we discuss a number of pretesting methods. Although they are presented as separate methods, they overlap and some can be combined in the same pretesting exercise. The methods can be grouped and categorised in different ways. This can be according to their timing in the research process (though this can vary), their cost, whether they involve participants or can be office based and whether they are by-products of other elements of the research process. An additional factor to consider is what the focus of the method is: conceptual, information perception and processing, interaction (between the participant and the interviewer or questionnaire) or the survey process. Campanelli (2008) suggests three stages of pretesting: developmental (during which the subject matter is understood and issues of language and culture are considered), question testing, and dress rehearsal where the questionnaire is tested in real survey conditions. The order in which we discuss each method reflects this later categorisation.

For each method we provide a brief description and indicate the kinds of information the method can produce. For a fuller description of these methods see, for example, Presser et al. (2004). A summary of the advantages and disadvantages of each method is provided in Figure 2.5 at the end of this section.

2.2.1 Depth interviews and focus groups

Depth interviews and focus groups are non-standardised, focused discussions that collect information about pre-specified issues using a 'topic guide'. Depth interviews are usually one-to-one encounters although they can involve pairs being interviewed in certain circumstances (for example friendship pairs when interviewing young people, see Highet (2003)). Focus groups involve typically 8 to 10 people coming together to discuss a topic, the discussion being moderated by a researcher or experienced facilitator. Both depth interviews and focus groups can be conducted face-to-face, online or by telephone, depending on the topic. Interactions are recorded (audio and or video) and data analysed from a verbatim transcript or from notes. Unlike cognitive interviews, depth interviews and focus groups are more exploratory and attempt to understand the world from the participant's perspective by capturing the participant's narrative.

These qualitative methods can be useful in the early stages of questionnaire development, helping you define concepts and decide on your content and structure, and the appropriate language to use to describe phenomena. In addition you can use these methods to look at other survey design issues, such as what might motivate people to take part in the survey and what barriers there might be to participation and to generate ideas about how these could be overcome.

You might want to use these methods to speak with members of the survey's target population. In addition you might also want to talk to data users such as analysts, policy-makers and practitioners, to better understand their needs. If the survey questionnaire is to be completed by vulnerable groups or special populations such as children or young people, older people, people with physical or mental health problems or disabilities, or employees then you might also want to consult gatekeepers such as parents, carers or senior managers within organisations.

Figure 2.1 sets out the issues to consider when deciding whether to use depth interviews or focus groups as a questionnaire development tool.

Sometimes focus groups are used to 'test' the wording of proposed survey questions. This is often done to save time and money. However, in our experience focus group testing can produce very different findings to those from cognitive

	Pros	Cons
Depth interviews	To understand individual circumstances, histories, attitudes, knowledge and understanding.	Can be costly and time-consuming, particularly if interviews are carried out in person and sample is dispersed.
	The topic requires a private and personal setting.	Not so good for generating ideas and problem solving.
	When the people you want to involve are geographically dispersed.	
Focus groups	Focus groups can be used where the topic is one which could be comfortably discussed in a group setting and where the discussion does not rely on an individual narrative (Ritchie and Lewis, 2003).	Can be dominated by one or two people with restricted input from other group members. The moderator's role is to encourage everyone to take part.
	Useful when you want people to share, develop and or discuss ideas, or come up with options or solutions to problems.	If face-to-face, participants have to travel to attend the group and this may make it difficult for some to attend. Offering to pay for travel/childcare can help.
	May be more appropriate for certain groups, e.g. young people, where it has been argued that the setting reduces the power and influence of the interviewer and therefore creates a less intimidating data collection environment (Eder and Fingerson, 2003).	Having too much variation or too little in terms of the characteristics and experiences of group participants can affect the 'group dynamic' and have a negative influence on how the group works together. Your sample design and recruitment are important.
	Time and cost-efficient: you can speak with a lot of people in a relatively short period of time.	

Figure 2.1   Issues to consider when deciding whether to use depth interviews or focus groups

interviews with the same population group. We found that using focus groups identified a narrower range of wording problems, that problems with comprehension can go undetected because focus group participants are less willing to reveal their ignorance in a group setting, and problems with question order and length may not come to light because the focus group context is very different to the survey context (d'Ardenne and Collins, 2013). For these reasons, we would not recommend questions are tested using focus groups.

2.2.2 Desk appraisal and other office-based methods

Although it is essential to test survey questions with participants, you can gain a great deal from a desk-based, systematic evaluation of the questionnaire. There are a number of tools available for this. The tool we have used is the Questionnaire Appraisal System (QAS) developed by Willis and Lessler (1999), but there are others (Statistics Netherlands have developed several: Snijkers (2002), Akkerboom and Dehue (1997) cited in Campanelli (2008)). These tools group problems into different types and suggest particular issues to look out for. For example, Willis and Lessler suggest eight problem types: reading, instructions, clarity, assumptions, knowledge or memory, sensitivity or bias, response categories, and other. For each of these the QAS asks the reviewer a number of questions, for example is the question double-barrelled, are the response categories overlapping, is it reasonable to assume the participant will have the knowledge necessary to be able to answer a factual question. In contrast the Snijkers (2002) tool focuses on four areas: question comprehension, retrieval of information, judgement and reporting (of answers), with the reviewer being asked a series of questions which cover similar areas to the QAS, for example around overlapping response categories and whether the participant would know the information 'by heart'.

Systematically using the 37-page QAS manual on every question in a questionnaire may be too time-consuming but it's possible to produce a cut-down version, focusing on a selection of issues of particular relevance to your study. Alternatively you could carry out a full systematic appraisal on specific questions which are new or are considered to be problematic.

The structured desk appraisal methods are very focused on the potential pitfalls of specific questions. Another type of desk appraisal is to review the questionnaire as a whole. This can be particularly useful on long-standing, repeat surveys where the content of the questionnaire, if not regularly reviewed and pruned, can end up becoming repetitive and may lose its flow. This type of review is best carried out by a researcher who has not previously been involved in the survey. The researcher would go through the questionnaire, looking at when different questions were added, topic flow, and interviewer feedback on the questionnaire. The purpose of this is to evaluate whether the structure and content which has evolved is fit for purpose and results in an interview which is interesting and makes sense to participants. The resulting recommendations may be challenging for clients and survey researchers to hear because changing question wording or order, or removing questions is never popular.

If time and money are tight then reading aloud the questions to yourself and interviewing colleagues or friends in mock interviews quickly identifies questions which are wordy or unclear (Campanelli, 2008; Czaja and Blair, 1996). If you are writing questions that will be read aloud by an interviewer it is useful to say them aloud and hear how they sound. The way you write a question that will be spoken is often different to the way a question will be phrased when it is to be read. This is also important to remember if you are borrowing questions from other surveys where questions were asked in different modes.

2.2.3 Expert review

'Expert review' is a process whereby a variety of experts are invited to form a panel to review the draft questionnaire or subset of questions (Campanelli, 2008; Czaja and Blair, 1996), with experts coming together as a group (face-to-face, by telephone or virtually) to discuss each question in turn or providing individual feedback (by email). If experts are reviewing a web questionnaire then it is possible to gather feedback with additional question fields included in the online tool being evaluated, for the experts to record their views (Gräf, 2002). However, collecting individual feedback loses the benefits of discussion between experts and the alternative approaches this can yield.

Experts are sent the draft questionnaire along with background information about the survey (e.g. mode, purpose, target population) to review. It can be useful to provide guidance to reviewers on the issues and/or questions you want them to focus on. This can help make the task more time efficient and ensure the whole questionnaire is reviewed. Example 2.1 provides an example of guidance for reviewers. In this case all the questions needed to be considered. The guidance provides information about the background and purpose of the questionnaires and the types of design issues to consider.

Example 2.1 Example guidance for expert reviewer

Refining questionnaires on care services for older people

Background to project

- The Department of Health and the Nuffield Foundation have funded NatCen to work with academic collaborators at the Personal Social Services Research Unit (PSSRU) at the London School of Economics and the University of East Anglia to develop a clear and robust module of survey questions about (social) care.

- Currently the information collected on this area is limited and patchy and the data do not provide sufficient detailed information for policy analysts. Existing questions are also now out of date.
- The survey questions will be suitable for use in longitudinal or cross-sectional population surveys and will cover *community-based* care and economic evaluations on:

  o receipt of care and support services by older people;
  o payment for social care for older people;
  o receipt of informal care by older people; and,
  o provision of informal care for older people.

- It is expected that the question module will last 10 minutes in a CAPI administered interview in whichever survey it is used in.

Worked carried out

- The question module development was informed by a literature review of current survey questions on this topic as well as in-depth interviews with service providers and focus groups with service users.

Our current involvement

- NatCen is now in the process of designing the question module which will be cognitively tested next month (round 1) and again early next year following integration of findings from round 1.
- Before round 1 testing occurs we want to make sure questions meet the needs of data users and that questions are framed in the most appropriate way possible.

Focus of the review

The review will focus on the following three areas:

- **Measurement priorities** What has been asked (task approach, what is being asked of participant and proxy participants, use of documentation and sensitivities).
- **Question wording** Issues related to question wording (general issues (tasks, professional carer and family carer, proxy participants) and question specific).
- **Administration issues** Applicability in different surveys.[1]

Reviewers can be subject experts with knowledge of the research topic of interest, policy experts who are commissioning the research or understand how the research will be used in the future, methodological experts with knowledge of questionnaire design or of the mode in which the survey will

---

[1] See http://www.natcen.ac.uk/our-research/research/social-care-questions-for-over-65s/ for more information about this study

be delivered (e.g. an online research expert), or the researchers running the surveys on which the questions will be placed. We find it useful to have a mixture of experts.

You will need to decide on the timing of your expert panel. Your questionnaire needs to be fairly well developed. We typically carry out an expert panel prior to cognitive testing. This is because:

- expert panels tend to be useful for identifying more obvious potential problems with the questions such as ill-defined terms, missing or overlapping response options or routing errors; whereas
- cognitive interviewing is a more effective method for identifying less obvious problems, which can often only be uncovered when people representing the survey population are exposed to the question stimulus.

However, sometimes cognitive interviewing highlights problems for which there are no obvious solutions and in such cases it can be valuable to consult experts on what approach should be taken.

2.2.4 Usability testing and eye-tracking technology

Usability testing is used as a method when testing web questionnaires and other data collection instruments on personal computers, tablets and mobile devices. Testing explores whether members of the target population are able to use the software and the device as intended. It involves observation and verbal reports, using the cognitive interviewing techniques of think aloud and probing. The testing of web data collection tools is complicated because there are so many additional elements to consider (Baker et al., 2004). The sorts of issues to explore in testing include:

- the target population's computer literacy;
- computer settings on individual computers/ tablets/ mobile devices;
- how the questionnaire looks on the screen;
- whether people (can) see whole question and answer options on the screen, without the need for scrolling;
- how participants assess their progress through the questionnaire.

It is not enough to focus on question wording; an understanding of usability is essential (Hansen and Couper, 2004).

The focus of cognitive interviewing is on the question wording and how people answer the questions but you cannot separate this from the participant's ability to navigate the questionnaire, read the question and answer options on the screen and be able to use the mouse or keys to select their answer. As a result, cognitive interviewing of web-based questionnaires also strays into and overlaps to some extent with usability testing, as Example 2.2 below illustrates.

Example 2.2   Cognitive testing and links with usability testing: testing a questionnaire with children and young people in Wales

The Sports Council for Wales conducts surveys about involvement in sport and other physical activity with pupils in primary and secondary schools. They wanted to convert their paper-based questionnaire into a web questionnaire to assist with routing and data capture, to allow more interesting images to be used and to capture the interest of participants who are increasingly used to computers. Web questionnaires for primary- and secondary-aged pupils were developed using existing questions from the paper instrument as well as some new content, with the design guided by the expertise of survey methodologists and a company specialising in web surveys.

The questionnaires were tested in schools by cognitive interviewers who used observation, think aloud and probing. The findings of the cognitive testing included not just recommendations for the survey questions but also a range of recommendations related to the technology, design and usability. For example, we made recommendations about the size of answer buttons, introduction of a progress bar, location of information on the screen and the size of the mouse provided to smaller children (McGee and d'Ardenne, 2009).

As the example above shows, cognitive interviewing can incorporate some elements of usability testing, where interviewers are appropriately briefed. However, there are more systematic approaches to usability testing which you can use separately from cognitive interviewing. Research has shown that when participants read information on a computer screen they tend to scan the text and their speed of reading on the screen is slower than on paper (Gräf, 2002). This has implications for questionnaire design since it means web questionnaires should probably be shorter than paper questionnaires, and researchers should not assume that participants will read everything on screen.

Eye-tracking technology is a technique that can be used during usability testing to assess what information the participant actually looks at on the screen (Galesic and Yan, 2011). In recent years eye tracking has been used by survey methodologists to explore how people read questionnaires as part of pretesting. For example, Galesic et al. (2008) have used eye tracking to examine whether participants exhibit satisficing behaviours (such as not reading definitions or all available answer categories) when completing web questionnaires. Eye tracking has been used to test the usability of the online American Community Survey (Ashenfelter and Hughes, 2011) and to explore whether people read questions differently if they are presented in different modes, for example on screen or on paper (Kaminska and Foulsham, 2013).

Eye tracking tends to take place in a lab using equipment that is calibrated for each individual participant although there are mobile options such as eye-tracking glasses that participants wear. The technique produces a great deal of data for

Heat map

Gaze plot

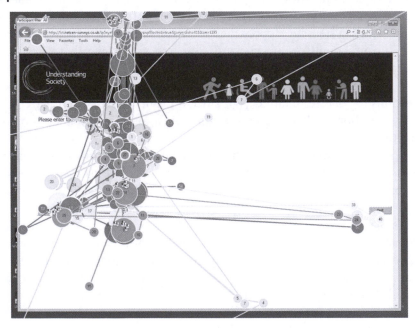

Figure 2.2 Example outputs from eye tracking

Screen shots taken from the IP user-testing that Jo d'Ardenne and Hayley Lepps conducted in 2012 on behalf of the Understanding Society Scientific Leadership Team at the Institute of Social and Economic Research, University of Essex. Permission to use these screen shots has been obtained from Jon Burton at ISER (the client).

analysis and it is therefore important to think carefully about what sorts of information you want to get and what kinds of data you will need. We have found, for our purposes, that heat maps and gaze plots, see Figure 2.2, are useful. Heat maps show you how long the participant(s) looked at a particular section of the screen for, ranging in colour from red (the areas they looked at for the longest amount of time), through yellow, to green (the areas they looked at for the least amount of time). You can produce a heat map of just one participant or for all participants. Gaze plots show you every point on the screen the participant(s) looked at in one image; each point is numbered and joined up by a line. You can also observe the gaze plot of just one participant, or for all of the participants in your test. If you choose to look at the gaze plots of more than one participant at a time the plots will be displayed in different colours so you can tell participants apart.

See section 2.3 for an example of a study that combined cognitive interviewing and eye tracking.

2.2.5 Piloting

A pilot examines the questionnaire in terms of length, flow, ease of administration and response, and acceptability and relevance of the questions to participants. Sometimes the pilot will be large, involving up to several hundred participants, and will rehearse the whole survey process. Not only would you test the entire questionnaire, but you may also want to test the sampling procedures, coding and editing processes and other procedures. This type of 'dress rehearsal' pilot typically mimics the actual survey conditions and will give you a feel for what might happen in the main survey and what kinds of data you will get back. Looking at your pilot data is recommended. It can help identify:

- any routing problems in your questionnaire;
- questions with high levels of item non-response, which may indicate a problem;
- answer scales that fail to adequately differentiate between participants; and
- scale items that can be dropped.

Pilots are rarely large enough to provide reliable estimates of survey response rates because sample sizes are not large enough. However, they can flag problems with the sampling procedures and the process of inviting sample members to take part.

Pilots can also be small-scale, involving interviews with between 10 and 50 participants and may focus on testing certain elements of the survey, such as a particular subset of questions or the protocol for collecting measurements or bio-samples, such as height or blood samples, rather than the whole questionnaire.

A hybrid of the two piloting approaches may be used, for example testing the whole questionnaire in the final mode but using a different sample or recruitment method from the eventual survey. Some form of piloting is recommended for all surveys. Cognitive interviewing is not an alternative to piloting.

> ## Checklist of things to consider when designing your pilot
>
> - What do you want to evaluate? The whole survey process or certain parts of it?
> - What is your target population for the pilot?
> - How will you get your sample?
> - Do you need ethical approval for your pilot?
> - Will you tell people that they are taking part in a pilot?
> - What materials will you require for the pilot? Invitation letters/emails, questionnaires, show cards, consent forms, information leaflets, etc.?
> - Do you want to code and or edit (clean) the pilot data?
> - Do you want to analyse the pilot data (run frequencies, crosstabs or more complex analyses)?
> - Will you write up a report on the findings from the pilot?
> - Will you document your recommendations and/or what changes were made post pilot?

There are a variety of techniques that can be incorporated into field piloting. While these are not a replacement for cognitive interviewing they do add to what researchers can learn about problems with the questionnaire during a pilot.

2.2.6 Interviewer debriefing

If you are piloting an interviewer-administered questionnaire it can be useful to bring all the pilot interviewers together at the end of the pilot fieldwork to talk about what went well and what was problematic. This 'debriefing' is an opportunity to discuss general problems with length and subject matter as well as to go through the pilot questionnaire question by question. The session, which may last several hours, is moderated by the researcher. To structure the feedback for the discussion or where a face-to-face debriefing is not possible, an interviewer debriefing questionnaire can be used, as illustrated in Example 2.3 below.

> **Example 2.3   Using an interviewer debriefing questionnaire to evaluate an Event History Calendar method on the English Longitudinal Study of Ageing**
>
> During a project which sought to evaluate an Event History Calendar method used as part of the English Longitudinal Study of Ageing (ELSA), we gave the interviewers who worked on the pilot a debriefing questionnaire. This questionnaire was designed to gain a sense of how the calendar worked, from the interviewers' perspective, and also to understand how they used this less standardised approach to data collection. It included questions about:

- how participants interacted with the calendar – whether and how often they looked at the calendar on the computer screen, which topics they followed;
- whether the participant had indicated that the visual calendar had helped them to date events;
- the order in which interviewers had asked questions and whether, in hindsight, this felt like the best order;
- whether there were particular topic domains that were difficult or easy for participants to remember and why;
- whether participants found parts of the interview upsetting and their general emotional state at the time of interview.

See http://www.census.gov/srd/papers/pdf/rsm2008–02.pdf

To guard against what Czaja and Blair (1996) describe as the experiences of the outlier and knowledgeable participants who may come to dominate discussion at debriefings you need to skilfully moderate the debriefing to ensure that all views are heard and triangulate this with information from the debriefing questionnaires.

The debriefing questionnaire should be given to interviewers prior to the debriefing (ideally at the start of the pilot). You can ask interviewers to complete one debriefing questionnaire for each interview in order to obtain case-by-case feedback on specific issues. Alternatively you can ask each interviewer to complete one questionnaire to cover all pilot cases. It should include open questions to allow interviewers to raise unanticipated problems as well as closed questions, asking for more specific information. This written format also allows the voice of quieter interviewers to be heard, as well as for less salient problems to be raised.

Finally, it can be valuable for clients or subject experts involved in the project to attend the debriefing to hear about questionnaire problems first-hand. The debrief can provide useful evidence on what the problems are and what impact they are having on the survey.

2.2.7 Respondent debriefing

Respondent debriefing is a method which can be added to field piloting to increase participant input. It is distinct from cognitive interviewing but at the edges there are overlaps and Willis (2005) refers to it as an example of 'field-based probing'.

Debriefing questions can collect information on the participant's overall impressions of the questionnaire and subject matter and on what participants were thinking when they answered particular questions. Respondent debriefing questions can be asked as soon as is practical after the pilot question has been answered (Converse and Presser, 1996) or at the end of the questionnaire (DeMaio and Rothgeb, 1996; Hess, 1995) – see Figure 2.3.

During the interview	At the end of the interview
You can capture what was in the participant's mind when they answered the question (they might not recall this later on).	Doesn't interrupt the flow of the questionnaire (Martin, 2004).
Certain types of debriefing question can flow naturally from the survey question (e.g. can I just check, did you include x in your answer to this question?).	Doesn't interfere with the assessment of length of the pilot questionnaire.
	It is the natural place to ask for views about the questionnaire overall – e.g. enjoyment, sensitivity of topics, relevance, etc.

Figure 2.3 Respondent debriefing

The questions can be open or closed but in our experience to yield useful information they need to be focused on specific issues, see Example 2.4 below. Asking general, open questions about what participants were thinking when they answered a pilot question rarely yields sufficiently detailed information to be of much use because survey interviewers do not have the skills or subject matter knowledge to probe effectively. However, if debriefing interviews are carried out by 'experts' then useful information can be obtained using more open questioning (see for example, Nichols and Hunter Childs, 2009).

Example 2.4   Respondent debriefing question used to evaluate the accuracy of a question about homework

As part of the development of the Longitudinal Study of Young People in England (first cohort questionnaire) we tested the following question using cognitive interviewing.

On weekdays, about how much time per day do you spend doing homework?

Findings indicated that the question was misinterpreted on occasions, with respondents giving a figure that represented the number of *evenings per week* they did their homework rather than *the number of hours per day* they spent doing it, which is what was required.

At the pilot a respondent debriefing question was asked, after this question, to check whether the answer given referred to the number of hours per weekday evening the respondent spent doing homework or the number of weekday evenings he or she spent doing it. This allowed us to get a better idea about how widespread this misinterpretation was.

Respondent debriefing questions can be asked in any data collection mode but are particularly valuable for self-completion questionnaires, where the only source of feedback is the respondent. Behr et al. (2012) have experimented with the use of respondent 'probe' questions as part of a web questionnaire. They found respondents did respond to 'category selection' probes within an online survey which ask respondents why they have selected a particular answer category from a closed question.

2.2.8 Behaviour coding

Behaviour coding is used to examine the interaction between survey interviewer and respondent during the administration of the questionnaire (see for example Fowler, 1995; van der Zouwen and Smit, 2004). These interactions are coded using a set of codes that capture aspects of behaviour of interest which are appropriate to the questions being asked. For example, the technique can be used to evaluate whether the survey question was read by the interviewer as worded, whether respondents requested clarification and whether inadequate answers were given. You decide what the unit of coding should be: each utterance or interaction over an individual question. Depending on the complexity of the coding schema and the unit to be coded, the interaction can be 'live coded' (a coder sits in on the interview and codes the interactions as they happen) or, more typically, the interactions are recorded, with participants' consent, and the coding takes place later. Behaviour coding provides quantitative data that indicates which questions have lots of problems.

Coding schemes can be very simple, but the temptation is to try to capture more detail, which can make the exercise time consuming and costly. Figure 2.4

Behaviour code	Description
(1) Interviewer codes	
FF (feed forward) item read as worded/ slight change	Interviewer read the item verbatim or made a minor modification that did not change the meaning.
*FF statement became a question	Feed forward statement is read as a question e.g. *'Last time you told us you had high blood pressure, is that correct?'*
*FF question became a statement	Feed-forward question is read as a statement e.g. *'And your date of birth was 25th May 1933'.*
*Other major change	Any change in wording that did or could change the meaning *e.g. omitting key words*.
*Omission	Data item missed out altogether.
*Inaudible interviewer/other	Recording inaudible or interviewer behaviour does not fit into any of the above categories.

(Continued)

(Continued)

(2) Respondent codes	
*Affirmed FF item – adequate	Respondent either acknowledged or did not dispute that they gave the information previously.
*Disputed FF item – adequate	Respondent challenged that they gave the information previously.
*Inadequate answer/elaboration	Initial utterance does not fit into any of the given response categories.
*Clarification	Respondent requests clarification of the data item.
Question re-read	Respondent requests that the item is read again.
Don't know	Respondent does not have the required information.
Refusal	Respondent refuses to give an answer/response.
*Inaudible respondent/other	Recording inaudible or respondent behaviour does not fit into any of the above categories.
(3) Outcome codes	
Adequate answer	Final response fits one of the given categories.
*Inadequate answer	Final response does not fit any of the response categories or is incorrectly coded.
Don't know	Respondent does not have the required information.
Refusal	Respondent refuses to give an answer/response.
*Inaudible/other	Recording inaudible or respondent behaviour does not fit into any of the above categories.

Figure 2.4 Behaviour code frame used on the English Longitudinal Study of Ageing to assess use of dependent interviewing

Notes: * indicates non-standard behaviour; FF = feed forward data.

This project was carried out by former colleagues Pascale and McGee. The code frame included here is based on the frame used by researchers during coding and adapted from that which is included in the article by Pascale and McGee (2008).

shows the behaviour code frame used on the English Longitudinal Study of Ageing. Each of the 48,000 first utterances recorded was coded using this detailed behaviour coding frame. Unsurprisingly the resulting analysis was extremely complex. However, this level of detail was required so that we could assess how dependent interviewing affects data quality (see Pascale and McGee,

2008). Dependent interviewing is a questioning technique whereby answers from a previous interview are 'fed forward' to a current interview (for example, 'Our records show that when we last interviewed you, you had a child called [Susan], whose date of birth is [1/1/1960]). Are these details correct?'). It is commonly used on longitudinal studies as a way of reducing seam bias (see for example, Moore et al., 2009).

An important decision you will need to make is what the problem threshold should be that would necessitate a change being made to the question. For example, if 15% of participants ask for clarification, should clarification be added to the question or should changes only be made if 25% of people have problems? Also, the quantitative information does not itself indicate the nature of the problem. A record is also needed of the nature of the clarification requested in order to actually deal with the problems.

2.2.9 Paradata

When questionnaires are administered using computer-assisted methods (interviewer administered or web) a considerable amount of 'paradata' are produced as a by-product of the data collection (Nicolaas, 2011). This includes information about keystrokes made by participants (when self-administered), and occurrences of consulting help keys. Another important type of paradata is the time taken to answer the whole questionnaire, sections of questions or even individual questions as set by 'time stamps'. Such data can be obtained from the main stage of a survey or from a pilot. These data can be analysed to provide clues as to which questions may be problematic or to assess questionnaire length and flow.

We routinely analyse the timing data to look at the overall mean and median length of an interviewer-administered pilot questionnaire as well as the maximum and minimum interview lengths for different groups because interview length determines to a large extent, survey cost. We use median length to judge whether the survey content is the length the client has paid for or whether cuts need to be made to the content. You can exploit timing data to explore participant burden, particularly in looking at the maximum length and which types of participants are having the longest interviews. For example, on the English Longitudinal Study of Ageing we checked to see whether the addition of new questions about social care use meant that older and less healthy people were receiving a much longer interview than the average because of detailed questions about health conditions and social care use, which younger, healthier people are not being asked.

2.2.10 Split ballot experiments

Split ballot experiments involve testing two or more versions of a questionnaire simultaneously on a large sample, with participants being randomly assigned to one of the test versions. The sample for the experiment needs to be designed to ensure it has sufficient statistical power to detect real differences rather than those that could occur by chance and to avoid confounding of the variables being manipulated in the experiment (see Krosnick, 2011). Typically this means samples need to be quite large: it is not uncommon for each test version to be fielded with 700 or more people, which is much larger than the size of a typical dress-rehearsal pilot (see section 2.2.5). An example of a study that makes extensive use of split ballot experiments is the UK Household Longitudinal Study, known as Understanding Society, funded by the Social and Economic Research Council and managed by the Institute of Economic and Social Research at the University of Essex. It has a separate 'Innovation Panel' designed explicitly to test out alternative ways of asking questions, collecting data and communicating with panel members. The results of its experiments are published on the study's website and are a rich source of information (see references at the end of this chapter for the current URL).

Split ballot experiments can be useful when you want to know what difference, if any, asking a different form of a question or order of questions will have on the estimates you obtain. However, these experiments cannot tell you which version is 'best'. Rather you can test hypotheses about what you might expect to see and based on the results decide which version to run with on the main survey, see Example 2.5.

Example 2.5   Illustration of a split ballot

Take an existing question and one that has been revised based on the results of cognitive interviewing.

The revisions to the question are designed to make the question clearer.

Hypothesis: If it is clearer we would expect to see a reduction in the number of people answering 'don't know'.

Does the revised question achieve this objective?

You undertake a split ballot test and here's what you find.

Version A (existing Q)	Version B (revised Q)
Yes 46%	Yes 48%
No 28%	No 39%
DK 26%	DK 13%

Results: The difference in DK responses is statistically significant at the 95% confidence interval and is not confounded with other variables. Based on this evidence you conclude that the revised question is an improvement and you decide to run with it on the main survey.

Method	Survey types it is suitable for	Advantages	Disadvantages	Combining with cognitive interviewing (CI)
Focus groups and in-depth interviews	All modes	Can capture the language people use to describe phenomena, which you can use when writing your survey questions.	Need a longer development period and additional resources.	Use early to help you to develop questions then test your questions using CI.
		Can explore concepts and their boundaries, which is useful prior to question development.	Can't tell you about the size or prevalence of issues or ideas which emerge.	Use after cognitive interviewing, to explore further any problems regarding questions with specific subgroups or with other stakeholders, such as survey coding and editing staff or interviewers.
		Can explore how people 'tell the story' or recall information, which can inform question or topic order and strategies for facilitating recall.	Can't tell you about what will happen in the field, in a survey context. Testing questions in a focus group produces very different findings to testing questions in a cognitive interview, as the presence of others influences focus group participants' responses.	
Desk appraisal	All modes	Cost-effective	Relies on researcher experience and judgement.	Prior to cognitive interviewing for new questions
		No respondent burden	Researchers may not identify all the problems that the target population will experience, or problems that specific subgroups may encounter.	Can be used prior to CI, to improve the draft questions and identify/prioritise questions for testing.

Figure 2.5 Comparison of pretesting methods

(Continued)

Method	Survey types it is suitable for	Advantages	Disadvantages	Combining with cognitive interviewing (CI)
Desk appraisal (continued)		Quick (compared with field-based methods)	Problems identified may not occur in the survey at all or not in a way that would compromise the usefulness of the survey data.	
Expert review panel	All modes	Cost- and time-effective	Different contributors may have different views so researcher has to make the decisions (consensus may well not be reached).	Can be used prior to CI to identify priorities for testing.
		No respondent burden	Can be hard to find a time when all experts can come together to discuss the questionnaire. Individual feedback can be collected but the value of the discussion is lost.	Can be used after (a first round of) CI, to review findings and make decisions on (final) wording/layout.
		Brings in a wider range of experience and knowledge than single person desk appraisal.	Does not provide evidence about how the survey target population, or specific subgroups, will interpret and respond to the questions.	Improves efficiency of CI by removing obvious problems before testing.
		When adoption of your questions by others (e.g. academics/ policy-makers) will rely on their buy-in involving them in the expert panel can be useful.	Subject experts may not be skilled in designing questions which respondents can answer. It's important to have a mix of subject and methodological expertise.	

Method	Survey types it is suitable for	Advantages	Disadvantages	Combining with cognitive interviewing (CI)
Expert review panel (continued)		Can make subsequent testing more efficient as it removes obvious problems with questionnaire.	Problems identified may not occur in the actual survey.	
Usability testing	Self-completion, particularly web	Provides objective, quantifiable data on user behaviour (e.g. eye-movements, mouse movements).	Can be expensive, particularly if eye tracking is involved. Special equipment is needed for eye tracking.	Basic usability testing can be incorporated within cognitive testing through appropriate training and briefing of interviewers.
		Findings can be generalised. Findings from intensive testing of question formats (such as grids) or placement of information (such as additional help) can be used to inform the design of other questionnaires.	Testing may not replicate the 'user' environment if a lab is used. Thought needs to be given to what the aims of the testing are and whether testing on the respondent's own computer/tablet/mobile device is required.	More detailed, focused usability testing can be undertaken as a separate exercise to assess specific design issues such as what information the respondent looks at on the screen and how they navigate through the questionnaire.
Field piloting	All modes	Tests questions in a survey context. Can be large enough numbers for some quantitative analysis to identify item non-response and routing problems or satisficing.	Rarely offers clues to the causes of problems.	CI can precede a pilot, helping to refine the questionnaire.

(Continued)

(Continued)

Method	Survey types it is suitable for	Advantages	Disadvantages	Combining with cognitive interviewing (CI)
Field piloting (continued)		Tests wider survey procedures (sampling, making contact, returning completed questionnaires to you etc.) not just the questionnaire.	Some problems may be hidden: respondents answer questions but don't fully understand them.	CI can take place after a pilot, to review questions that have been found to be problematic.
			Can be expensive and slow to set up, depending on scale.	
Respondent debriefing	All modes	Allows greater respondent input than a straight field pilot but at little extra cost.	Writing debriefing questions that yield specific detail about aspects of the question and answer process can be challenging.	Findings from CI can be used to inform your decision about which survey questions to follow up on with respondent debriefing questions and what the focus of those questions should be.
		Can assess whether problems still persist and what impact they might have on data quality.	If embedded in the questionnaire, debriefing questions can add to its length and to respondent burden. This could compromise other measures that your pilot is designed to collect.	
Behaviour coding	Interviewer-administered	Quantitative and objective, it can indicate the extent of problems with a question.	Coding can be complex and time-consuming (though does not have to be). Coders need training and coder reliability must be measured.	Can be used to assess the effectiveness of post CI changes to questions, as part of a pilot.
		Can identify problems with interviewer delivery of questions as well as problems with respondents being able to provide an answer.	Does not describe the cause(s) of problems with specific questions, especially where coding schemes are kept simple.	

Method	Survey types it is suitable for	Advantages	Disadvantages	Combining with cognitive interviewing (CI)
Paradata (especially timing data)	All modes but most useful and straightforward for computer-assisted modes	Set up time can be minimal as most computerised questionnaires collect timing and other paradata automatically (though you may need to check what the default settings are and customise these as required).	You can end up with a lot of data, which needs to be organised and analysed with care and skill.	Since CI does not allow for any assessment of eventual interview length, it is good practice to combine CI with a pilot in which data on survey length is collected.
		Provides objective data on interview length; interviewer and respondent impressions are subjective.		
		Paradata can be used for a variety of purposes (flexible).		
Split panel experiments	All modes. Expensive except in web surveys	Provides quantitative information to compare survey questions.	Typically you need large sample sizes to have sufficient statistical power to detect effects. This can make such experiments expensive and impractical (if sample is finite).	Could be used to evaluate whether the new/revised questions proposed after CI are better.
		Experimental designs allow you to assess the size and direction of impact of changes in question order, wording and layout.	You may not have sufficient understanding of the underlying causes of the differences you observe in your experiments to interpret the results.	CI can be used afterwards to gain a deeper understanding of differences found between the different experimental groups.
		Can be useful on a survey which provides time series data to explore impact of changes to the questionnaire on the data.		

Figure 2.5 Comparison of pretesting methods

Split ballot experiments can be expensive, although if you are testing questions designed for web surveys then such experiments can be run relatively cheaply using high-quality web panels.

2.3 Combining cognitive interviewing with other methods

2.3.1 How much pretesting is needed

Czaja and Blair (1996) ask the question 'how much pretesting is enough'? There is no definitive answer to this but a good starting point is to think about what level of evidence you (and the study sponsor) feel is necessary to be confident that the survey's measurements will be valid, reliable, unbiased, useful and sufficiently complete in terms of measuring the concepts of interest to meet the research aims and objectives. The amount of money the survey will cost and the costs (both financial and political) if the survey data are inaccurate will shape, to some extent, the amount of effort invested in pretesting. A good example is the decennial population census. It costs millions of pounds to collect the data and the data are used to make important decisions about how public money is spent. New questions and modes of data collection are subject to extensive pretesting using a variety of methods to ensure the resulting data are robust.

Given the range of pretesting and piloting tools available to researchers, the possibilities for combining methods are endless. Most of us carry out research in a setting in which budgets and time constrain what is possible and so a test plan must be devised carefully. It is not sensible to use all the methods available, instead the optimum combination must be chosen. Apart from the inevitable time and budget constraints, the considerations which can guide your choice of methods include:

- how much is already known about the topic;
- whether you are adopting or adapting questions or whether you are designing them from scratch;
- the target population for the survey and the extent to which their characteristics may present challenges;
- whether you are using questions in a new mode;
- the extent of routing, looping and other complexities in the questionnaire structure;
- the complexity and difficulty of concepts in the questions;
- the sensitivity of the topic;
- the size and cost of the main survey for which you are testing;
- whether the questions are to be asked once or whether they are going to form part of an ongoing time series or be included in multiple surveys;
- the skills of the research team and the additional resources available to undertake any pretesting.

2.3.2 Examples of multiple pretesting methods in practice

Below we describe how we have combined multiple pretesting methods on two different projects – Examples 2.6 and 2.7. In both cases funding was obtained from a research funder (the Nuffield Foundation) for projects which were devoted to developing and testing the survey questions. We therefore had the luxury of more time and money than may be available at the start of a project where the funder's main concern is getting the survey into the field and receiving a report of findings.

Example 2.6   Developing a question on household spending

Traditionally, measures of household income have been used to measure material well-being on UK general population surveys. This has sometimes been supplemented by information about people's consumption of key material goods (which can be used to identify material deprivation). Only special expenditure surveys tend to collect information on expenditure and this is done in great depth using a long interview or a diary. Research by the Institute for Fiscal Studies has shown that, particularly at the lower end of the income distribution, the link between income and expenditure can be unexpected. They therefore wanted to develop a simple question (or questions) about household expenditure which could be asked with the other demographic questions on surveys where the main focus was a different topic such as health or lifestyles.

The resulting research project had four stages, which are listed below.

- **Focus groups** (d'Ardenne and Blake, 2012a) to explore:

  - key terms and definitions used by people when talking about spending;
  - how people group their spending into categories; and
  - how it is easiest for them to report on their spending (for example by adding up spending or by taking spending to be their income minus any savings left at the end of the month).

- **Expert review** with international collaborators, government departments running surveys of expenditure and income and the research team to explore whether the draft questions would produce data which could answer their research questions.

- **Cognitive interviewing** (two rounds) (d'Ardenne and Blake, 2012b; d'Ardenne and Blake, 2012c) to test:

  - different ways of asking about expenditure.

- **Split sample experiment** (using Understanding Society Innovation Panel) to test the two possible approaches developed so far:

  - with a larger number of participants;
  - in the context of a larger survey with other more general content.

Example 2.7   Testing questions about the use of social care services

The way in which social care services are delivered and paid for in England has been evolving, and existing survey questions did not provide enough information to fully understand the range of care services people use and how they pay for them. Therefore, academics with a special interest in social care worked with survey methodologists to develop a new set of survey questions on social care use which could be included on relevant surveys about health or older people. The methods used are described below.

- **Focus groups** with care users (Balarajan et al., 2009), to explore:
  - o how people describe the services they use;
  - o their level of understanding of care funding; and
  - o whether an initial focus on their needs or who provides the care would be most effective.

- **Key informant interviews with stakeholders** such as local authorities and private care providers to explore:
  - o what they felt the key research issues were; and
  - o how they think users understand and describe services.

- **Cognitive interviewing** (Balarajan et al., 2010):
  - o the first round tested the initial draft questions; and
  - o the second round tested the revisions that were made to the first round questions on the basis of the cognitive interview findings, explored how the complex routing worked in CAPI, and tested the questions with groups who had not been fully represented in the first round.

- **Expert Panels** were held at various points in the project:
  - o before the first round of cognitive testing;
  - o between cognitive testing rounds; and
  - o after the cognitive testing was completed to consider the final questions and how they could best be implemented on specific surveys.

- **Piloting** was then carried out on the individual surveys implementing the survey questions to see how well the questions worked in the context of each survey's questionnaire and with their respective target populations.

http://www.natcen.ac.uk/our-research/research/social-care-questions-for-over-65s/

2.4 Chapter summary

Cognitive interviewing is one of a number of pretesting methods available to you. It has strengths and limitations and to offset these it is a good idea to use a combination of pretesting methods and triangulate your results. Cognitive interviewing is not a replacement for a standard field pilot, and some form of pilot is almost always required prior to the fielding of the main survey to check that everything is working as it should.

Some pretesting methods are more complex and costly than cognitive interviewing, while others are cheaper and quicker. There are methods which can be used before cognitive interviewing or after, some of which are office-based while others involve participants.

The way in which methods are combined to test the questions on any given project will depend on the time and the budget, the skills and equipment available to the team and, importantly, the characteristics of the questions being tested and the surveys on which they will be asked.

References

Akkerboom, H. and Dehue, F. (1997) 'The Dutch model of data collection development for official surveys', *International Journal of Public Opinion Research*, 9(2): 126–45.

Ashenfelter, K.T. and Hughes, T.R. (2011) 'United States Census Bureau, results from iterative usability testing of the American Community Survey (ACS)'. Paper presented at 4th European Survey Research Association conference, Lausanne, Switzerland.

Baker, R.P., Crawford, S. and Swinehart, J. (2004) 'Development and testing of web questionnaires', in S. Presser, J. Rothgeb, M. Couper, J.T. Lessler, E. Martin, J. Martin and E. Singer (eds), *Methods for Testing and Evaluating Survey Questionnaires*. Hoboken, NJ: Wiley and Sons. pp. 361–84.

Balarajan, M., Gray, M., Blake, M., Green, S., Darton, R., Fernandez, J-L., Hancock, R., Henderson, C., Kearns, D., King, D., Malley, J., Martin, A., Morciano, M., Pickard, L. and Wittenberg, R. (2009) *Developing Social Care Questions: Findings from Qualitative Research with Service Users*. London: National Centre for Social Research. Available at: http://www.natcen.ac.uk/social-care-questions-for-over-65s

Balarajan, M., Gray, M., Blake, M., Green, S., Darton, R., Fernandez, J-L., Hancock, R., Henderson, C., Kearns, D., King, D. Malley, J., Martin, A., Morciano, M., Pickard, L. and Wittenberg, R (2010) *Cognitive Testing of Social Care Questions for People Aged 65 and Over*. Available at: http://www.natcen.ac.uk/social-care-questions-for-over-65s

Behr, D., Kaczmirek, L., Bandilla, W. and Braun, M. (2012) 'Asking probing questions in web surveys: which factors have an impact on the quality of responses?', *Social Science Computer Review*, 30(4): 487–98.

Campanelli, P. (2008) 'Testing survey questions', in E.D. de Leeuw, J.H. Joop and D. Dillman (eds), *International Handbook of Survey Methodology*. New York: Taylor and Francis Group. pp. 176–200.

Converse, J.M. and Presser, S. (1996) *Survey Questions: Handicrafting the Standardised Questionnaire*. Newbury Park, CA: Sage.

Czaja, R. and Blair, J. (1996) *Designing Surveys: A Guide to Decisions and Procedures*. Thousand Oaks, CA: Pine Forge Press.

d'Ardenne, J. and Blake, M. (2012a) *Developing Expenditure Questions: Findings from Focus Groups*, IFS Working Papers, No. W12/18.

d'Ardenne, J. and Blake, M. (2012b) *Developing Expenditure Questions: Findings from R1 Cognitive Testing*, Working Paper 12/19, Institute for Fiscal Studies. Available at: http://www.ifs.org.uk/wps/WP1219.pdf

d'Ardenne, J. and Blake, M. (2012c) *Developing Expenditure Questions: Findings from R2 Cognitive Testing*, Working Paper 12/20, Institute for Fiscal Studies. Available at: http://www.ifs.org.uk/wps/WP1220.pdf

d'Ardenne, J. and Collins, D. (2013) 'Horses for courses: why different question testing methods uncover different findings and implications for selecting methods'. Paper presented at 5th European Survey Research Association 2013 conference, Ljubljana, Slovenia.

d'Ardenne, J. and Lepps, H. (2012) *IP5 Usability Testing Summary Report*. Prepared for the Institute of Social and Economic Research, University of Essex and NatCen Social Research survey management teams.

DeMaio, T. and Rothgeb, J. (1996) 'Cognitive interviewing techniques: in the lab and in the field', in N. Schwarz and S. Sudman (eds), *Answering Questions: Methodology for Determining Cognitive and Communicative Processes in Survey Research*. San Francisco, CA: Jossey-Bass. pp. 177–95.

Eder, D. and Fingerson, L. (2003) 'Interviewing children and adolescents', in J. Holstein and J. Gubrium (eds), *Inside Interviewing: New Lenses, New Concerns*. Thousand Oaks, CA: Sage. pp. 33–53.

Fowler Jr, F.J. (1995) *Improving Survey Questions: Design and Evaluation*. Thousand Oaks, CA: Sage.

Galesic, M. and Yan, T. (2011) 'Use of eye tracking for studying survey response processes'. in M. Das, P. Ester and L. Kaczmirek (eds), *Social and Behavioural Research and the Internet*. Routledge: London. pp. 349–70.

Galesic, M., Tourangeau, R., Couper, M. and Conrad, F. (2008) 'New insights on response order effects and other cognitive shortcuts in survey responding', *Public Opinion Quarterly*, 72(5): 892–913.

Gräf, L. (2002) 'Assessing internet questionnaires: the Online Pretest Lab', in B. Batinic, U-D. Reips and M. Bosnjak (eds), *Online Social Sciences*. Gottingen: Hogrefe and Huber Publishers. pp. 49–68.

Hansen, S.E. and Couper, M. (2004) 'Usability testing to evaluate computer-assisted instruments', in S. Presser, J. Rothgeb, M. Couper, J.T. Lessler, E. Martin, J. Martin and E. Singer (eds), *Methods for Testing and Evaluating Survey Questionnaires*. Hoboken, NJ: Wiley and Sons. pp. 337–60.

Hess, J. (1995) *The Role of Respondent Debriefing Questions in Questionnaire Development.* Working Papers in Survey Methodology. 95:18. Washington DC: US Census Bureau.

Highet, K. (2003) 'Cannabis and smoking research: interviewing young people in self-selected friendship pairs', *Health Education Research*, 18(1): 108–18.

Kaminska, O. and Foulsham, T. (2013) 'Real-world eye-tracking in face-to-face, web and SAQ modes'. ISER working paper No 2013–07. Available at: https://www.iser.essex.ac.uk/publications/working-papers/iser/2013–07.pdf

Krosnick, J.A. (2011) 'Experiments for evaluating survey questions', in J. Madans, K. Miller, A. Maitland and G. Willis (eds), *Question Evaluation Methods: Contributing to the Science of Data Quality.* Hoboken, NJ: Wiley. pp. 215–38.

McGee, A. and d'Ardenne, J. (2009) *'Netting a Winner': Tackling Ways to Question Children Online. A Good Practice Guide to Asking Children and Young People about Sport and Physical Activity.* Sports Council for Wales and NatCen. Available at: www.sportwales.org.uk/media/351853/netting_a_winner_-_english.pdf

Martin, E. (2004) 'Vignettes and respondent debriefing for questionnaire design and evaluation', in S. Presser, J.M. Rothgeb, M.C. Couper, J.T. Lessler, E. Martin, J. Martin, and E. Singer (eds), *Methods for Testing and Evaluating Survey Questionnaires.* Hoboken, NJ: Wiley and Sons. pp. 149–71.

Moore, J., Bates, N., Pascale, J. and Okon, A. (2009) 'Tackling seam bias through questionnaire design', in P. Lynn (ed.), *Methodology of Longitudinal Surveys.* Chichester, England: John Wiley. pp. 76–91.

Nichols, E. and Hunter Childs, J. (2009) 'Respondent debriefings conducted by experts: a technique for questionnaire evaluation', *Field Methods*, 21: 115. Available at: http://fmx.sagepub.com/cgi/content/abstract/21/2/115

Nicolaas, G. (2011) Survey *Paradata: A Review.* London: ESRC National Centre for Research Methods Review paper.

Pascale, J. and McGee, A. (2008) 'Using behaviour coding to evaluate the effectiveness of dependent interviewing', *Survey Methodology*, 34: 2.

Presser, S., Rothgeb, J., Couper, M., Lessler, J.T., Martin, E., Martin, J. and Singer, E. (eds) (2004) *Methods for Testing and Evaluating Survey Questionnaires.* Hoboken, NJ: Wiley and Sons.

Ritchie, J. and Lewis, J. (eds) (2003) *Qualitative Research Practice.* London: Sage.

Snijkers, G. (2002) *Cognitive Laboratory Experiences on Pre-testing Computerised Questionnaires and Data Quality.* Heerlen: Statistics Netherlands. [See Table 10.2.]

Understanding Society – information on split ballot experiments can be found at https://www.understandingsociety.ac.uk/documentation/innovation-panel

van der Zouwen, J. and Smit, J.H. (2004) Evaluating survey questions by analysing patterns of behaviour codes and question-answer sequences: a diagnostic approach', in S. Presser, J. Rothgeb, M. Couper, J.T. Lessler and E. Martin, J. Martin and Singer, E. (eds), *Methods for Testing and Evaluating Survey Questionnaires*. Hoboken, NJ: Wiley and Sons. pp. 109–30.

Willis, G. (2005) *Cognitive Interviewing: A Tool for Improving Questionnaire Design*. Thousand Oaks, CA: Sage.

Willis, G.B. and Lessler, J.T. (1999) *QAS: Questionnaire Appraisal System*. Rockville, MD: RTI. Available at: http://appliedresearch.cancer.gov/areas/cognitive/qas99.pdf

PART II

HOW TO CONDUCT A COGNITIVE INTERVIEWING PROJECT

THREE

PLANNING A COGNITIVE INTERVIEWING PROJECT

JO D'ARDENNE

3.1 Introduction

The aim of this chapter is to assist you in designing, planning and carrying out a cognitive interviewing project. Project planning is important and in this chapter we discuss the main decisions and issues you should consider. Specifically, we discuss:

- When to use cognitive interviewing
- What stages you will need to consider when planning a cognitive interviewing project
- How long the overall process takes and timetabling considerations
- Who will do the interviewing
- Where the interviews should take place
- Special considerations when interviewing different groups
- Ethical issues.

3.2 When to use cognitive interviewing

Before deciding to conduct a cognitive interviewing project it is important that you have a clear rationale for why you are using this method. In this section we describe the types of information that can be collected using cognitive interviewing and why this information is important. Consider whether cognitive interviewing will provide you with evidence that will allow you to answer your research questions and whether other pretesting methods are needed, in addition to or instead of cognitive interviews (see Chapter 2, sections 2.2 and 2.3). Also bear in mind the limitations of cognitive interviewing (refer to Chapter 1, section 1.5).

3.2.1 What types of information can be collected in cognitive interviews?

Cognitive interviewing can help improve data collection instruments by providing evidence on whether participants:

- *understand* questions in the intended way (and suggesting alternative wordings if questions are misunderstood);
- are *able* to provide the requested information (and if not whether this can be overcome by changing the data collection approach);
- are *willing* to provide information (and if not how co-operation can be improved);
- can *respond* using the answer options provided (and if not refining the list of answer options available);
- find self-administered questionnaires *user-friendly*, in terms of visual appearance, placement of instructions and so on (and if not how usability can be improved).

Cognitive interviewing can form part of the questionnaire development process, helping you to develop new questions or revise existing questions to make them suitable for a particular survey context, for example for use with a different population group or use in a different survey mode (see Chapter 10). It can also be a useful method for exploring why existing questions have problems, for example why they underestimate or overestimate behaviour.

In addition to testing questionnaires, cognitive interviewing is increasingly being used as a method to test the effectiveness of other types of documents and we discuss this in Chapter 12. In this context the types of research question you can address with cognitive interviewing can be expressed more broadly as:

- Does your target audience *understand* the information provided in the intended way?
- Are your target audience *able* to act on the information provided?
- Do your target audience seem *willing* to act on the information provided?
- Is any information *missing* from the materials you have developed?
- Are your materials *user-friendly* in terms of their visual appearance and layout?

The principles outlined in this guide apply to both question-testing projects and projects where you are testing other types of written materials.

3.3 The five stages of a cognitive interviewing project

A cognitive interviewing project involves five stages. In this section we will look at each of these stages in turn and describe the factors that influence how long each stage will take.

Design and development

The design and development stage is the first part of any cognitive interviewing project. This is when all key decisions about the project are made. In the design and development stage you will need to:

- finalise the materials you are going to test and your testing objectives;
- decide *who* you are going to test questions on and how you are going to recruit people to take part – you will need to design any recruitment documents you need such as screening questionnaires or advertisements (see section 4.3 for more details);
- decide *how* you will test your questions. You will need to design your interview protocol (see Chapter 5).

The length of time required for the design and development stage will vary depending on the complexity of what you are testing and the context in which you are working. For example, if you are testing a relatively short questionnaire and you have a small number of well-defined testing objectives, designing a protocol will be relatively straightforward. However, if you hope to test multiple, long or complex sets of questions you may find the process of defining and prioritising test objectives and designing test protocols more time consuming.

If you are testing questions that have been designed by other people you will need to build in additional time to familiarise yourself with the measurement aims of the questions and the context in which the question will be used in the actual survey. If you require a supervisor or a funder to comment on the protocols you design, you will need to set aside time for this. Similarly, time should be built in to submit an ethics review application, if this is required (see section 3.9).

Recruitment

In the recruitment stage you will need to sign up people to take part in the study. The amount of time this will take will depend on the number and types of people you wish to recruit. In some cases you may have to recruit via advertising or through a gatekeeper. In these cases recruitment will take longer compared to if you have direct access to your target population (see Chapter 4 for more detail).

Fieldwork

In the fieldwork stage you will be carrying out cognitive interviews. Fieldwork may start before recruitment is complete. The length of time needed for field-work will depend on the number of people you wish to interview; how dispersed your sample is; how much variation there is in when people are willing to be interviewed; and whether you are doing all the interviews yourself or with oth-ers. If multiple interviewers are working on the project you will need to build in time for an interviewer briefing to make sure everyone understands the testing objectives and how you want the interviews carried out (see Chapter 6).

Data management

In the data management stage you will need to collate, organise and reduce all the information you have gathered into a format conducive to systematic analysis.

The length of the data management stage will vary depending on the number of interviews you have conducted and what your strategy for data management is. For example, if you are planning on getting your interviews transcribed you will need to allow time for this compared to if you plan to work from interview notes (see Chapter 7).

Analysis and reporting

The analysis and reporting stage is the final stage of a cognitive interviewing project. In the analysis and reporting stage you will review the data collected in the interviews and make recommendations based on the key findings. Depending on the context you are working in you may have to produce a formal report illustrating your research methodology and explaining the rationale behind any suggested changes. In other contexts a formal report may not be required. The length of time required for analysis and reporting will vary depending on the amount of material you are testing and the types of output you wish to produce (see Chapters 8 and 9 for further details).

3.4 Multiple rounds of cognitive interviewing

For some projects you may wish to carry out multiple rounds of cognitive inter-viewing. This may involve testing different materials at different rounds, for example because you have too much material to test in one round. Alternatively, you may want to carry out iterative testing on the same material. Under this model the original materials are tested, refined, re-tested and refined further until you are happy that the materials are as good as they can be (see Figure 3.1).

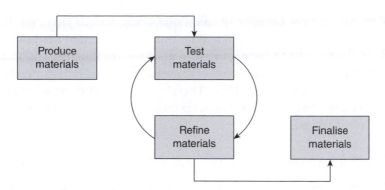

Figure 3.1   Iterative testing

There are a number of pragmatic issues to consider when deciding whether to undertake iterative testing. The most important of these is that iterative testing, in its purest form, has no set 'end date'. Testing continues until the point the researcher decides the materials can no longer be improved. Furthermore, as the number of iterations of testing is not known in advance, it is difficult to plan resources. The iterative testing process can be time-consuming because each stage of the project has to be repeated multiple times.

If you are working in a commercial research environment there can be an issue with conducting iterative testing in terms of project budgeting. For instance, you may provide costs for projects based on a set fee per interview. However, with iterative testing you cannot anticipate the number of interviews you will be conducting in advance. This makes it hard to provide information up front on how much it will cost to complete a project. For this reason commercial organisations tend not to offer completely open-ended iterative testing. Rather they will usually set a cap on the number of rounds and the number of interviews that will be conducted per round in advance of the project commencing.

If you plan to conduct multiple rounds of testing you will repeat some of the stages described above. For example, if you carry out two rounds of testing you will have to conduct two rounds of fieldwork, data management and so forth. You may also need to review and alter your testing objectives to accommodate findings from earlier rounds.

3.5 How long does it take to run a cognitive interviewing project?

The length of time it takes to complete a cognitive interviewing project is dependent on a number of factors including the ease of recruitment of the target population, the number of rounds of testing, the number of interviews to achieve in each round and the number of questions being tested. However the main driver will be *how much time is actually available*. Although, methodologically speaking, we may want to conduct testing until we are satisfied documents can no longer be improved, in practice every researcher works within practical constraints in terms of budget and time. Therefore the main thing to remember is that *some question testing is better than no testing at all and a lot can be achieved in a relatively short space of time*.

3.5.1 Timetabling cognitive interviews within the survey process

Cognitive interviewing is often a small component of a much larger project. Before you begin cognitive interviewing, you should have, at the very least, a firm idea of the aims of the survey, a working draft of the questionnaire you are going to test and a view on how the questionnaire will be administered in practice. If you are using cognitive interviewing to test something other than a questionnaire similar principles apply. For example, if you are testing a leaflet you will need a firm understanding of the aims of the leaflet, a working draft of the leaflet and an appreciation of how and when people will receive the leaflet before you begin to plan the cognitive interviewing.

When planning a cognitive interviewing project the main time constraint will be the deadline by which the materials you are testing need to be finalised. This deadline will be determined by when the final documents (questions, letters, leaflets, etc.) are needed so that the next stage of the process can start.

If the next stage is a pilot (see section 2.2.5) then you will need to allow time after the cognitive interviewing to make any changes to the questionnaire and get any paper documents printed and any computerised questionnaires programmed before pilot fieldwork starts.

TOP TIP

When designing a cognitive interviewing timetable it can be easier to work backwards from the survey launch date to work out when different test stages need to occur.

It is possible to conduct cognitive interviews at the same time as the survey pilot is being conducted. This generally occurs when the entire survey has to be completed within a short timescale and there is not enough time for the cognitive interviews to be completed prior to the pilot. In these circumstances results from both the pilot and the cognitive interviews are considered together to inform the design of the final survey questionnaire.

Cognitive interviewing can also be conducted after the survey pilot or after the main survey has taken place. This generally occurs when a particular problem has been observed (for instance, participants not answering certain questions or providing inconsistent answers) and there is a requirement to find out more about why this issue occurred and how it can be remedied before the survey takes place again. In this instance cognitive interviewing may have to be conducted within a narrow window in order for the survey fieldwork to start on time. The aims of testing in these instances are focused on trying to explain and resolve whatever problem was identified.

3.5.2 Other timetabling considerations

It's sensible to consider whether there are any events that might affect your ability to recruit and interview people in your suggested timeframe. For example, if you plan to conduct interviews in schools there will be periods when the school will be closed (half-term and school holidays). Exam periods may also be best avoided along with times when staff members are particularly busy (e.g. the start of the school year). If you are conducting interviews within businesses offices may be closed over public holidays. Similarly, certain industries may have peak seasons when they will be less willing to take part in research. Think about your research audience and try, where possible, to set fieldwork dates that will maximise the number of people who will be willing and able to take part.

3.6 Who will do the interviewing?

When planning a cognitive interviewing project you will need to decide who will conduct the interviews. In this section we discuss whether cognitive interviews should be conducted by the person who designed the materials being tested and how many interviewers may be needed to work on the project. Chapter 6 provides guidance on the skills and qualities needed to be a cognitive interviewer.

3.6.1 Should cognitive interviews be conducted by the person who designed the document being tested?

You can conduct the cognitive interviews to test the document you designed yourself and there are some advantages to doing this. For example, if you are the question designer you will know what the measurement objectives are and the rationale for the questions being the way they are. There may also be practical reasons why you would conduct the interviews yourself, for example you may not have the resources or be in a position to involve others as interviewers.

There are, however, disadvantages to testing a questionnaire you have designed yourself. You may be too close to the test material and you may not be able to distance yourself from it sufficiently during the interviews to allow participants to feel comfortable providing honest feedback, and you being the only interviewer may limit the number and geographical spread of the interviews.

3.6.2 How many interviewers should work on a cognitive testing project?

The decision as to how many interviewers will be required to work on a cognitive interviewing project will depend on the time and resources you have available. The main advantage of having multiple interviewers is that you can complete more interviews in a shorter period of time. Other benefits to involving more than one interviewer include having:

- extra 'pairs of eyes' to spot problems;
- increased flexibility over when and where interviews can take place; and
- possible cost savings, if interviewers are located close to where interviews will take place.

If multiple interviewers are working on the project you will need to ensure that interviews are carried out consistently and in accordance with the procedures you have designed. We provide guidance on how to achieve this in section 6.3.

Finally, if multiple interviewers are working on a project you should consider running a debriefing meeting once fieldwork is complete. A debriefing is a meeting attended by all interviewers and anyone involved in conducting analysis of the findings. The purpose of the debriefing is to provide an opportunity for all interviewers to present the top-level findings uncovered by their interviews prior to a more formal analysis being conducted. A debriefing also provides an opportunity for interviewers to provide feedback on how well the interview protocols worked in practice and whether they could have been improved. This feedback can help you improve your procedures in future cognitive interviewing projects.

TOP TIP

You can invite survey funders or stakeholders to the debrief, so that they can get an early taste of the issues emerging from the debrief. However, be aware that interviewers can exaggerate or give undue weight to individual comments.

3.6.3 Using survey interviewers as cognitive interviewers

Survey research organisations, like NatCen Social Research, are fortunate to have a large pool of survey (or field) interviewers who are trained in survey interviewing methods. Survey interviewers can be successfully trained to undertake cognitive interviewing projects. DeMaio and Landreth (2004) found that survey interviewers can make good cognitive interviewers so there is no reason not to consider this as an option, provided that interviewers are provided with appropriate training prior their first cognitive assignment (see section 6.2.1 for points to think about when training survey interviewers).

3.7 Where should interviews take place?

Cognitive interviews are typically conducted face-to-face (see section 10.5 for a discussion of conducting cognitive interviews by telephone). If you plan to conduct face-to-face interviews you need to consider where these should take place. Interviews should ideally be conducted in an environment that is quiet, comfortable and free from distractions. The interview should be conducted somewhere private, where there is minimal likelihood that the conversation could be overheard by people not involved in the research project. If possible the venue should be convenient for both the participant and the interviewer.

3.7.1 Naturalistic vs. controlled interview environments

There are two different approaches to interview location. One is that interviewing should take place in a naturalistic environment. By this we mean an environment that the participant is familiar with, local to, and willing to be interviewed in. This could be the participant's home, the participant's office, a school or another suitable public venue, such as a library or a community centre. The advantage of this is that participants may feel more comfortable taking part in a naturalistic environment. This could make recruitment for your study easier and, more importantly, increase the diversity of people who are willing to take part in your research. Certain groups may find the idea of taking part in an interview in an unfamiliar location off-putting.

However, the disadvantage is that, as a researcher, you have less control over a naturalistic environment. There could be other people in the proximity who compromise the privacy of the interview. There could be other potential distractions. Background noise is a particular issue as in most cases cognitive interviews need to be audio recorded. If your chosen venue is noisy you may have problems listening to your audio recordings and getting the interview transcribed. This means you will not be able to fully review the interview after it is completed. However, there are strategies that you can use to maximise control of a naturalistic setting and we discuss these in section 6.4.2.

The other approach to location is that cognitive interviewing takes place in a controlled environment. By this we mean a venue chosen by the research team that is set up to have 'ideal interview conditions'. This environment could be a meeting room or interview room. It could also be a 'laboratory' environment. Social science laboratories have specialist equipment for conducting research interviews (no white coats are required). For example, labs have equipment to assist in observational techniques such as discreet video recording or two-way mirrors. The advantage of these is that multiple researchers can (with the participant's consent) unobtrusively observe the interview. This is useful for quality control and for providing feedback as part of interviewer training. If you plan to use behavioural coding (see section 2.2.8) alongside cognitive interviewing then a lab setting can be particularly useful for undertaking 'live' coding.

The downside of controlled environments is that they could put off some people from taking part in the research. Generally speaking naturalistic environments place a lower burden on participants, as the interview takes place in a location that is more familiar and convenient for them. Conversely, controlled environments place a lower burden on researchers as you can maintain complete control over the interview environment. An additional complication is that participants may behave differently in a naturalistic environment compared to a controlled environment. For example, it is feasible that participants may take greater care completing a questionnaire if they are in a quiet environment, or if they know they are being video-recorded or observed through a two-way mirror. Therefore, another disadvantage of the controlled environment is that it is unrealistic; when people are asked to take part in a survey in real life they may be doing so in an environment with noise and distractions.

A summary of the advantages and disadvantages of naturalistic and controlled interviewer environments is shown in Figure 3.2.

	Naturalistic environment	Controlled environment
Examples	• Participant's home • Participant's workplace • Community venue	• Interview room • Laboratory
Advantages	• Convenient for participants • Easier to recruit a diverse range of people • Mimics survey context	• Quiet / distraction-free • Private • Access to specialist equipment
Disadvantages	• Less control over noise and distractions • Less control over privacy • May be impractical to use specialist equipment	• Participants could find the environment off-putting • Could impact on ease of recruiting a diverse group of people • Does not mimic survey context

Figure 3.2 Advantages and disadvantages of different interview environments

For the most part we conduct our interviews in a naturalistic environment in order to make taking part more appealing to a more diverse group of participants. A controlled environment might be preferred when specialist equipment is required to address the research aims (and it is impractical for this equipment to be used outside of a controlled environment). For example, we have conducted testing on web questionnaires that combined cognitive interviewing techniques with eye-tracking (see Chapter 12 for more details). In this case interviews were conducted in a laboratory environment as the eye-tracking equipment being used was not very portable. However, most cognitive interviewing projects do not require specialist equipment and can therefore take place in a naturalistic environment.

3.7.2 Other considerations when picking a venue

We often give participants a choice over where they wish to be interviewed (e.g. their own home or a public venue convenient to them). When letting participants decide on a venue we explain that the interview should ideally be conducted somewhere quiet and suitably private. In our experience most participants are able to pick a suitable environment provided expectations are made clear upfront. It is worth bearing in mind that different groups of participants may have different needs when it comes to selecting an interview location. For example, people who live in communal residencies (e.g. halls of residence or sheltered accommodation) may not have access to a quiet, private room in their home other than a bedroom. In these situations it may be more comfortable for both the participant and the interviewer to meet in a different location.

If you are responsible for sourcing an external venue (not the participant's home or workplace) you need to make sure participants are able to easily get to the venue. Remember that not all participants will have access to a car. Is your venue convenient to get to using public transport? You should also consider whether the venue will be accessible to the participants you are interviewing. For example, is there wheelchair or step-free access to the venue you have chosen? By considering these issues in advance you will be able to pick an appropriate venue that meets the needs of the people you are interviewing.

If you are planning to test online materials (for example a web questionnaire or a website) you need to be careful about selecting an interview venue. You cannot assume that an internet connection will be available in a participant's home and you should check this before you arrive. In addition, you should consider having an 'offline' version of the materials you want to test if this is possible. This will ensure you will still be able to conduct your interviews if internet reception is patchy or slow.

3.8 Who are you interviewing?

When planning your cognitive interviews you need to think about who will be taking part, and how you can make the interviews appropriate for your target audience. This section looks at extra considerations to keep in mind when interviewing different groups.

3.8.1 Interviewing children and young people

Questionnaire-based research with children under the age of seven is not advisable. When conducting research about young children there is a high reliance on collecting information from proxies (such as giving questionnaires to parents or teachers) or using observation methods (de Leeuw et al., 2004).

With special care, children from the age of seven can be expected to complete simple questionnaires (de Leeuw et al., 2004). Cognitive interviewing can be used to test survey questions with children and we have carried out interviews with children as young as seven (McGee and d'Ardenne, 2009). Some authors have conducted cognitive interviews with children as young as five. For example, Rebok and colleagues (2001) conducted cognitive interviews to test questions on self-reported health with children aged five to 11. They concluded from their testing that the five-year-olds did not have the language skills required to understand the questions tested, the six- to seven-year-olds varied in whether they understood questions, and the eight-year-olds did understand the key words. It should be noted that although the authors concluded that the questions they were testing were not appropriate for the five-year-old group, the cognitive interviews with this age group were useful to demonstrate the age limitations of the questions being tested.

When involving children and young people in any type of research you should pay particular attention to the following ethical issues.

- Seek consent from the child's parent, guardian or carer prior to conducting the interview.
- Explain the study in a simple way and always ask the child if they have any questions and understand what participation involves.
- Obtain informed consent from the child prior to their taking part in the research. Consent from a parent or guardian is not a replacement for consent from the child (see section 3.9).
- When interviewing younger children you need to be realistic about the amount of material you can cover as they may have shorter attention spans compared to teenagers or adults.
- You should consider having shorter interviews, including a range of short activities to help make the interviews more engaging, and allowing breaks mid-interview.
- When producing your test materials and interview protocols you will need to make sure you use child-friendly language.

- Depending on the age of the child, the interview content and the interview location you should consider whether a parent, guardian or friend should be present during the interview to put the child at ease.

3.8.2 Interviewing employees, employers and businesses

Sometimes you may be testing survey questions and other materials that are designed to be answered by people in paid work. For example, we have conducted cognitive interviews to test questions on work–life balance and employer–employee relations. To do this we needed to talk to people who worked within a variety of business sectors (e.g. retail, construction, transport) and in a range of roles, including managers and business owners.

 Many professionals have constraints on their time, and for this reason may be put off from taking part in an interview. Therefore, you will need to consider strategies that will make it easier for busy people to take part.

TOP TIP

Make participation easier for workers by offering:

- evening and or weekend interview appointments;
- to conduct interviews at the participant's place of work; and
- to conduct cognitive interviews by telephone (see section 10.5).

In some cases you may wish to test questions for use in establishment surveys. Establishment surveys collect information about businesses or organisations rather than individuals. For example they could collect information on the structure, policies, outputs or finances of businesses. We have carried out cognitive interviews with establishments to test questions that measure self-assessed economic impact (see Collins et al., 2011; McGee et al., 2009a; McGee et al., 2009b). Establishment surveys can be more complex to administer than surveys of individuals. This is because multiple people within an organisation may need to contribute in order to provide all the information requested. In addition, some of the information requested may only be accessible via company records or databases such as employee details or company accounts.

TOP TIP

Consider the following things when planning cognitive interviews for establishment surveys.

(Continued)

(Continued)

- Which person (or people) within the organisation would complete the questionnaires in practice and how will these individuals be identified? To what extent will it be possible for you to replicate the participant selection procedures in your cognitive interviews?
- Will survey participants need to check company records or databases in order to answer the survey questions? If so, how will this work in the context of the cognitive interview (if at all)?

It may be impractical to replicate the survey conditions during a cognitive interview. For example, businesses may be unwilling or unable to allow an interviewer to observe their employees accessing company files or computer systems to extract information. Therefore, it may not be possible for you to incorporate certain cognitive techniques (such as observation and think aloud) into your protocols. If this is the case you should consider the use of *hypothetical or rhetoric probes* (Willimack, 2013) to explore areas you are not able to observe or probe on directly. For example, you could ask the following.

- Would you, or someone else in your organisation, be able to provide this information if you received this questionnaire?
- How easy or difficult would it be for your company to retrieve the information requested using your existing systems?

Hypothetical probes can generate some useful information about whether or not the questionnaire would work well within the participant's organisation. However, a word of caution: participants may make inaccurate assumptions about how they would find the process. In practice the required information may be more difficult (or more easy) to extract than the participant first presumes. Therefore you should also consider collecting further information about the process retrospectively, after some participants have completed the questionnaire. This information could be collected using depth interviews or respondent debriefing techniques (refer to sections 2.2.1 and 2.2.7 respectively).

3.8.3 Interviewing people with health conditions and disabilities

Your prospective cognitive interview participants may have long-term health conditions or disabilities and you will need to ensure that your interview protocol facilitates their participation. We have conducted a number of cognitive interviewing projects that targeted people with long-term health conditions or disabilities (for example, Balarajan and Blake, 2009; Balarajan et al., 2010; and Gray et al., 2009).

People's needs vary greatly depending on their individual circumstances.

Develop a strategy that will help you establish whether you will need to make modifications to the interview protocol to facilitate the participation of prospective participants in advance of the interview taking place.

- You may need to include a question as part of recruitment questionnaire to establish this, refer to section 4.3.
- Alternatively you may want to establish this when you set up the interview, if this is not being done as part of the recruitment process.
- If the interview is taking place in a controlled setting (discussed in section 3.7.1) you will need to ensure it will be accessible.
- You may need to establish whether the prospective participant will need a helper, friend or family member present during the interview to assist them in their participation.
- Will you need the services of a signer, with specific language skills (e.g. Sign Supported English, British Sign Language or sign language in another language)?
- Will large print documents or documents in Braille be required?
- Will you need to offer breaks, or split the interview into shorter chunks that are carried out on different days?

You will need to decide what levels of support you will be able to offer based on your budget.

3.8.4 Disclosure and Barring Service checks

If you live in the UK and are planning on conducting interviews within certain groups, you may require a Disclosure and Barring Service (DBS) check (previously known as a Criminal Record Bureau/CRB check). For example, if you are planning to conduct cognitive interviews with children in schools, the school may require you to have a DBS check. Similarly, hospices, care homes, foster homes and prisons have rules about visitors who conduct work on their premises. Talk to the institutions you will be working with well in advance of conducting any interviews so you know what standards they will require and what checks you may need.

If you work within a research organisation a DBS check is recommended if your work entails *regular unsupervised* contact with children or other potentially vulnerable groups. Your employer will generally arrange this, although they will require you to authorise this and provide the required information.

Disclosure checks take time and this can vary, depending on the level of check that is required. If you require a DBS check make sure you allow adequate time for this to be processed when planning your project. The organisation you should approach to carry out these checks will vary depending on the country you reside in (see Figure 3.3 for the contact information on relevant agencies).

For further information on disclosure checks please see the resources below.

England and Wales
In England and Wales disclosure checks are processed via the Disclosure and Barring Service.

Website: www.gov.uk/disclosure-barring-service-check
Telephone: 0870 909 0811

Scotland
In Scotland disclosure checks are processed through Disclosure Scotland

Website: www.disclosurescotland.co.uk
Telephone: 0870 609 6006

Northern Ireland
In Northern Ireland disclosure checks are processed by Access NI

Website: www.nidirect.gov.uk/accessni
Telephone: 0300 200 7888

Figure 3.3 Where to get further information on disclosure checks

3.9 Ethical issues in cognitive interviewing projects

Ethical considerations should be at the heart of the design of any research project. This section provides an overview of the ethical considerations you need to consider when designing a cognitive interviewing project.

3.9.1 Gaining fully informed consent

It is important that potential participants are given enough information for them to make a *fully informed* choice on whether they wish to take part or not. You will need to think about how you describe the study to participants in a way that is meaningful and provides them with all the information they might need to make this decision.

- Always give an accurate description of the purpose of the study and what taking part involves. As part of this you should tell participants: who is conducting the research; what types of subject matter will be discussed; roughly how long the interview will take; how you will be recording the interview; and what the information collected will be used for.
- Always stress that taking part is voluntary. Participants must be told that they do not have to take part if they do not wish to. Participants should also be informed that they can skip any question they do not want to answer and can withdraw from the study at any time.

We recommend that full information is provided at both the recruitment stage (see section 4.3) and (if there is any gap between recruitment and interviewing) at the start of each interview (refer to section 6.5). We also recommend that participants are provided with some form of study information leaflet when they are recruited. This is a written document confirming the details of the study and the contact details of the research team, so recruits have a point of contact if they have any questions or if they change their mind about taking part (refer to section 4.3.1).

When designing your protocol for gaining informed consent you need to take into account the needs of your target population. The way you describe the study should be appropriate to the people you are interviewing, taking into account things like their age, language ability and cognitive ability. For example, if you plan to interview children you may need to explain the study using very simple language compared to if you are interviewing industry professionals. Different groups may want different types of information to decide if they wish to take part. You should try to pre-empt what concerns different people may have and address these in your recruitment procedures.

In some cases you may be recruiting people through third parties such as gatekeepers or recruitment agencies (see section 4.3.4). If you are recruiting via a third party you will need to carefully brief them about how you want them to describe the study to potential recruits. You should also carry out checks to see if your recruitment procedures are being adhered to. Again, it is recommended that information about the study is repeated prior to the start of each interview to ensure there have been no miscommunications during the recruitment stage.

If you work for a research organisation you may have access to a list of potential research participants (e.g. people who have taken part in a study before and who have given permission to be contacted again). In these cases you will still need to go through the consent processes described above. A general interest in being involved in more research is not sufficient to infer fully informed consent for a specific project.

Be aware that different organisations have different codes of practice in regards to collecting informed consent. For example, some organisations will ask you to collect written consent from all research participants whereas other research organisations will say verbal consent is sufficient. Make sure you are aware of your organisation's policy on this when designing your consent procedures.

3.9.2 Minimising participant burden

It is important not to make unreasonable requests of participants and to be realistic about the amount of material that can be covered in a single interview. Only collect information that is necessary for the research. Do not overburden participants by collecting more detailed information than you require.

Ideally interviews should last no more than an hour. In practice there will be some variation in interview length depending on how much your participants have to say. You should be aware of the needs of the participant and offer breaks in longer interviews if this is possible. If your interviews regularly exceed 90 minutes this indicates you are trying to investigate too much using a single protocol.

For some projects you may know in advance that the interview will cover sensitive topics. In these cases you will need to consider what steps you will take in the eventuality of a participant become uncomfortable or upset, and how you will minimise the likelihood of this occurring (see section 6.7.1 for tips on managing difficult interviewing situations). It is important to be upfront regarding what topics will be covered as part of the process of gaining informed consent. It is also important to emphasise that participants can provide as much, or as little, information as they choose. When interviewing participants on sensitive topics you may wish to re-emphasise the voluntary nature of the interview at different points throughout the interview, in addition to at the start.

You should always seek to end the interview on a positive note and direct people to sources of advice if this is appropriate, refer to section 6.8.

3.9.3 Using incentives

Depending on the context in which you are interviewing you may wish to offer incentives to people taking part in your interviews (for more information on this see section 4.5). Even when offering incentives it is important to minimise participant burden. Incentives, when used appropriately, are meant to thank people and to reimburse them for their time. They should never be used to coerce or pressurise people into taking part in an activity they would not otherwise engage in. If you are using incentives you should make it clear to participants that they are under no obligation to take part and that they can skip any questions they would prefer not to answer. Alternatives to cash incentives should be considered if you are interviewing groups where having cash may increase vulnerability (e.g. active substance abusers or problem gamblers).

3.9.4 Preserving confidentiality and anonymity

It is important that you always maintain participant confidentiality. The identity of participants (and people who are approached to take part during recruitment) should be protected throughout the research process. Names, contact details and any information that could potentially identify people should be stored securely. Only people who are working on the research project, and who need to know this information as part of their assigned role, should be able to view this information. For more details on how to store data safely please refer to section 7.8 on data security.

Details that could potentially identify participants should not be included in any report, presentation or other output you produce. Participants' identities should only be shared with sponsors or clients if participants have given their consent for this information to be passed on. The information provided by people should only be used for the purposes you have described in your consent procedures. People's contact details should not be kept after the project completion date unless, again, participants have given their explicit consent to be contacted again in the future.

3.9.5 Protecting interviewers

In addition to considering how you will protect participants you also need to think about steps you can take in order to protect interviewers working on your project. Interviewers need to be supported and made aware of what procedures they should follow in regards to their own safety and well-being. Section 6.9 provides more details about interviewer safety.

3.9.6 Ethical review boards

Many academic and professional research institutions require research projects to be submitted to an ethics review board before the project can start. A cognitive interviewing project is no exception to this. Make sure you are familiar with the procedures in place at your organisation with regards to ethical reviews and what information they may require from you in order to make a decision on your application for approval. For example, will they want to see copies of proposed recruitment documents and interview protocols? When planning your cognitive interviewing project ensure you allow sufficient time for this process.

3.10 Chapter summary

Before deciding to conduct a cognitive interviewing project it is important that you have a clear rationale for why you are using this method. Once you have decided on your research aims there are a number of practical issues you need to consider.

- There are five stages to a cognitive interviewing project (design and development, recruitment, fieldwork, data management and analysis). You will need to consider how much time you have and what resources are at your disposal when planning each stage of the project. The length of time it takes to complete a cognitive interviewing project is variable. Some form of testing is better than no testing at all.
- You will need to decide who will conduct the interviews. You may want to carry out all the interviewing yourself or involve others in the process. There are pros and cons for both options but your decision will largely be driven by the resources and time you have available.

- You will need to decide where the interviews will take place. You can either opt for a naturalistic environment (such as the participant's home) or a controlled environment (such as a laboratory). There are advantages and disadvantages to both approaches.
- Different groups may have different needs when it comes to taking part in an interview. You need to think about who will be taking part and how you can make the interviews appropriate and accessible for your target audience. If you live in the UK and are planning on conducting interviews within certain groups, you may require a Disclosure and Barring Service (DBS) check prior to fieldwork commencing.
- You will need to consider ethical issues in advance of conducting your research. This includes how you will gain informed consent, how you will minimise participant burden and how you will maintain participant confidentiality. You will also need to consider interviewer safety. A submission to an ethics review board may be required and you should allow sufficient time for this when planning your project.

References

Balarajan M. and Blake M. (2009) *Community Mental Health Survey Developing Survey Questions for Mental Health Service Users: Findings from the Cognitive Interviews*. Working Paper prepared for Care Quality Commission. Available at: www.nhssurveys.org/survey/931

Balarajan, M., Gray, M., Blake, M., Green, S., Darton, R., Fernandez, J.-L., Hancock, R., Henderson, C., Kearns, D., King, D. Malley, J., Martin, A., Morciano, M., Pickard, L. and Wittenberg, R. (2010) *Cognitive Testing of Social Care Questions for People Aged 65 and Over*. NatCen Working Paper. Available at: www.natcen.ac.uk/social-care-questions-for-over-65s

Collins, D., Balarajan, M. and Bryson, A. (2011) *Survey Questions for Impact Evaluations which Rely on Beneficiaries Self-assessment: Evidence and Guidance*. London: Department for Business, Innovation and Skills.

DeMaio, T.J. and Landreth, A. (2004) 'Do different cognitive interview techniques produce different results?', in S. Presser, J.M. Rothgeb, M.P. Couper, J.T. Lessler, E. Martin, J. Martin and E. Singer (eds), *Methods for Testing and Evaluating Survey Questionnaires*. Hoboken, NJ: Wiley. pp. 89–108.

de Leeuw, E., Borgers, N. and Smits, A. (2004) 'Pretesting questionnaires for children and adolescents', in S. Presser, J.M. Rothgeb, M.P. Couper, J.T. Lessler, E. Martin, J. Martin and E. Singer (eds), *Methods for Testing and Evaluating Survey Questionnaires*. New York: John Wiley & Sons. pp. 409–430.

Gray, M., Cripps, H. and Johal, A. (2009) *British Social Attitudes Survey – Attitudes Towards the Rights of Disabled People: Findings from Cognitive Interviews*. London: Department for Work and Pensions, Research Report No 588. Available at: http://webarchive.nationalarchives.gov.uk/20130314010347/http://research. dwp.gov.uk/asd/asd5/rports2009–2010/rrep588.pdf

McGee, A. and d'Ardenne, J. (2009) 'Netting a Winner': Tackling Ways to Question Children Online. A Good Practice Guide to Asking Children and Young People about Sport and Physical Activity. Sports Council for Wales and NatCen. Available at: www.sportwales.org.uk/media/351853/netting_a_winner_-_english.pdf

McGee, A., Andrews, F., Legard, R. and Collins, D. (2009a) Self-assessment as a Tool to Measure the Economic Impact of BERR Policies: Findings from Stage One Cognitive Testing. London: Department for Business, Innovation and Skills.

McGee, A., Andrews, F. and Legard, R. (2009b) Self-assessment as a Tool to Measure the Economic Impact of BERR Policies: Findings from Stage Two Cognitive Testing. London: Department for Business, Innovation and Skills.

Rebok, G., Riley, A., Forrest, C., Starfield, C., Green, B., Robertson, J. and Tambor, E. (2001) 'Elementary school-aged children's reports of their health: a cognitive interviewing study', Quality of Life Research, 10(1): 59–70.

Willimack, D.K. (2013) 'Methods for the development, testing and evaluation of data collection instruments', in G. Snijkers, G. Haraldsen, J. Jone and D.K. Willimack (eds) Designing and Conducting Business Surveys. Hoboken, NJ: John Wiley.

FOUR

SAMPLING AND RECRUITMENT
DEBBIE COLLINS AND MICHELLE GRAY

4.1 Introduction

The aim of this chapter is to provide you with a guide to designing a suitable sampling and recruitment strategy for your cognitive interviewing project. It identifies the decisions you will need to make and the factors you will need to consider in making those decisions. Sample design is crucial in ensuring that questions are adequately tested. It is important to clearly establish early on in the design process the types of people you need to test your questionnaire or questions with, before actually going out and recruiting your participants (Gobo, 2004).

In this chapter we:

- Describe the sampling approach used in cognitive interviewing – that of purposive sampling – and discuss how to design a purposive sample
- Look at how to define your sample population, develop and prioritise your sampling criteria and set quotas
- Discuss the practicalities of recruitment, looking at six commonly used recruitment strategies
- Set out the kinds of recruitment documents you may need
- Discuss the use of incentives.

4.2 Sampling for cognitive interviews

The goal when designing a sample for a cognitive interviewing study is to ensure that the test questions are fully evaluated. In practice this means recruiting participants who reflect the target population for which the questions are designed and ensuring that your sample includes a variety of different kinds of participants. We are not attempting to design a statistically representative sample, rather we use purposive sampling methods to capture this diversity and the rest of this section sets out how this is achieved.

4.2.1 Purposive sampling

Cognitive interviewing is a qualitative technique (see section 1.5) and typically studies involve relatively small numbers of participants (from fewer than 10 to 50 or more), who are purposively selected. Purposive or criterion sampling, as the name suggests, is about deliberately selecting particular types of people who 'represent' the characteristics of interest to your research objective(s) in a qualitative sense (Bryman, 2012; Ritchie et al., 2003). Example 4.1 illustrates how a purposive sample design might be used in a cognitive test of health questions.

Example 4.1   Purposive sample design

Your study involves testing questions to be asked on a general health survey. In designing a purposive sample one of the key characteristics you would want to include is some form of proxy indicator for general health, such as whether or not participants have a long-term health condition. Another characteristic you would probably want to include is age; it may be that your age influences how you answer certain questions (levels of physical activity, for example). Included within the test questionnaire are a number of items which relate to smoking, which indicates that you would probably want to select participants who vary in their smoking behaviour or habits.

The characteristics or criteria you choose to purposively select on are important for two reasons. Firstly, they ensure that all key characteristics of relevance to the way the questions could be interpreted and answered by the survey's target population are covered. Secondly, they ensure diversity within the sample so that differences in interpretation can be explored. So in the case of our survey of general health, we might want to explore whether questions are being consistently understood across all participants – those with and without health conditions and those with different smoking behaviours. In addition, we may wish to assess this within and between age groups (the age groups reflecting those that may be used in the analysis and reporting of the survey data) so that we can assess the validity of answers obtained.

In the next section we look further at how to define the sampling criteria.

4.2.2 Defining the sample population and sampling criteria

The **first step** in designing your purposive sample is to define the population of interest. The starting point is to think about who the questions will be asked of in the survey itself. For example, the survey might collect information about people's income and expenditure from adults, aged 18 and over, living in private households. However, the questions you are testing are about the cost of childcare, and are asked only of parents or guardians of dependent children (aged 0–17) who live with them as part of their household. It is this group who are the population of interest.

Once you have defined your population of interest, the **next step** is to review the aims of the cognitive interviewing. The sample design needs to help you meet those aims. Thinking of the childcare costs example, one aim might be to check that the questions work for all the kinds of childcare arrangements participants might have. If the questions do not cover all arrangements then this will cause problems for participants.

The **third step** is to consider if there are likely to be differences within the survey population that will affect how participants will go about answering the questions. If the answer to this is 'yes', it will be important for your sample to reflect this diversity. So thinking about the childcare questions again, childcare costs will vary depending on:

- the number of children parents have;
- the age of those children; and
- the type of childcare used (formal or paid vs. informal or free childcare).

In testing questions designed to collect information on childcare you would therefore need to ensure that the questions were tested with parents who:

- have different numbers of dependent children;
- have children of different ages (0–4, 5–10 and 11–17); and
- use different childcare providers (e.g. day nurseries, child minders, after school clubs, grandparents, etc.).

But how do you know which participant characteristics to use as sampling criteria in your purposive design? Sometimes you will know this because you are testing questions where there is already data – quantitative or qualitative – that can tell you how people's answers might vary. This evidence may come from:

- the literature, or pre-existing knowledge, on the topic of interest which may point to reasons why certain participant characteristics, or subgroups, should be included within the sample;
- feedback from survey interviewers or participants that suggests that (similar) questions do not perform as well with particular subgroups of the survey population. This feedback might come from interviewer or participant debriefing, see section 2.2.7; or
- findings from secondary analysis of survey data, which indicate that response patterns vary across subgroups (e.g. that parents of pre-school children use fewer types of childcare provider than those with school-age children).

In other cases you may need to make an educated guess, thinking through the kinds of characteristics that could have a bearing on how the test questions are understood or answered. And of course sampling criteria may also reflect the different versions of questions that you are testing. For example, you may be testing two different versions of the same question to assess whether they are understood in the same way. The question version is a criterion and you will need to ensure you undertake a sufficient number of interviews with each version. We discuss how to estimate the number of interviews needed in section 4.2.3.

When thinking about the different types of participant you need to include when testing all your questions, you can quickly end up with a long list of sampling criteria. The more sampling criteria you have, however, the more complex recruitment will become and the scale of the project can become unmanageable if too many criteria are given equal priority (Ritchie et al., 2003). To guard against this it is almost always necessary to prioritise sampling criteria.

TOP TIP

- Start by going through each sampling criterion, critically thinking about why you want to include it and if it is really needed.
- Go back to the aims of the cognitive interviewing and the evidence sources which informed your initial list of sampling criteria (see above) and think about which are essential and which are nice to have.

This process of prioritisation will help you to identify your primary and secondary sampling criteria. It is at this point that you can start to set quotas. Quotas are the number of interviews you wish to achieve with each type of participant in your purposive sample (i.e. parents of pre-school-aged children) and are discussed in more detail in the next section). Example 4.2 describes how you might go about developing your list of sampling criteria, using the example of a study of lone parents and barriers to work.

Example 4.2 Developing sampling criteria

You have been asked to test some questions designed to measure the barriers lone parents face in entering or re-entering paid work. The target population for the survey questions is lone parents with dependent children (aged 0–15 and 16–17 in full-time education). However, you need to think about what kinds of lone parents to include in the test. You conduct a cursory review of the literature and this indicates the following.

- Lone parents who have worked before having children are more likely to work again after having them than those who have never worked.
- Those with lower levels of educational attainment are less likely to (re-) enter the labour market after having their children than those with higher levels of attainment.
- Those with pre-school children are less likely to (re-)enter the labour market than those with older children.

(Continued)

(Continued)

Your sampling criteria might therefore include lone parents with differing labour market participation histories (those who have never worked, and those who have worked prior to having children); educational attainment levels (using the proxy of age left compulsory full-time education for simplicity or a more sophisticated breakdown if necessary); and age of the youngest child (see Collins et al., 2006).

4.2.3 Setting quotas and determining sample size

Now you have defined your sample population, listed and prioritised the sampling criteria, the next step is to consider the number of individual quotas to set, which will in turn help you decide on how many interviews to carry out. In an ideal world you would not set a pre-specified limit on the number of interviews to be achieved. Instead you would set out to keep interviewing until you observe the same problems occurring over and over again *but* where you are not finding any new discoveries – i.e. data saturation has been reached (Bryman, 2012; Guest et al., 2006). It is also worth noting that research suggests that a larger number of interviews may produce more stable occurrences of the number of individual problems across the sample when compared with a smaller number of interviews (Blair and Conrad, 2011). Whilst in practice, for reasons we go on to discuss, it may not always be feasible to interview a large number of participants, it is worth noting that a small sample may fail to detect all potential problems with a question, and this is a criticism of the method, see section 1.5.

In practice, there will be a number of factors that will impact on the size of your sample.

a) *The number of selection criteria* (or quotas) will determine how large your sample needs to be. In general, the more quotas there are, the larger the sample will need to be.
b) *What the budget will allow for.* It is likely that you will need to specify upfront how many interviews you intend to do, so that the total cost can be calculated.
c) There may be a limit set on resources in terms of *available research staff*, and in particular interviewers, meaning you would not want to set your overall number of interviews to achieve too high.
d) *Who the questions are asked of?* Are some the test questions only to be asked in certain circumstances, meaning that some questions are not asked of everyone? If this is the case, you will need to ensure that you include adequate numbers of participants in such circumstances so as to ensure that those questions are properly tested.
e) *The time available* will often define how many interviews can take place, especially if a pilot is planned and there is a desire to use the findings from cognitive interviews in finalising the pilot questionnaire.

So what is an adequate sample size? A useful starting point is to consider whether you want any of your quotas to be 'interlocked' or 'nested'. Interlocking quotas involves linking the sampling criteria and stipulating that a certain number of interviews need to be obtained within each quota cell – a cell being a group of people with specific characteristics. For example, each interlocking quota could stipulate that a certain number of the total number of interviews with adults aged 18 and over must be carried out with men aged 18 to 24 years.

An alternative to interlocked quotas is to have parallel quotas: those which are not linked in any way. Using the same example, you might just specify that a certain number of interviews need to be with men and a certain number of interviews need to be with people aged 18–24.

4.2.4 Interlocked quota sample design

Let's start by looking at interlocked quotas and consider Example 4.1 – testing questions for a general health survey. In this example it is reasonable to suppose that people's rating of their general health and well-being is likely to vary by age and presence of a long-term health condition. So you may want to ensure that you capture this diversity in your cognitive interviews. Using three binary criteria that are interlocked – gender (male, female), age (18–64 and 65 and over) and long-standing health condition status (with and without) – eight quotas are produced:

a) men aged 18–64 with a health condition;
b) men aged 18–64 without a health condition;
c) men aged 65+ with a health condition;
d) men aged 65+ without a health condition;
e) women aged 18–64 with a health condition;
f) women aged 18–64 without a health condition;
g) women aged 65+ with a health condition;
h) women aged 65+ without a health condition;

You need to decide how many interviews will be needed in total. One way to do this is to start by considering how many interviews should be conducted within each quota (e.g. how many with men aged 18–64 with a health condition, and so on). This will be influenced by several factors: the likely diversity within that quota group; ease of finding and recruiting such participants; and time and money available for the study. By thinking about the number of interviews to conduct within each quota you will be able to come up with a total number of interviews. Let's look at how you can do that.

4.2.5 Sample matrix for interlocked quotas

An effective way to check that your proposed interlocked quota design is practical and fit for purpose is to draw a sample matrix. The sample matrix is a table, containing the primary sampling criteria. Each cell represents the number of interviews planned for that quota.

By thinking through how many interviews you need to do in each interlocked quota (cell) you will also establish how many interviews you need in total for the project. Figure 4.1 illustrates the sample matrix for testing questions with participants for the general health survey (Example 4.1).

Men				Women			
18–64		65+		18–64		65+	
With health condition	Without health condition	With health condition	Without health condition	With health condition	Without health condition	With health condition	Without health condition
8	10	10	10	8	10	10	10

Figure 4.1 Sample matrix for interlocked quotas for general health survey testing

The likelihood, as we mentioned above, of finding younger women and men with long-term health conditions is low as such conditions are rarer among this age group, so in this case you may decide, for practical reasons, to do fewer interviews with these groups. Your design means that you will carry out 76 interviews in total. At this point you may want to step back and reflect on whether you have sufficient resources and budget to conduct this scale of testing. Is this level of interlocking necessary? If an aim of your testing is to explore whether different subgroups understand the test questions in the same way then your answer will be 'yes'. You then need to ask yourself whether you feel confident that your quota cell sizes are sufficiently large enough to cover the diversity in the target population. If the answer is 'no' then you may need to increase the target number of interviews in each quota cell. Alternatively, if you have insufficient resources you may need to reconsider the aims of your test. Can you reduce the number of groups you compare, for example, and so reduce the number of interlocked quotas you need? There is a degree of subjectivity around how many interviews is 'enough' when the option of interviewing until data saturation is reached is not possible, so be guided by what you know about the target population and the factors that might influence their answers to your test questions.

Even if your resources limit the scale of interviewing you can undertake; interlocking quotas can be a good way to ensure you interview a variety of people.

4.2.6 Parallel or non-interlocked sample designs

It does not always make sense to interlock quotas, for example when you have to make an educated guess about what the sampling criteria should be, when you are uncertain about how easy it will be to find certain subgroups or when subgroup analysis is not required. In these circumstances the process of determining the total number of cognitive interviews to undertake is often driven by practical constraints – chiefly time and money. Let's think about Example 4.2 – the barriers to work questions for lone parents. You may decide that the priority sampling criteria are labour market participation history, educational attainment levels and age of youngest child. You may also decide that you want to ensure the sample reflects minority ethnic groups since you suspect that patterns might differ accordingly.

You decide that you don't want to interlock quotas but you want to specify the diversity that needs to be achieved in terms of number of interviews with different types of people within the survey population. Figure 4.2 shows how your sample matrix might look.

Main sampling criteria	Quotas Of your 20 interviews, you will interview	Quota Cell Ref
(A) Labour market history	**10** lone parents who have never worked	A1
	10 who worked prior to children	A2
(B) Education	**10** lone parents who left school at or before 16	B1
	10 who left school at 17+	B2
(C) Age of youngest child	**At least 6** lone parents whose youngest child is under 6	C1
	At least 6 whose youngest child is aged 6–10 years	C2
	At least 6 whose youngest child is 11+	C3

Figure 4.2 Example of a sample matrix for parallel, non-interlocked, quotas

Source: Collins et al. 2006.

Note that in the non-interlocked design, shown in Figure 4.2, the main sampling criteria are independent of each other. So a lone parent might fit in quota cells A1, B2 and C3; she has never worked, left school at 17 and her youngest child is 12, for example. The number of interviews to achieve with lone parents with youngest children of different ages is specified as a minimum number to achieve. This ensures you will obtain a good mix but provides some flexibility in recruitment, which will make the recruitment task a bit easier.

Pros and cons of interlocked and parallel quotas

Interlocking quotas can make the task of recruitment more specific and focused, and can also ensure that you have enough participants with certain characteristics to carry out subgroup analysis. Parallel quota samples, on the other hand, can only ensure that a certain number of interviews are carried out overall for each sampling criterion. Consider the general health survey example (Example 4.1). You might interlock age, gender and health condition and set a target number of interviews to achieve in each quota cell (10 interviews with women, aged 65 and over with a long-standing health condition, for example). Alternatively you could use a parallel quota design, where you set broader targets, such as 10 interviews with people with a long-standing illness, who could be either male or female of any age. You could set separate, independent targets for the number of interviews to achieve with men and women, and for different age groups. With the parallel design there is a risk that you might end up with rather homogenous quotas. For example, the people recruited to your long-standing health conditions quota are (almost) all 65 years of age and over; long-standing illness being more common among this age group. There is a risk in this situation that not all potential problems with the questions will be identified because your sample does not include younger people with long-standing illnesses, for example. The circumstances of young people with long-standing illness and the nature of those illnesses might, for example mean that they interpret the test questions differently to the older people in your sample.

Whilst interlocking quotas have their benefits, they can easily result in a difficult recruitment task. If you set out to recruit a set number of participants who fit particular quota cells (males, aged 18–24, with long-term health conditions for example), you can end up investing lots of time and effort to find such people. It is also essential to consider whether you are likely to find adequate numbers of people fitting a particular quota cell. For instance, you are likely to have difficulty if you set yourself the task of finding specific types of younger participants with long-term health conditions since such people, in the wider population, are rarer. You'll need to use your judgement and decide if interlocking (all) quotas is practical and necessary.

In summary, when deciding on the size of your sample there are a number of issues that should be taken into account. These are listed below.

- *Who the questions are asked of* – You need to ensure that all the questions you want to test will be asked of your test participants. Consider the questionnaire's navigational rules when designing your sample and make sure your sample contains enough people with different characteristics to ensure all your questions are tested.
- *The number of selection criteria (quotas)* – The more quotas there are, the larger the sample should be.
- *The budget and resources available* – Sample size will depend on how much money is available for cognitive interviewing in the budget. Factors to bear in mind are how easy or difficult it will be to recruit participants, who will be doing the interviews and their availability.
- *Whether to interlock or have parallel quotas* – This will depend to some extent on the aims of your test. Consider how rare your quota groups are and therefore how easy or difficult they will be to recruit.

4.2.7 Other factors affecting sample design

Geographical coverage

You need to consider where your testing is going to take place. For example, is it adequate and efficient to do the testing all in one location or area, or is geographical spread necessary and/or desirable? This decision, in part, will be influenced by whether you feel there is any geographical component to the diversity you want to include, for example testing questions about access to certain health services where you know there are urban/rural differences. Other factors will also help you make your decision around where the interviews will take place. How feasible is it to send interviewers to interview people in different areas for example, (time, budget and interviewer availability will determine this) and which recruitment strategy or strategies (see section 4.3) are being used?

Reserve sample

Think about whether you will need a reserve sample, so that you can replace prospective participants who drop out. You will need to estimate the number of reserve cases you will need. The types of participants you are aiming to interview will shape your decision.

TOP TIP

In our experience we would advise including at least three or four reserves: more if your target population are particularly busy and likely to break appointments.

4.3 Recruitment

Having decided on the sampling criteria (the chosen characteristics you will include), set your quotas (interlocked or parallel) and decided on your sample size (so you know how many people you will aim to interview), the next step is to establish how you will find people to interview.

TOP TIP

Allow plenty of time for recruitment as in our experience it can be one of the most time-consuming stages of the project.

There are a number of different recruitment methods you could adopt: the one you choose will depend on the types of participants you need and the resources you have available. The most commonly used recruitment methods are listed below:

- face-to-face recruitment;
- snowballing or chain sampling;
- using advertisements – posters, flyers, email adverts, postings on social media and online forums;
- recruiting via organisations or groups;
- the use of recruitment agencies;
- using a pre-existing sampling frame or panel of participants.

You may use one or a combination of different recruitment methods to find suitable and eligible participants for cognitive interviews. Although you and/or the research team will ultimately design the recruitment strategy, you may well involve others to actually carry out the task, for example a third party recruitment agency. Where there is a need to involve others in this process, it will be important to ensure that they are well briefed to carry out the exercise correctly, appropriately, and within the allocated time. To help you decide which recruitment method(s) you will use, the next section outlines the six methods shown above and discusses some of the strengths and weaknesses of each approach.

4.3.1 Direct recruitment

This method of recruitment covers all approaches whereby people are recruited to take part in cognitive interviews, face-to-face, by telephone, SMS or email. The recruiter could be you, other members of your research team or other people assisting with the task, for example representatives from a recruitment agency (see section 4.3.6). Direct recruitment involves:

- approaching prospective participants;
- providing an initial, brief introduction about the study and the recruitment task.

A short questionnaire (often referred to as a 'screening questionnaire') is used to collect information about people, which establishes eligibility and, if people meet the sampling requirements for the study, fill quotas. There are two main ways you can approach people using face-to-face recruitment:

- knocking on doors; and,
- having a physical presence at a location where you expect to find potential participants, for example within a shopping centre, outside a museum or in the cafeteria at a university campus.

The face-to-face recruitment method you use will very much depend on what kinds of people you are trying to find. You need to think about *where* you are likely to come across the right kinds of people, without going to too much effort or spending more time than is necessary.

Going door to door is effective when your sampling criteria are fairly uncomplicated, for example, and you need to interview a mix of men and women from different ages, with some that work and some that don't. Where you are using door knocking as a means of finding potential participants, you can use local area data to give you more information about the kinds of households that reside in certain areas. This will help you target your recruitment in areas which are already known to contain the kinds of people you are looking for, for example families with young children or people from certain ethnic minority groups. However, if the sampling criteria are more specific then a more targeted approach to recruitment may be more efficient. For example, if you want to recruit people actively looking for work you might want to stand outside Jobcentres rather than going door-to-door.

Whichever way you decide to approach people, you will need to introduce yourself and explain what the study is about, who it is for and what taking part involves. It is good practice to also give people an information leaflet (refer to section 6.8).

Having established that people are willing to answer your screening questions, the next step is to ask the questions so that you can establish their eligibility. This is usually done using a *screening questionnaire*.

Screening questionnaires

This questionnaire should be short and succinct, so as to not put off prospective participants from participating in the study. Think carefully about the questions you use. Are they similar to any of the questions you will be testing? If so, is there any risk that in asking the screening questions this might influence the way in which people respond to the test questions? If the answer is 'yes' you may need to ask a different kind of screening question. Also, consider whether your screening questions will make it obvious what kinds of participants you are looking for. Will this risk biasing your recruitment, for example, because people think you are only interested in speaking to certain kinds of people when actually you want to speak to a wide range? In addition, consider what information you will be able to collect as part of the screening process.

- What information do you need to collect to identify the people you want to include in the test and to fill your quotas?
- Can this information be collected directly from your target population or will you need to involve a gatekeeper (such as a parent or carer)?
- Can this information be collected easily, in a few simple questions?
- Can it be collected in an appropriate way from people who have been stopped on the street or who are stood on the doorstep?

Follow good questionnaire design principles when writing your screening questions. You may need to use show cards, if response options to your screening questions are long, for example, or the questions are asking for potentially sensitive information.

Informed consent is usually obtained once someone has been 'screened in', i.e. you or whoever is doing the face-to-face recruitment has identified them as someone who is eligible to take part.

Screening questionnaires are often used to establish eligibility across a range of recruitment methods, not just in direct recruitment.

Gaining agreed access to carry out face-to-face recruitment

Whilst you do not need agreement from anyone to approach people for your study by knocking on doors, it can be useful to inform the authorities (for example, local police, or housing estate managers) that you will be working in the area and provide them with information about the study.

TOP TIP

Ensure recruiters carry photographic identification with them that contains information on their affiliation and that they can provide members of the public with a telephone number that they can call to check their bona fides.

If you plan to undertake recruitment in public spaces such as shopping centres or outside schools or colleges you will need to check if you require permission. Allow time for this.

4.3.2 Snowballing or chain sampling

This method involves asking participants who have already been recruited and/or interviewed to identify other people they know who might fit the sampling criteria. The sample appears to grow like a rolling snowball. Snowballing, or chain sampling, is a useful approach to implement when you need to find quite specific, or even hidden, populations. Snowballing can be very effective but it relies on the motivation of already recruited participants to be the main engine for recruitment. Consider whether you have enough time to enable your sample to grow via the snowballing approach.

We tend to use snowballing as a supplementary approach to the main recruitment method. For example, we have used it to supplement doorstep screening to recruit parents of children aged 11–15 years and we have used it in addition to advertisements (see section 4.3.3) to recruit people who gamble.

When snowballing is used, it is essential that you think about *how* new recruits will be put into contact with you. It is often inappropriate, for example, for already recruited participants to simply provide you with the contact details of potential new participants. Instead you could arrange for an information leaflet to be passed on to potential participants, which sets out what the study is about and provides contact details so that they can express their interest in taking part (opt in) or gain further information about the study. It's also important to consider what implications there may be for participant confidentiality if you are asking participants to help with snowballing. Will the act of telling others about the study reveal information about their own circumstances, for example that they have a long-term health condition?

Steps usually need to be taken to ensure that the sample includes a diverse range of participants, reflecting the heterogeneity of the target population so that you don't end up recruiting people who are very similar to each other. One strategy is to ask participants to recruit people who are in some way different to themselves but who still meet the sampling criteria (Ritchie et al., 2003). This is often achieved by asking the original participant to ask someone he or she knows to recruit a new participant, who is not an immediate friend or family member of either the original participant or the recruiter.

It is essential that you explain the study to all new recruits, even if they may have received an information leaflet. This will ensure they understand the study and what taking part involves and have not been coerced. Their eligibility should also be checked before they are recruited, using a screening questionnaire.

4.3.3 Advertisements

Sometimes the groups you are looking for can be recruited by the use of advertisements. Advertisements can be physical: posters put up on notice boards of local libraries, for example, or in other places where they may catch people's eye; distributing leaflets or flyers; or advertising in newspapers and newsletters. Advertisements can also be virtual (i.e. online), for example advertising on websites, online forums that are used by people in particular circumstances (pregnant women, for example) or via social media. Advertisements can be a useful way to recruit very specific groups. For example, we had huge success recruiting transgender people using online advertisements, but that success was in part because we knew that transgender communities have a strong online presence. When choosing *where* you will advertise, think about who will be excluded if you use particular media – people who don't use the library or pregnant women who are not online and participating in mother and baby forums, for example. These people are likely to have different characteristics. How will you ensure that your sample includes these people? What additional recruitment strategies will be needed?

Your advertisement should contain:

- a succinct description of the project;
- who you are looking for;
- what taking part involves;
- how the data will be used;
- how, and by what deadline, to get in contact with the research team.

Use good design principles when designing your advertisements. The language and presentation of the advertisement should be tailored to the population you are hoping to attract. Including the research funder's logo or survey branding can give credibility to the advert. A free phone number and/or a study email address are helpful as it makes it easier for would-be recruits to get in touch.

If you plan to advertise at specific venues, you will need to gain permission from the venue (or its head office). If you have a very limited budget, and if the population is general and unspecific, you might want to consider advertising amongst people you may know (for example, your fellow students or work colleagues). Be mindful, however, that you are going to risk interviewing very similar kinds of people if you choose this route.

Again, as with previously discussed methods, you will probably want to use a screening questionnaire to check whether people who respond to your advert are eligible, to help you fill your quotas and to check where they live. This last point is important because your advertisement may be seen by people who are outside the geographical area(s) your cognitive interviewing study is covering.

It is also important to be aware that by using advertisements to recruit test subjects you may be recruiting more motivated and articulate participants than if you used another method. Depending on the purpose of the test, this may or may not be an issue.

4.3.4 Recruitment via organisations or groups

Sometimes you may want to recruit specific people who are members or users of, or affiliated with, particular groups, organisations or services. For example, if you were testing questions about satisfaction with and costs of social care you could contact local support groups for carers and/or local support services to ask for their assistance.

If you are going to involve organisations or groups in the recruitment process then there are a number of steps you will need to take.

- You need to get their permission to help you. You will need to identify the right person to speak to who can make that decision and provide them with information about the study and what exactly you would need their staff/volunteers to do (e.g. put up posters, pass on details of those interested to you). This may involve you liaising with various intermediaries and the decision may need to be referred to a board of trustees and/or ethics panel for approval.

TOP TIP

A face-to-face meeting with the right person within the organisation or group early on can be useful to help get them on board.

- You may be required to provide copies of the recruitment materials, and organisations may make their participation conditional on you making changes to your recruitment strategy and/or documents. You will need to consider whether such changes can be accommodated.
- You may be required to provide funding, in the form of a donation, to cover the costs incurred to the organisation in helping you with recruitment.
- Once you have approval you may need to brief individual staff who will be under-taking the recruitment, for example staff at individual sites. Be aware that organisa-tions may be staffed by volunteers and people might not necessarily always be around.

Whilst organisations or groups can be a resource for helping you to meet your recruitment goals there are a few points to consider.

- The organisation/group may want to influence the research design. Think about to what extent this may be possible.
- The organisation/group may suggest certain individuals for you to interview, for example people they class as helpful or willing. Whilst this could save you time, this could compromise your recruitment. Think about how you can ensure a wide variety of people are included in your study.
- Think about how you will ensure that recruits do not feel pressured into taking part just because they have been identified as people who might be happy to help. You will still need to gain informed consent from would-be participants.

4.3.5 Pre-existing sampling frames and recruitment panels

Using a pre-existing sample frame can be a very efficient recruitment method because you potentially already know at least some information about the people you are going to approach. At the very least you should have their name and contact details as without this you will be unable to make contact. However, in some situations you could be fortunate enough to know more about the people on the list: their age; benefits they are in receipt of; health problems and condi-tions that they have, for example. Pre-existing sampling frames are useful, if not essential, if your task is to interview a very specific group, such as people par-ticipating in a particular government training scheme.

Pre-existing sampling frames may include **administrative records** (such as benefits records, doctors' surgery lists, recipients of a particular grant or service), **previous research participants** who have given consent to be re-contacted about future studies, or people who sit on **a research recruitment panel**.

95

There are several things to note, however, if you want to use these resources.

(a) You will need to check what the conditions are for using this information and how you should approach people.

(b) You will need to establish whether people know that you might be contacting them: have they given their consent to be contacted?

(c) You may need to check contact information for sample members, depending on when the source was last updated.

(d) Information useful to fill sample quotas may need to be checked with the prospective participant to ensure it is correct during recruitment – i.e. through the use of a screening questionnaire.

Let's look at each of these issues in more detail.

Conditions of use

Make sure you are able to use the sample source for your research and that you are contacting people to take part in your study who have provided consent to their details being passed on to you. If your organisation is not the owner of the data, check that the people on the sampling list have consented to their details being used by a third party (you) for research purposes. In short, make sure you are compliant with the Data Protection Act and that you ensure the data you are using for sampling purposes are treated securely. The UK Social Research Association and Market Research Society provide useful guidance for researchers around this (see Market Research Society/Social Research Association, 2013).

Opt in or opt out?

You may need to carry out an opt-out or opt-in exercise first, before you can contact people about your study, and even if there are no such requirements it is ethical and good practice to make written contact with people prior to contacting them more directly.

- An 'opt-in' exercise involves writing to prospective participants to tell them about the study and asking them to get in touch with you if they wish to be interviewed. Response rates to opt-in exercises are much lower than to opt-out exercises.

■ TOP TIP ■

Make sure you have a large sample: at least 10 times the number of cases you need to achieve your target number of interviews, but more may be required depending on the target population and the nature of the questions you will be testing.

- An 'opt-out' exercise involves writing to prospective participants to tell them about the study and to let them know that they may be contacted unless they get in touch within a specified time period (usually two weeks) to say they do not wish to take part. In our experience around 8–15% of cases will opt out depending on the topic and funder, so factor this in when deciding how many people to initially contact.

Opt-ins are typically used when the sampling list is owned by a third party and they feel it is more appropriate for them to make initial contact with people. If you find yourself in this position, you will need to ensure that informed consent is obtained. Make sure you are involved in the drafting of the opt-out letter and any other recruitment material.

In addition to what has been said so far, your sample should contain **at least three times** as many people as you intend to interview as not everyone will be contactable, suitable or willing to take part in the study. Irrespective of whether you use an opt-in or opt-out your sample may need to be larger if:

- a screening stage is required to identify eligible participants in the sample (and/or you are looking for quite specific types of people);
- if you are using administrative records where contact details are not regularly checked (we assume a mover rate among the general population living in private households of around 10 per cent per year).[1]

Checking contact information and additional screening

It is important that the records in the sample list contain up-to-date contact information for individuals, i.e. full name, address and ideally telephone numbers and/or email addresses. The latter are very useful as this means recruitment could take place by telephone or via email rather than face-to-face, which is cheaper and more efficient, particularly for samples that are fairly geographically dispersed. As noted already, you may need to carry out additional screening before you can recruit people (i.e. by using a screening questionnaire).

Other considerations

If you are planning to use a pre-existing sampling frame or list, there are some additional issues you need to consider. These are set out below.

- Accessing the list may take time – sometimes months – depending on who 'owns' it.
- Once you physically have your list you will need to keep a record of who was contacted. The sampling frame owner may wish to be informed as to who was contacted.
- Sometimes, the owner of the list may make it a condition of use that they sign off all fieldwork documents prior to use. You will need to allow time for this.

4.3.6 Recruitment agencies

If you do not have the time or the resources to do your own recruitment, then one option is to commission a recruitment agency to do the recruitment for you. There are many specialist qualitative recruitment agencies around.

---

[1]In 2008/09 9% of all households in England had moved to their current homes within the previous 12 months (Randall, 2011).

▰▰▰▰▰▰▰▰▰▰▰▰▰▰ TOP TIP ▰▰▰▰▰▰▰▰▰▰▰▰▰▰

- Make sure the recruitment agency fully understands what you want them to do. You will need to provide them with written instructions and talk them through the recruitment protocol.
- Find out from the agency how they plan to recruit participants, and if you have a preference let them know, for example if you would like them to avoid using a panel.
- Provide the agency with written details of the sampling criteria, your quotas and the ethics you wish to be observed on your study.
- Provide them with a written recruitment script, the screening questionnaire, quota sheets and any specific recruitment instructions, as appropriate.
- Discuss the use of incentives with the recruitment agency (see section 4.5).

Some recruitment companies have a list of people on their books who are happy to take part in research and whom they continuously go back to with requests. These panel members may be 'professional participants' and may be very different to the target population for your test questions. Check with the agency how they plan to recruit participants for your test and let them know if you don't want them to use their panel. We usually ask agencies to recruit participants using face-to-face recruitment methods.

4.4 Recruitment documents

We have mentioned various recruitment-related documents that you will need throughout this chapter: Figure 4.3 summarises these.

- Recruitment instructions
- Quota sheet
- Recruitment screening questionnaire, including introductory script
- Consent forms
- Information leaflets or sheets for respondents
- Recruitment posters
- Instructions for individuals within organisations/groups
- Interview confirmation letter or email

Figure 4.3   Recruitment document checklist

The interview confirmation letter or email thanks participants for agreeing to take part, provides a succinct explanation of the study and confirms what will happen next. If at the time of recruitment a date and time for the interview has been arranged, this should also be included in the letter or email. If this has not yet been arranged, then it is good practice to explain who will be in touch to arrange a convenient time and place in the letter or email. The text should also give details of the person to contact if the participant has any queries or cannot make the appointment. If you are offering an incentive this should also be mentioned (see section 4.5).

TOP TIP

Include the name of the interviewer in the confirmation letter.

4.5 The use of incentives

Many organisations offer financial incentives to potential participants, to assist with recruitment. The incentive also acts as a token of appreciation and acknowledges the time and effort involved in taking part. The ethical issues to consider when using incentives are discussed in section 3.9.3.

We usually provide a small incentive (typically £20) to thank people for participating in an interview. The form of the incentive – cash, voucher, etc. – varies depending on the type of people we are interviewing and the project sponsor. Incentives tend to be money – cash or some kind of gift voucher. However, we have used gifts and donations to a charity of the participant's choosing in certain situations, where cash was not deemed appropriate. When a financial incentive is given, we usually ask the participant to acknowledge receipt.

If you are inviting participants to come to a location of your choosing to take part in an interview, you should consider whether or not you should reimburse participants for travel or other expenses and whether this should be in addition to any incentive you offer.

4.6 Chapter summary

Sampling for cognitive interviewing is purposive in nature, with people recruited to reflect the different kinds of people who will be asked the questions when the survey takes place.

In designing a sample for a cognitive interviewing study, you will need to go through the following steps:

- Define the population of interest.
- Develop your sampling criteria and prioritise as appropriate.
- Set quotas: this will help you to determine your sample size.

- Decide whether your sample will contain interlocked or parallel quotas.
- Decide where you will conduct your interviews – in which areas, for example in different regions and/or urban and rural locations.
- Ensure you have a reserve sample.

Recruitment for cognitive interviews can be a lengthy process, so allow sufficient time.

Decide on which recruitment methods you will use: personal recruitment; snowballing; advertisements; recruitment via organisations; recruitment agencies; or pre-existing lists.

Use a screening questionnaire to establish people's eligibility and to help you fill your quotas.

Offering a small incentive can help with recruitment.

References

Blair, J. and Conrad, F.G. (2011) 'Sample size for cognitive interview pretesting', *Public Opinion Quarterly*, 75: 636–58.

Bryman, A. (2012) *Social Research Methods* (4th edition). Oxford: Oxford University Press.

Collins, D., Gray, M., Purdon, S. and McGee, A. (2006) *Lone Parents and Work: Developing New Survey Measures of the Choices and Constraints*. London: DWP Working Paper No. 34: Corporate Document Services.

Gobo, G. (2004) 'Sampling, representativeness and generalizability', in C. Seale, G. Gobo, J. Gubrium and D. Silverman (eds), *Qualitative Research Practice*. London: Sage. pp. 435–56.

Guest, G., Bunce, A. and Johnson, L. (2006) 'How many interviews are enough? An experiment with data saturation and variability', *Field Methods*, 18: 59–82.

Market Research Society/Social Research Association (2013) *Data Protection Act 1998: Guidelines for Social Researchers*. Available at: http://the-sra.org.uk/wp-content/uploads/MRS-SRA-DP-Guidelines-updated-April-2013.pdf

Randall, C. (2011) 'Housing', *Social Trends 41*. London: Office for National Statistics.

Ritchie, J., Lewis, J. and Ellam, G. (2003) 'Designing and selecting samples', in J. Ritchie and J. Lewis (eds), *Qualitative Research Practice A Guide for Social Science Students and Researchers*. Sage: London. pp. 77–108.

FIVE

DEVELOPING INTERVIEW PROTOCOLS
JO D'ARDENNE

5.1 Introduction

The aim of this chapter is to provide practical guidance on how to design a cognitive interview protocol. Interview protocols provide the cognitive interviewer with all the information he or she needs to carry out the interview. The purpose of a protocol is to:

a) highlight the aims of the testing;
b) explain how test questions should be administered; and
c) indicate which cognitive interviewing techniques should be used (e.g. think aloud and/or probing), and where appropriate, which scripted cognitive probes.

In this chapter we will discuss:

- The importance of defining measurement objectives and testing aims prior to designing the protocol
- How to decide which questions to test
- How to administer the test questions
- How to train participants to think aloud
- How to write different types of cognitive probes
- The factors to consider when deciding on which cognitive interviewing techniques to use in your test.

Example interview protocols are shown at the end of this chapter.

5.2 Define and clarify measurement objects

Before you start designing your cognitive interviewing protocol it is imperative that you are familiar with the measurement objectives of the questions you are testing. One purpose of cognitive interviewing is to test whether survey questions work in the way intended by the researcher. This means that participants *understand* the questions in the intended way and are *willing* and *able* to provide the required information. However, the above assumes that you, the researcher, have a clear idea of what the intended meaning of the question is and what information is required. If you are not clear about what the question is trying to measure how will you be able to test whether the question is meeting its measurement objectives?

It is very easy to write survey questions that initially appear straightforward but that become ambiguous on closer inspection. Let us look at the following example:

> Q1. Have you visited your doctor in the last month?
>
> *Yes* ☐
> *No* ☐

On the face of it this question looks relatively simple. However, on closer inspection a number of ambiguities arise.

- Should participants only include times when they visited the doctor about their own health or should they include taking their children or other dependants to see the doctor?
- Should participants include visits to the doctor's surgery, even if their appointment was not to see the doctor (for example, if they went to see the practice nurse)?
- Should participants include times a doctor has visited them, for example on a home visit?

If you are designing your own research project you need to ensure that each question has a well-defined measurement objective and that you have an appreciation of what you want participants to include and exclude when answering. To do this you may want to go back to your original research aims and objectives and reflect on how each question relates to these and to the analysis you would like to carry out once the survey data have been collected.

If you are working within a research organisation, conducting research on behalf of other people, you may need to return to the project's sponsor to clarify exactly what they see as being the measurement objectives. Be aware that the sponsor may not always have fully defined measurement aims. Therefore time should be built into the questionnaire development process to discuss the precise purpose of each question prior to testing commencing.

Including the measurement objective of each question with the test question, as shown in Figure 5.1 will help you to formulate your cognitive probes. In addition,

Q1. Have you visited your doctor in the last month?

Yes   ☐

No   ☐

[**Q1 Measurement objective:** To capture whether the respondent has seen a doctor, either on behalf of themselves or someone else, in the last month. This could be a GP or a consultant. Visits to other health practitioners (nurses, opticians, dentists) should be excluded.]

Figure 5.1   Example measurement objective

you will be able to revisit this document when writing up the findings from your cognitive interviews (see Chapter 9).

5.2.1 Understanding concepts within questions

Survey questions often involve the use of concepts. Sometimes you will be the question designer and therefore you will (or should) know how concepts are being defined. However, there may be occasions when you are being asked to test someone else's questions. In these circumstances it is helpful to check concept definitions. Let's look at another example.

Q2. How many portions of fruit and vegetables did you eat yesterday?

0   ☐
1–2   ☐
3–4   ☐
5+   ☐

Q3. How many units of alcohol did you drink yesterday?
_____ units

Questions 2 and 3 contain the concepts 'portion of fruit' and 'unit of alcohol'. These concepts have a specific meaning and in testing the questions you may want to check that participants understand them in the way the question designer intended. Knowing what the definitions are will help you design probes that explore participants' understanding of them.

5.3 Setting cognitive interviewing aims

Once you are clear about the measurement objectives of the questions you are testing, you can start to formulate your test aims. Cognitive interviewing aims are typically a list of all the areas you would like to explore in order to check that the question is working as intended. Areas to investigate are often based on the four-stage model of survey response (Tourangeau, 1984) described in detail in Chapter 1.

Figure 5.2 shows how the four stages of Tourangeau's model can translate into cognitive interviewing aims.

Area of investigation	Aims of cognitive interviewing
1. Comprehension	• To explore comprehension of key terms within the question, such as 'doctor'. • To explore comprehension of the question as a whole, for example that respondents understand that they have to count up all the times they have been to the doctor in the past month.
2. Retrieval	• To establish whether respondents can recall the required information (e.g. visits to the doctor in the past month). • To establish whether respondents restrict their recall to the specified reference period (e.g. the last month).
3. Judgement	• To explore respondent strategies when answering. For example, do respondents try to recall each time they visited the doctor during the past month or do they just take a guess? • To explore the boundaries of what respondents include and exclude within their answers. For example, how they define 'visit'.
4. Response	• To explore whether the question is considered sensitive or embarrassing and the impact this may have on the data collected. For example, could respondents edit their answers or refuse to provide an answer? • To explore whether respondents are able to map their 'in mind' answer onto the answer categories available. • To check whether any answer categories are missing from the list provided. • To establish whether respondents consider answer categories to be mutually exclusive (if only one category can be selected).

Figure 5.2 Using the four-stage model to formulate cognitive interviewing aims

Now let's apply the four-stage model to the visiting a doctor question and set some aims for the testing of this question. Figure 5.3 shows the interview protocol – the test question, the measurement objective of the question and the aims for the cognitive interviewing.

The aims of testing will vary depending on the nature of the question being tested. For instance, in Figure 5.3 there is no aim related to testing answer categories. This is because 'Yes/No' answer categories are considered relatively straightforward and therefore testing these may not be a priority. If you were testing a question with a longer list of answer categories or a visual answer scale, setting an aim to explore response would be more important.

Not all cognitive interviewing aims are related to testing specific questions. Cognitive interviews can also explore more general factors related to the survey experience. For example, additional aims in a cognitive interview might be to:

Q1. Have you visited your doctor in the last month?

Yes ☐

No ☐

[**Q1 Measurement objective:** To capture whether the respondent has seen a doctor, either on behalf of themselves or someone else, in the last month. This could be a GP or a consultant. Visits to other health practitioners (nurses, opticians, dentists) should be excluded.]

Aims of testing Q1

- To explore **comprehension** of the phrase 'visited the doctor' and whether it is in line with the measurement objective.
- To explore whether respondents can **recall** if they visited a doctor in the last month.
- To explore which **judgements** respondents make when deciding what to include/exclude within their answer.
- To explore sensitivity and whether respondents are **comfortable** answering this question.

Figure 5.3   Aims of testing

- explore what factors could increase people's willingness to take part in the survey;
- establish whether participants are able to accurately provide factual information or whether the survey would benefit from a request to see documentation (such as employer pay slips or household bills);
- explore whether participants think any important topics are missing from a question-naire. For example, if your questionnaire aims to measure satisfaction with a service, participants may be able to think of areas they want to give feedback on (related to their satisfaction) that you have not thought to include. This can happen even if you have carried out questionnaire development work (such as depth interviews or focus groups) prior to designing your questions (see Chapter 2);
- [for self-administered questionnaires] collect opinions on the attractiveness of the questionnaire and how this could be improved;
- [for self-administered questionnaires] collect opinions on the usability, in terms of the instructions, layout and flow of the questionnaire and how this could be improved;
- [for paper questionnaires] establish whether participants are able to follow naviga-tional instructions and, if not, how these can be made clearer.

We recommend that all interviewing aims, both those related to specific ques-tions and more general aims, are recorded on the interview protocol. This will help keep the interview focused if spontaneous probes are used.

5.4 Deciding which questions to test

If you are testing a long questionnaire it may not be possible to test every ques-tion in a single cognitive interview. The average length of a cognitive interview is around one hour and this includes the introductions, the administration of the survey questions and subsequent probing.

Don't be tempted to test too much in one go. Taking part in a cognitive interview requires a sustained amount of concentration from participants. If interviews last for longer than one hour participants may get fatigued. This means that the questions you test towards the end of the interview may not be explored as fully as you would like.

There is no golden rule about the maximum number of questions that can be tested in one cognitive interview. The total number of questions you can test is dependent on:

- the complexity of the questions;
- whether participants will be asked all the questions or whether some questions will be asked only of those who provide a particular answer at a previous question;
- the extent of cognitive probing envisaged; and
- whether you are hoping to explore any other issues in the interview, for example views on the visual presentation of the questions.

We have found that typically in a one-hour cognitive interview you will be able to test around 15–20 individual questions. When assessing how many questions you want to test, be aware that irrespective of question numbering, a question is one request for information. So a series of 10 agree/disagree statements should be treated as 10 questions. If your questionnaire contains more than 20 questions you will need to decide how this will be managed in testing. You can either:

a) prioritise testing certain questions over others; or
b) **create two (or more) different interview protocols**. For example, if you have 40 questions you wish to test, you could create one protocol to test the first 20 questions and another protocol to test the second 20 questions. Each individual interview will therefore only involve the testing of 20 questions (with participants being allocated to the first or second protocol).

If you decide you would prefer to produce just one protocol there are a number of ways you can prioritise which questions to test. Priorities include:

- **New questions that you have written from scratch** rather than those you have adapted from existing sources. That said, it is worth noting that just because a question has been used in a survey before does not mean it has been tested. Additionally, if the question has been tested with one audience it does not mean it will still be suitable if you use it with a different audience. Context can also have an impact on how partici-pants understand questions. For example, a question which aims to measure long-standing illness, disability and health conditions is likely to give different estimates when asked on a health survey to when it is asked in a survey about employment.
- **Questions that aim to measure unusual or technical concepts**.
- **Key filter questions**. By this we mean questions that determine subsequent questions participants are asked.
- **Questions presented in an unusual or innovative format,** for example questions with pictorial answer categories.

Questions that are less of a priority for testing may include those that:

- **need to be retained in their current form for comparison purposes**; and
- **have been tried and tested in a similar context**.

But how will you know if questions have been tested before? There are a number of online resources that list both existing survey questions and question testing reports (see below).

Useful online resources

The UK Data Service: www.ukdataservice.ac.uk

The UK Data Service provides access to data collected from a range of major UK and cross-national social surveys. Questionnaires can be downloaded from most of the archived surveys. Technical reports (detailing what questionnaire pretesting was done) are provided in some instances and not others.

Q-Bank: www.cdc.gov/qbank

Q-Bank stores questions that have been tested and used primarily in US Federal surveys. A search function allows users to identify questions on different topics and all questions are linked to a question evaluation report. A list of cognitive testing reports is also available.

It is worth noting that just because questions are in the public domain does not mean they have been tested. Similarly, even if they have been tested the results of testing are not always easily accessible. Question testing findings, if published at all, are often only included as an appendix or a technical annex.

If you are working for a research organisation, conducting research on behalf of other people, you will need to discuss testing priorities with the funder. It is important to manage expectations about the amount of material that can be tested in one interview. One way to set priorities is via an expert review (see section 2.2.3).

You may need to include some additional questions in your cognitive protocol on top of the questions you wish to test. For example:

- **Demographic questions.** We often include demographic questions at the start of an interview, to ease people in to the interview and to provide contextual information. Often, these demographic questions may have already been asked as part of the screening process (see section 4.3.1). However, even if they have been asked before you may wish to include them again to check that the information you have is correct. This is particularly important if you have used a third-party recruiter (such as a gatekeeper or a recruitment agency).

- **Contextual questions.** Questions may appear to have a different meaning if they are viewed in isolation. If you want to add a couple of new questions to an existing questionnaire module or series you should consider asking participants some or all of the existing questions in that module or series. This is done to replicate the context in which the questions would be asked/read in the actual survey.

Even though these demographic questions and context questions do not need to be probed on they will still take up some time in the interview. The time it takes to administer these questions needs to be taken into account when planning your interview protocol. Figure 5.4 presents a scenario we encountered where it was important to include contextual questions.

Study background

We were asked to test some new questions designed for use in the Smoking, Drinking and Drug Use survey (SDD). SSD is an annual survey conducted in schools across England with young people aged 11–16. Respondents are asked to complete a self-completion questionnaire under 'exam hall' conditions. The new questions we were testing were on how young people obtain cigarettes, and exposure to second-hand smoke.

Designing interview protocols

- We did not want the test respondents to complete the entire SDD questionnaire booklet during the cognitive interview as this contains of over 200 questions. Many of the existing questions were not related to the new questions we were testing (for example questions about alcohol and drug-use).
- However, we didn't want to test the new questions in isolation because we felt this could influence the way they were viewed by young people. For example, earlier questions had set the context of what to include as 'smoking' and had contained navigational instructions so that smokers were asked additional questions.
- Therefore we created a shorter test version of the questionnaire. This contained the original cover page, instructions and approximately 30 questions (12 of these were the new test questions and the rest were contextual questions from the existing smoking module).
- The visual presentation and formatting of the new questions was in keeping with the existing questionnaire.
- The interview protocol described how the interviewers should introduce the questionnaire. For example, interviewers were asked to explain to participants that in the real survey young people would fill in the questionnaire at school under 'exam hall' conditions, that their name is not included on the questionnaire and that no one would be able to see their answers.
- Interviewers observed participants, with their consent, completing the questionnaire.
- If consent to being observed was given, participants were asked to complete the test questionnaire whilst thinking aloud. If permission was not given participants were allowed to fill in the questionnaire privately.
- After completing the test questionnaire participants were asked additional probes about the new questions to collect further details about comprehension, perceived sensitivity and so forth.

Figure 5.4 Adding context questions and placement instructions to an interview protocol

Contextual questions mean that participants do not view the text questions in isolation but rather as a part of a larger survey experience.

5.5 Administering the test survey questions

The interview protocol should make it clear how the test questions should be administered. In a real-life survey setting questions are administered in a standardised way. By doing this researchers can be confident that variations in answers reflect real differences between participants rather than artificial differences caused by the questions being presented in different ways. In cognitive interviews it is important to replicate survey conditions in terms of the way questions are administered. How this is done will vary depending on the survey mode of questionnaire you are testing (see section 10.4). Your cognitive interview protocols will vary depending on whether the survey questions you are testing are meant to be *interviewer administered* (read out by an interviewer with supplementary written material if required) or *self-completed* (where the participant fills in a questionnaire either on paper or on a computer).

5.5.1 Interviewer-administered questions

When testing *interviewer-administered* survey questions a copy of the test questions should be included in the protocol. The test questions should be read out **exactly as worded** and in the way the questions would be asked in the actual survey. This means you need to specify in the protocol:

- If pre-specified answer options should be read out;
- Whether single or multiple answers can be coded for each question; and
- Any questionnaire navigation instructions, for example showing if additional survey questions need to be asked based on the participants' answer to a previous survey question.

Figure 5.9, at the end of this chapter, shows a protocol for testing interviewer-administered questions.

5.5.2 Self-administered questionnaires

The protocols for testing *self-administered* questionnaires (either paper questionnaires or web questionnaires) differ slightly to protocols for testing interviewer administered questions. When testing self-administered questionnaires participants should be asked to fill out the questionnaire. This can either be the whole questionnaire (containing all the survey questions, including those that are not the focus of the testing) or a test questionnaire containing only the questions you are testing and any necessary instructions/questions to set the context.

When writing protocols for testing self-administered questionnaires you need to consider *how* you will give the test questionnaire to the participant and what you will say. Chapter 10 provides more details.

5.6 Cognitive interviewing techniques

There are a number of different cognitive interviewing techniques that you can use, either on their own or in combination, to test your questions or questionnaire. In this section we look at features of these techniques that should be documented in your interview protocol.

5.6.1 Observations

When testing self-administered questionnaires you may want to observe participants whilst they complete the form. Observation is helpful in framing spontaneous (unscripted) probes to ask at a later point in the interview, without interrupting the participant as they complete the questionnaire. Examples of spontaneous observational probes include:

> I noticed you skipped question seven. Can you explain why that was?

> You changed your answer at question nine, why was that?

Without including a checklist it is easy to forget areas to follow-up on later in the interview. An observation checklist, such as the one shown in Figure 5.5, can be a useful tool onto which you, as the interviewer, can record observations.

It is worth noting that we include observational checklists as an aide-mémoire to help subsequent probing, rather than as a source of numerical data to be used

Observation	Details
☐ Did the respondent skip any questions?	
☐ Did the respondent change an answer at any point?	
☐ Did the respondent ever select two answer categories when only one was required?	
☐ Did the respondent ever trigger an error message? *[Web questionnaire only]*	
☐ Did the respondent ever click the 'help' button? *[Web questionnaire only]*	

Figure 5.5 Observation checklist

in analysis. Therefore, when reporting our findings we would focus on the reasons why a question was skipped rather than the number of times it was skipped.

5.7 Using think aloud

Think aloud allows you to examine the participant's own reactions, views and thought processes in real time with minimal prompting from the interviewer. There are pros and cons of the think aloud method for collecting cognitive data (see Figure 5.6).

Advantages	Disadvantages
• It is relatively easy to train participants to think aloud. In our experience most participants will be able to provide some information via this method. • Thinking aloud collects participant-initiated rather than interviewer-initiated data. Reports of problems initiated by participants may be more reliable compared to problems elicited by probing (see Conrad and Blair, 2009). • Think aloud data is collected at the point at which the question is answered. When data is collected retrospectively (e.g. through probing) participants may be more likely to forget or over elaborate on problems they encountered.	• Not all participants feel comfortable thinking aloud. Think aloud data can vary in quality between individuals. • Thinking aloud could interfere with the task being undertaken. • Participants may not be providing an actual 'stream of consciousness' when thinking aloud. Their monologue may be edited and refined prior to verbalisation. This means problems could still be overlooked. • The think aloud data, in itself, may not address all the research questions you wish to explore.

Figure 5.6   Advantages and disadvantages of the think aloud method

When deciding on whether think aloud is an appropriate technique to use on your study, ask yourself the following questions.

- Are the questions you are testing likely to be very sensitive? Will participants feel comfortable having to think aloud their answers? In these circumstances probing may be more appropriate, to check understanding of the questions without needing to refer to the answers provided.[1]
- Will the act of thinking aloud interfere substantially with how participants go about answering the questions or filling in the questionnaire? For example, we were once asked to test a number of questions designed to assess memory. The decision was made not to use think aloud for testing these questions as the act of verbalising thoughts out loud may have interfered with the task (see Example 5.1).

---

[1]We used this approach when testing questions on sexual behaviour, which were to be included in a self-administered module in the National survey of Sexual Attitudes and Lifestyle (Natsal). Please see refer to Example 10.3. in Chapter 10 for further details.

Example 5.1   Testing memory assessment tasks: a rationale for not using think aloud in certain cases

Study background

We conducted cognitive interviews to test a battery of cognitive functioning items to be used in Understanding Society, a large, longitudinal survey following the lives of individuals in private households in the UK funded by the Economic and Social Research Council. The cognitive functioning items included tests on prospective memory and immediate and delayed word recall. Items on working memory and numerical ability were also tested.

The aim of the cognitive interviews was to ascertain whether the test instructions were clear. The cognitive functioning items were to be used in a survey context where a large number of respondents do not speak English as a first language. Therefore one aim of the cognitive interviewing was to establish whether performance in the memory tests was influenced by language ability rather than not being able to remember things per se.

Study design

- We conducted 43 interviews with people in their own homes. Of these 21 interviews were conducted with people who primarily spoke English at home and 22 interviews were conducted with people who primarily spoke a different language at home. Participants also varied in terms of their age, sex, ethnicity and self-rated English proficiency.
- In total we tested seven types of cognitive functioning task. The memory tasks tested included:

  o *A prospective memory test: prospective memory can be described as 'remembering to remember'. Prospective memory was assessed using a 'clipboard' task (see Huppert et al., 2006). Participants, at 'time one' were shown a clipboard. They were then told that at some point during the interview this clipboard would be handed to them and, when this happened, they needed to write their initials on the top right-hand corner. Later in the interview (at 'time two') participants were handed the clipboard. Interviewers were instructed to record whether the participant remembered to write their initials and, if so, whether they remembered to write them in the correct position.*
  o *A word recall test: participants had a list of words read out to them by the interviewer. Straight after this they were asked repeat back all the words they could recall. At a later point in the interview participants were asked which words from the original list they could still remember. Performance in both the immediate word recall test and word delayed recall test was recorded.*

- The decision was made not to collect think aloud data. This was because we thought that thinking aloud could actively interfere with completing the tasks. For example, on the prospective memory test we thought participants may be more likely to remember instructions if these were verbalised during the think aloud process. For both the prospective memory and the word recall task we thought thinking aloud could increase the amount of time between 'time one' and 'time two'. This would effectively increase the task difficultly for people who were more loquacious think-alouders.

- Consideration was given to when probing should occur in order to mini-mise the impact of probes on task performance. For the most part probes were conducted concurrently (after each task was completed). If a task was conducted in two stages (e.g. with a 'time one' and a 'time two' stage) probing was not conducted until both stages of the task were complete.
- When designing the probes the main focus was to investigate comprehen-sion of instructions. Other elements of the question and answer model (e.g. recall, judgement and response categories) were not explored in probing in any detail.

Study findings

- We found that performance could be influenced by language ability. For example, there were instances of people failing the prospective memory task as they did not understand the word 'initials'. Subsequently the pro-spective memory task was dropped from the survey and the instructions for other tasks were edited to aid comprehension.
- For more information on this study please refer to Gray et al. (2011) and Uhrig et al. (2011).

Your interview protocol should specify whether or not think aloud techniques should be used and how you would like think aloud to be introduced. There is no hard and fast rule about how the think aloud should be introduced. However, in our experience it is often necessary to tailor the way you introduce the think aloud, depending on the participant you are talking to. Here are some general pointers.

- **Keep explanations of think aloud simple.** You might wish to say one or more of the following.

'When you answer the questions I would like you to tell me what you are thinking...'

'Please say 'out loud' anything that comes into your head whilst you are answering...'

'Please tell me what is going through your mind as you work out each of your answers...'

- **Provide a simple practice example.** We sometimes use the 'windows example' described by Gordon Willis (2005), which involves the participant counting up how many windows they have in their home. This example is useful as it can be applied to nearly everyone you are likely to meet: your participants are likely to live somewhere with windows but are unlikely to know 'off-the-top-of-their-head' how many windows there are. An example of how to introduce the think aloud using the windows example is shown in Figure 5.10 at the end of this chapter.
- **Use praise** and **positive feedback** to encourage reticent participants to continue talk-ing during the practice.

In some cases participants will be able to think aloud perfectly naturally without much prompting. In other cases you may have to demonstrate the think aloud example by doing it yourself for the participant, to indicate what you mean.

It is possible to conduct cognitive interviews where participants are instructed to think aloud in some parts of the interview and not others. For example, we have designed protocols that include a large number of contextual questions that are not the focus of the testing. In these instances we have successfully instructed participants to only think aloud at certain points (e.g. the test questions and not the contextual questions). If you plan to use think aloud in some parts of your interview then let participants know this at the outset. Your protocol should clearly indicate when think aloud should and should not be used.

5.8 Probing

Think aloud, by itself, may not provide you with all the information you need to meet your test aims because:

- not all participants may be comfortable thinking aloud and therefore may not provide sufficient information; and
- even participants who are naturally good at thinking aloud may not verbalise all of their thought processes.

In this section we provide examples of different types of probes you may wish to include. We will discuss using scripted versus spontaneous probes, general probes and probes that are theory-driven. A summary of best practice when probing is provided in section 5.8.3.

5.8.1 Scripted vs. spontaneous probes

When designing your interview protocol you will have to decide whether you are going to include scripted probes or whether you will rely solely on spontaneous probes.

- **Scripted probes** are designed pre-interview and are included in the cognitive interviewing protocol.
- **Spontaneous probes** are not included in the protocols. They are generated *during* the interview. Spontaneous probes still need to address the research aims but there is more flexibility in how they are framed and they are more responsive to specific areas mentioned by participants.

One advantage of using scripted probes is that you can ensure they conform to the best practice principles discussed in section 5.8.3 (e.g. they are phrased in a neutral manner, that they are simple and so on). It is far more difficult to ensure that these best practice principles are being adhered to if you are required to compose probes 'on the hoof'. In addition, it will be easier for you to ensure that you address all your testing aims if you have a list of scripted probes to follow.

Another advantage of using scripted probes is that you can ensure that the same areas are being explored with every participant in a consistent way. This will make the data management phase of the analysis much more straightforward (see Chapter 7) and can be helpful when carrying out cognitive interviews in cross-national, cross-cultural and multilingual settings (see Chapter 11).

However, despite this we believe that to get the most useful information cognitive interviewers should have freedom to generate their own (spontaneous) probes during the interview. This allows you to:

a) explore relevant issues that arise, even if these issues have not been predicted in the protocols; and

b) seek clarification on what the participant has already said if the meaning is initially unclear.

In addition, we believe that, as a cognitive interviewer, you should be able to tailor the probes you ask dependant on the participant. Participants will vary in terms of their language skills and their ability to express themselves verbally. You should tailor the language you use when probing as appropriate in order to facilitate communication.

Therefore we recommend that the probing part of the interview should be *semi-structured* and involve both scripted probes and opportunities for spontaneous probing, in line with what Beatty (2004) and Beatty and Willis (2007) recommend. If multiple people are involved in conducting the interviews, all interviewers should be trained in how to generate good-quality probes (that are open, balanced and clear – see section 5.8.3). Likewise, all interviewers should always be briefed on the aims of the question testing to ensure that any spontaneous probes collect relevant and useful information. The use of unscripted probes is not without its risks, and their use needs careful consideration when undertaking cognitive interviews in different languages (see Chapter 11).

5.8.2 Respondent-driven vs. theory-driven probes

Probes can vary in terms of their specificity.

Respondent-driven probes are general probes that aim to gather participants' initial reactions to a question. They are called respondent-driven probes because they allow participants to comment on any aspect of the question they chose: Examples of respondent-driven probes might be:

How did you find answering these questions?

Were they easy or difficult? Why do you say that?

The advantage of using respondent-driven probes is that you can gain an insight into how questions function from a participant's point of view, without any potential bias caused by the interviewer. In this sense data collected from general probes is similar to findings generated by think aloud. Respondent-driven probes are non-directive as participants can discuss any issues they wish, including unanticipated problems.

The disadvantage of respondent-driven probes is that they may not yield full information about how a question is performing. This can occur when participants are not motivated to provide detailed responses to general probes. In addition general probes can result in problems going **undetected**. For example, after a general probe a participant may describe how he or she found a question easy to answer and provide some form of justification of why this was the case. However, on further probing it may transpire that the same participant has misunderstood a key word and not realised it.

Theory-driven probes seek to investigate specific problems that might have occurred based on the researcher's pre-existing knowledge about the measurement aims of the questions.

Figure 5.7 illustrates several examples of theory-driven probes based on the four-stage mode of survey response (Tourangeau, 1984).

It is worth reminding ourselves that Tourangeau's four-stage model is not the only theoretical framework that can be used to explore the question and answer process. For example, Willis (2005) has developed a framework for writing probes based on his Questionnaire Appraisal System. Under this framework probes can be formulated to explore:

a) Instructions
b) Clarity
c) Assumptions
d) Knowledge/ Memory
e) Sensitivity/ Bias
f) Response categories
g) Other issues.

Whichever model you choose the advantage of using theory-driven probes is that all potential areas of concern can be explored in a systematic way. By looking at the question prior to testing you can start to predict what types of problem it might have and then draft probes to establish whether or not these problems arise in practice.

The disadvantage of using theory-driven probes is that they may lead to artificial or 'artefact findings'. Artefact findings occur when participants start to think about questions in a new way as a result of the cognitive interviewing. Directive probing can influence participants' perceptions of a question (Conrad and Blair, 2009). Let us return to the example used earlier in this chapter of visiting your doctor as an illustration, shown in Example 5.2.

Area of investigation	Aims of cognitive interviewing	Example probes
1. Comprehension	• To explore comprehension of key terms within the question.	• What did you understand by the term 'X' when answering this question? • What does the term 'X' mean to you?
	• To explore comprehension of the question as a whole, for example to see whether comprehension is influenced by the questions' length or sentence structure.	• In your own words what do you think this question is trying to ask? [This type of probe is known as 'Paraphrasing']
2. Retrieval	• To establish whether respondents can recall the required information.	• How easy or difficult was it to remember 'X'?
	• To establish whether respondents restrict their recall to the reference period specified in the questions. For example; In the last seven days how many units of alcohol have you drunk?.	• What time period were you thinking about when answering? From when until when? • When did you last do 'X'?
3. Judgement	• To explore respondent strategies when answering. For example, do respondents use an accurate calculation strategy or just take a guess?	• How did you work out your answer to this question? • How accurate would you say your answer is?
	• To explore whether the question is considered sensitive or embarrassing and the impact this may have on the data collected. For example, do respondents edit their answers or refuse to provide an answer?	• How did you feel about being asked this question? • How comfortable would you feel answering this question in a telephone survey about 'X'? Why?
4. Response	• To explore whether respondents are able to map their 'in mind' answer onto the answer categories available.	• How easy or difficult was it to select an answer from the options provided? Why? • Why did you tick that particular box (choose that particular answer), rather than one of the others?
	• To check whether any answer categories are missing from the list provided.	• Are there any categories missing from the options provided or do they cover everything? What is missing?

Figure 5.7 Examples of cognitive probes based on the four-stage model of survey response

Example 5.2   Probes and artefact findings

Q1. Have you visited your doctor in the last month?

Yes ☐
No ☐

[**Q1 Objective:** To capture whether the participant has seen a doctor, either on behalf of themselves or someone else, in the last month. This could be a GP or a consultant. Visits to other health practitioners (nurses, opticians, dentists) should be excluded.]

Aims of testing Q1:

* To explore **comprehension** of the phrase 'visited the doctor' and whether it is in line with measurement objective.

Suggested probe:

What did you understand by the word 'doctor'?

In this example it might be that a participant only thinks about their GP when the survey question is first asked (in line with measurement objectives). However, on hearing the probe *'what did you understand by the word "doctor"?'* the participant might start to think of a broader range of things compared to when he or she first answered the question. For example, the participant might start considering allied health professionals (who should be excluded) as a result of reflecting on the probe. For this reason, it is important that probes are framed to discover what the participant was thinking about *when answering the question.* An improvement of the above probe would therefore be:

Suggested probe:

When answering this question what did you understand by the word 'doctor'?

In practice we typically use a combination of respondent-driven and theory-driven probes in cognitive interviewing protocols. Respondent-driven probes should come before more specific theory-driven probes, as this allows participants to articulate their initial views on a question without any steer from the interviewer and improves error detection (Conrad and Blair, 2009). Theory-driven probes can then be used to investigate additional areas that have not been previously discussed.

5.8.3 Writing cognitive probes

Cognitive probes need to collect information that is unbiased, clear and that addresses the research aims. This section describes a number of best practice principles to adhere to when writing cognitive probes.

Firstly, a good probe (like a good survey question) should be neutrally phrased. Biased probes can increase the likelihood of problems going undetected. For example, if a probe reads '*Was that easy?*' or '*How easy was it to remember X?*' participants may be naturally inclined to respond in the affirmative, regardless of how they found the question. Similarly, probes can encourage participants to report problems that may not have occurred, for example in the following wording: '*You seemed puzzled, was it difficult?*' Even if it seems clear to you that the participant was experiencing difficulties you should not make assumptions. This could lead you to detecting problems that do not occur in practice or exaggerating problems that do occur. Probes should be either:

- **Neutral**, where no particular mental state should be inferred in the question, e.g. '*How did you find that?*'; or
- **Balanced**, where any states inferred should be balanced with reference to an opposite state, e.g. '*Did you find it easy or difficult?*'

Secondly, the ideal scenario for cognitive interviewing is that participants should be doing roughly 80% of the talking, with the interviewer (you) doing the remaining 20%. To ensure participants do most of the talking you should use open probes that require more than a single word answer. Following up a closed answer to a probe with '*Why?*' or '*Why do you say that?*' is a straightforward way to encourage participants to give more expansive responses.

Thirdly, probes should be kept relatively simple. Probes that are long-winded or double-barrelled (where a single probe asks about multiple things) or have multiple clauses are likely to be misunderstood, in the same way a complicated survey question can be misunderstood. Again, if probes are misunderstood there is a danger that the cognitive interviewing could create artificial findings in that participants describe confusion as a result of the probes, rather than the question you are testing.

Finally, when writing probes you should always refer back to the aims of the cognitive testing. By doing this you can check that all your aims are being directly addressed in the probes you write, and that there are no superfluous probes collecting information irrelevant to your aims.

A summary of best practice when writing probes is shown in Figure 5.8.

Good probing	Bad probing
✓ Neutral/balanced	✗ Leading
✓ Open	✗ Closed
✓ Simple	✗ Complicated or double-barrelled
✓ All testing aims are covered	✗ Some testing aims are overlooked
✓ Relevant to testing aims	✗ Irrelevant to testing aims

Figure 5.8   Summary of good (and not so good) probing techniques

5.8.4 When to probe

As well as considering what probes to include, some thought needs to be given to the placement of the probes.

Concurrent probing is when probes are administered directly *after each survey question*. The advantage of concurrent probing is that participants should be able to recall what they were thinking about when answering the question. The disadvantage of probing after each question is that it breaks up the natural flow of the survey questions. When testing self-administered documents it is difficult to carry out concurrent probing without continually interrupting the participant.

Retrospective probing is when probes are administered *once all the survey questions have been answered*. The advantage of using this type of probing is that the probes do not interfere with the flow of the survey questions. This type of probing means that the experience of answering the questions more closely mirrors the context of an actual survey. The disadvantage of retrospective probing is that participants may not be able to remember what they were thinking about when they answered each question. This can lead to participants post-rationalising their survey answers, leading them to describe things that were not actually thought about when they first answered.

The decision as to whether to use concurrent probing, retrospective probing or a combination of both will vary depending on what you are testing. The following factors should be considered when deciding on when to probe.

a) **Questionnaire structure.** If the questionnaire you are testing has distinct sub-sections on different topics you may wish to probe after each sub-section rather than at the end of the questionnaire.

b) **Question similarity.** If you are testing a number of questions containing the same word or phrase comprehension probes should only be asked after all the questions containing the repeated phrase have been administered. For example, if you are testing two questions using the phrase 'general health', probing on understanding of 'general health' should occur after both questions have been administered, otherwise there is a danger that probing could influence understanding of the second question.

c) **Questionnaire mode.** This is discussed in section 10.4.5.

As discussed previously, we want to try and minimise the occurrence of artefact findings when probing. When reviewing your protocol you should consider whether the placement of your probes could influence how participants react to the questionnaire. If probes could influence the understanding of later questions or the navigation of the questionnaire their positioning should be reconsidered.

5.9 Using different cognitive interviewing techniques together

If a decision has been made to use think aloud and probing within the same interview, you will need to consider how your interview protocol will be arranged in terms of which technique the interviewer should use first. It may be that you wish to do either, or a combination, of the following.

a) Think aloud and probing for individual questions.
b) Think aloud for certain questions but probing for others.
c) Think aloud exclusively for certain sections.
d) Only probing for certain sections.

When using think aloud and probing to explore a question (1), think aloud should be encouraged first (before any probes) and *during* the question administration (before or whilst the survey answer is being provided). This is because, as already noted, think aloud is a respondent-driven technique and information elicited via it should not be influenced by the interviewer in any way. Once the participant has finished thinking aloud, probes can be administered. This arrangement of the techniques should be clearly explained to participants at the start of the interview.

If interviewers are to only use think aloud or only probing (2) for a question or during a section of the interview protocol (3 or 4), then this should be explained to participants.

5.10 Other information to include in the protocol

Your interview protocol should provide some information on how to introduce the interview to participants. For example, protocols should set out what the interviewer should say when introducing the study at the start of the interview and in obtaining participants' informed consent to take part. More details on how to introduce a cognitive interviewing study are given in section 6.5.

Similarly, your protocol should also summarise any extra steps you need to carry out at the end of each interview. For example, protocols should contain reminders to give participants incentives (if these are being used), check if participants have any questions and direct participants to further sources of information (see section 6.8).

121

5.11 Testing the protocols

It is recommended that you conduct a 'test' cognitive interview before you finalise your protocol. These test interviews can happen early on, in advance of the main fieldwork, with volunteers from within your organisation or university, or even with a colleague or a friend. A lot will be learned through doing some early interviews and they will help you to revise the probes, write the instructions and pre-empt what to do about unexpected issues that may arise.

A test interview will allow you to check the length of the interview. In general, we recommend that the maximum length of a cognitive interview should be about one hour. After an hour participants may begin to tire, and the information they give you will be less useful. If your test interview shows that your protocols are too long you have two options.

a) **Drop some of the material from the protocol.** You may need to drop some questions from the test or not probe on particular questions. This will involve you revisiting your testing priorities and reviewing your testing aims.

b) **Develop two (or more) versions of the protocol** and test different versions on different participants (see section 5.4).

Testing the protocol will also enable you to see whether there are any missing or unclear instructions or poorly phrased probes. Getting a sense of how the interview flows is very helpful at this stage and will help you to fine tune the interview protocol and develop appropriate guidance for other cognitive interviewers working on the project.

5.12 Chapter summary

Your cognitive interviewing protocols should:

• highlight the measurement objectives and the question-testing aims;
• explain how the test questions should be administered; and
• suggest which cognitive interviewing techniques to use and when.

We recommend using a combination of all or some of the following in your protocols: observations, think aloud and respondent-driven and theory-driven probes. The four-stage model of survey response (Tourangeau, 1984) or alternative question and answer models can be used as a starting point when writing theory-driven probes.

When writing probes you need to make sure they are neutral, open, simple and relevant to your testing objectives. Scripted probes can be supplemented with spontaneous probes to clarify what participants have said and to explore issues that are not predicted by the protocol.

5.13 Examples of cognitive interview protocols

Some examples of cognitive interview protocols are shown in this section.

- Figure 5.9 shows how you might train the participant to think aloud.
- Figure 5.10 shows an example protocol from testing interviewer-administered questions.

Think aloud training

- First, train the respondent to think aloud.
- *You may use the windows example or another example of your choice.* An example script is shown below if this is required.
- For this project we would like respondents to think aloud for **all** of the test questions

Example script

- Let me explain a little bit more about how the interview will work. I'm going to read ask/give you some questions. When you hear them, I want you to tell me whatever comes into your mind. This is called 'thinking out loud'.
- We've found that it helps to have some practice at doing this. So let me give you an example. Let's say I was asked a question about 'how many windows are there in my house'.
- If I was thinking out loud, I would say… *[GIVE EXAMPLE] '…well, there's one window in the kitchen …and then in the living room, there are two windows. Well I say windows, they are panes of glass – they don't open. Not sure if I should include those. I think I will. And then … (etc., etc.)'*
- Now, let me ask you the same question. Think about how many windows there are in your house. As you count up the windows, tell me what you are seeing and thinking about.

Further prompts if required:

- **Please say, out loud, what you are thinking….**
- **What's going through your mind?**

Note: In some cases you may want to design protocols that only use think aloud at certain points.

Figure 5.9 Protocol for think aloud

Testing questions on 'visiting the doctor'

Q1. Have you visited your doctor in the last month?

Yes ☐ → *GO TO Q2*
No ☐ → *GO TO PROBES*

Q2. How many times did you visit your doctor in the last month?

_____ *times*

> Provide space for interviewers to record the respondents' answers as well as any routing or administration instructions

> Use formatting conventions to distinguish survey questions from probes. In this example a grey box indicates the start of a probe section.

Aims of testing Q1–Q2:

- *To explore **comprehension** of the phrase 'visited the doctor'.*
- *To explore whether respondents can **recall** if they visited a doctor in the last month.*
- *To explore sensitivity and whether respondents are **comfortable** answering this question.*

> Provide a brief summary of the testing aims for each question at the start of each probe section.

Suggested probes

General

- How easy or difficult did you find these questions? Why?

Comprehension

- What did you understand by the term 'visited your doctor' when answering these questions?

Recall

- How easy or difficult was it to remember whether you visited a doctor in the last month?

Comfort

- How comfortable would you feel answering this question in a telephone survey conducted by your employer?

> Provide a list of scripted probes. We call these 'suggested probes' as interviewers are encouraged to tailor these and add their own probes based on any observations and respondent utterances).
>
> Organise suggested probes under headings to facilitate subsequent data management.

Testing questions on 'local services'

Q3. Which of these services have you used over the last 12 months?
[SHOW CARD A. Code all that apply. Prompt 'what else']

Local Hospital ☐
Local police station ☐

Figure 5.10 Example cognitive protocol for interviewer-administered questions

Your protocols should also provide details on how you want the interview to be introduced and closed. We recommend that you test your protocol before it is finalised.

References

Beatty, P. (2004) 'The dynamics of cognitive interviewing', in S. Presser, J.M Rothgeb, M.P. Couper, J.T. Lessler, E. Martin, J. Martin and E. Singer (eds), *Methods for Testing and Evaluating Survey Questionnaires*. Hoboken, NJ: John Wiley & Sons. pp. 45–66.

Beatty, P. and Willis, G. (2007) 'Research synthesis: the practice of cognitive interviewing', *Public Opinion Quarterly*, 71: 287–311.

Conrad, F. and Blair, J. (2009) 'Sources of error in cognitive interviews', *Public Opinion Quarterly*, 73(1): 32–55.

Gray, M., d'Ardenne, J., Balarajan, J. and Uhrig N. (2011) *Cognitive Testing of Wave 3 Understanding Society Questions*. Understanding Society Working Paper Series, No.2011–03 available at: https://www.understandingsociety.ac.uk/research/publications/working-paper/understanding-society/2011–03.pdf

Huppert, F.A., Gardener, E. and McWilliams, B. (2006) 'Cognitive function', in J. Banks, E. Breeze, C. Lessof and J. Nazroo (eds), *Retirement, Health and Relationships of the Older Person in England: The English Longitudinal Study on Ageing (Wave 2)*. London: Institute for Fiscal Studies. pp. 217–30.

Tourangeau, R. (1984) 'Cognitive science and survey methods: a cognitive perspective', in T. Jabine, M. Straf, J. Tanur and R. Tourangeau (eds), *Cognitive Aspects of Survey Design: Building a Bridge Between the Disciplines*. Washington, DC: National Academy Press. pp. 73–100.

Uhrig, N., Gray, M., McFall, S., d'Ardenne, J. and Balarajan, M. (2011) *Say What? Testing of Cognitive Functioning Tests with Non-Native English Speakers in the UKHLS*. Paper presented at 4th European Survey Research Association conference, Lausanne, Switzerland.

Willis, G. (2005) *Cognitive Interviewing: A Tool for Improving Questionnaire Design*. Thousand Oak, CA; Sage.

SIX

CONDUCTING COGNITIVE INTERVIEWS
MICHELLE GRAY

6.1 Introduction

The aim of this chapter is to provide you with a guide as to how to conduct a cognitive interview. It provides guidance and practical tips on:

- Conducting cognitive interviews
- The skills necessary to be a successful cognitive interviewer
- Ensuring consistency, where interviews are conducted by more than one person.

We have already discussed in some detail how to write probes (Chapter 5). This chapter focuses on other considerations when conducting a cognitive interview.

- How interviews should be introduced
- Dealing with participants' questions
- Interviewing logistics, such as recording the interview, how much time to leave between each interview, and taking control of the interview environment
- Managing difficult situations
- Interviewer safety.

We start by looking at what qualities and skills a cognitive interviewer needs and how to ensure consistency when more than one interviewer is involved.

6.2 What makes a 'good' cognitive interviewer?

As a cognitive interviewer you need to possess a mix of personal qualities and interviewing skills. In many ways a cognitive interviewer requires the same skills as a qualitative interviewer but we would argue that there is also a need for the cognitive interviewer to be familiar with the conventions and practices of survey interviewers. This helps in the administration of the test questions or materials, for example in knowing that questions are to be read out as worded, in coding answers and in following 'interviewer instructions' included in the test question, such as whether answer options are to be read aloud or coded based on the participant's spontaneous answer.

Figure 6.1 lists the qualities and skills we look for and train our interviewers to have.

Qualities	Skills
✓ Friendly ✓ Professional ✓ Inquisitive ✓ Putting people at ease ✓ Flexible ✓ Calm ✓ Organised	✓ Listens ✓ Asks open probes ✓ Asks non-leading probes ✓ Asks survey questions as worded ✓ Focuses respondents on what they were thinking when they were answering the test question ✓ Asks for clarification rather than making assumptions

Figure 6.1   Qualities and skills needed for cognitive interviewing

Listening skills are very important. So much of the success of a cognitive interview relies on the ability of you, as the interviewer, to follow up on things the participant says or does to reveal any problems or issues experienced.

In our experience it is also helpful to:

- have an appreciation of the principles of questionnaire design in terms of how the structure, wording, terminology and response categories of survey questions can influence the answers participants provide;
- have an understanding of the cognitive interviewing method – what cognitive interviewing can and can't do, and how the techniques are used to explore the survey response process;
- know who the target population is, who will be asked the survey questions, and any specific definitions or rules that are used. If you were testing questions about receipt of state benefits, for example, it would be useful to know what the eligibility rules are for each state benefit so that you could follow up with spontaneous probes (and this may form part of the interview protocol, see Chapter 5); and
- be able to tailor your interviewing style to the needs of different test subjects – for example, children and young people, the elderly, disabled people, and business and other professionals.

Of course as the designer of the cognitive test you may well know all of these things and you may be the only person who will carry out the interviews. However, if you are going to involve others in carrying out interviews then you may want to think about how you ensure that they have this knowledge, for example through training. This information can be drawn upon during the interview and used to help interviewers decide if they need to probe further, for example. In the rest of this section we look at the issues to consider if you are going to use survey interviewers as cognitive interviewers.

6.2.1 Survey interviewers working as cognitive interviewers

As described in section 3.6, if you are working as for a survey organisation you may wish to ask survey interviewers to conduct the cognitive interviews. This practice has been successfully adopted by a number of survey agencies (e.g. DeMaio and Landreth, 2004). Whilst it can be beneficial to use survey interviewers to conduct cognitive interviews, because of the reasons outlined above, there are some very clear distinctions between what makes a good survey interviewer and what qualities make for a good cognitive interviewer. If you are using survey interviewers in cognitive interviewing projects, it is important to note the following and build in protocols (i.e. through training and monitoring) to avoid any pitfalls.

The pace of the interview

Survey interviewers will be used to a fast pace of interviewing, whereby they know they have to get through a certain number of questions in the shortest time possible to keep participants engaged and minimise participant burden. In contrast, the pace of a cognitive interview should be slower, so that participants can articulate their thoughts.

Polished vs. draft instruments

Survey interviewers are familiar with working with very refined and polished instruments. They will be used to administering questionnaires that have fully detailed instructions, and are professionally designed and formatted. Questionnaires that are tested in cognitive interviews are often in very early draft forms and are therefore quite different. Additionally, survey interviewers may be used to pre-programmed computer-assisted questionnaires, where they need not worry about skip patterns or navigation. In cognitive interviews, they will often be working on paper (even if eventually the questionnaire is programmed using a computer) so they may need to familiarise themselves with how to navigate their way through a paper test questionnaire.

Sticking to the script

Survey interviewers are trained to follow the questionnaire as a script, not deviating from the standardised instructions contained within it. Cognitive interviewers, however, need to be at ease with going off script, to spontaneously use expansive or re-orienting probes and be able to judge when to do so.

Helping the participant arrive at their answer

In survey interviewing, interviewers are often required to code the participants' answers to the predefined response options and may, in some situations find that they need to reword ambiguous questions, or provide extra clarification to help participants to provide an answer that is codable. In cognitive interviewing, the goal is to highlight any flaws in the questions, and therefore cognitive interviewers need to explore (and make note) of reasons why participants can't answer the question rather than providing help or clarification. Likewise they need to note where participants' initial answers do not correspond with the predefined response options, for example where response categories are missing or overlapping.

6.3 Ensuring consistency in interviewing

You may do all the interviewing yourself but if you are going to involve other interviewers then you will need to ensure consistency in the way the interviews are carried out, particularly concerning when and how spontaneous probes are asked, when more than one interviewer is involved. One of the most well cited criticisms of cognitive interviewing is the variation in practice and approach (Willis and Beatty, 2007). In the rest of this section we set out some steps that you can take to achieve consistency in the interviewing, starting with interviewer briefings for individual cognitive interviewing projects.

6.3.1 Interviewer briefings

Even where individuals have undergone some formalised cognitive interview training, we have found that project specific training or briefings have an important part to play in the success of a cognitive interviewing project. Briefings provide the opportunity for all interviewers who will be working on the project to come together, learn about its aims, become familiar with the protocols to be used and to ask questions.

A briefing can also present a good opportunity to invite and involve the client. We always give our clients the opportunity to be involved in briefings, asking them to provide some background about how the survey data from the test questions will be used and their motivations for testing the questions.

You can brief interviewers face-to-face, by telephone or online using online conferencing or sharing facilities.

However the briefing is going to be carried out, there are a number of areas which should be covered.

- Background information on why the questions are to be tested using cognitive interviewing methods, and the overall aims of the testing (for example, to test new questions, to assess the performance of existing questions).

- How sampling and recruitment has/or will be carried out, making clear what kinds of people you want to test the questions with, and the importance of informed consent.
- The questions being tested and their measurement objectives (see Chapter 5).
- The interview protocol, including how the test questions are to be introduced and administered (e.g. face-to-face, telephone, self-completion), the cognitive interviewing techniques being used and specific points to note about probes.
- Practical sessions/role play.
- If appropriate, how the findings are to be reported. We often ask interviewers to write up notes on their interviews.
- Practical issues: interviewer safety, incentives, data security.

Usually we would have somebody who has been involved in the design of the cognitive interviewing project introduce the session and provide the background to the testing. As mentioned earlier, this could be the client. It may be that the sample has been recruited for the interviewers already but even if this is the case, they will still need to be told how this process was carried out so that they can answer any questions participants may have. If interviewers are being asked to do their own recruitment, then you will need to build in some time to talk through the way in which you want recruitment carried out: refer to section 4.3 for more details on recruitment.

In our experience, a walk-through of the test questionnaire is a useful way to structure the main part of the briefing. You will need to ensure that interviewers have copies of the actual questions/questionnaire being tested at the briefing. You might want to have those who will be interviewing take it in turns to read out the test questions and probes, so that they start to become familiar with them and ask any questions.

Ensure that you leave plenty of time for practice slots. Even the most confident and experienced interviewers require practice of a new cognitive interview protocol. Pair the interviewers up with each other, or use volunteers from within your organisation/department for them to practice asking the test questions and probes with. If you are able to, observe the interviewers during the practice slots and provide feedback.

TOP TIP

If you will be doing all the interviewing yourself:

- Find someone to practice on.
- Record the interview.
- Play back the recording and critique your interview:
    - Did you cover all the points in your introduction (see Figure 6.3)
    - Did you ask the survey questions as worded, following the protocol?
    - Did you probe on all the areas you should have, at each question?
    - Did you use open, non-leading probes?

- o Did the interview flow well?
- o Was the participant always clear on what they were being asked to do (i.e., when they were being asked a survey question and when they were being asked a cognitive probe)?

- Identify any improvement you can make to your interviewing style and use of probes. Highlight key points on the guide to act as reminders for future interviews.
- Make any changes to the probe sheet or interview protocol.

Remember, if you are testing a questionnaire that has been programmed on a computer (either to be asked by an interviewer or self-completed by the participant), you will need to ensure that the interviewers have access to the questionnaire programme. Ensure that if it needs to be, the questionnaire programme is loaded onto interviewer laptops either in advance of, or at the briefing. That way you can incorporate this into the questionnaire walk through, and/or the practical role play sessions. Figure 6.2 provides a checklist of the kinds of documents you might need to produce for a briefing.

- Project background and instructions
- Test questionnaires and interview test protocol
- Sampling and recruitment information
- Consent forms, if applicable
- Respondent leaflets or information sheets
- Interview arrangement and confirmation information
- Incentives and respondent thank-you letters/leaflets
- Other information about the fieldwork such as who to contact with queries and the date of the debriefing

Figure 6.2   Checklist of briefing documents

6.3.2 Quality checking

Briefing the interviewers so that they share a common understanding of the cognitive interviewing protocols to be used on your project is one way of ensuring quality. Another is to provide interviewers with written documentation: recruitment scripts and instructions; screening questionnaires (see Chapter 4); and interview protocols (see Chapter 5). Another step is to quality check interviews. We do this by taking a sample of interviews conducted on a project and listening to the recordings of these interviews. Members of the research team listen to each other's interviews. As well as being useful at the analysis stage in terms of getting closer to the data, this will fulfil two purposes relating to ensuring quality. It will:

a) gain a sense of whether the interviewers were consistent in their approach, whether the interview test protocol was followed and where interviewers deviated, which could have implications for the kinds of conclusions being drawn

b) provide feedback to interviewers about their interviewing skills, style and practice, which is essential for their ongoing development.

TOP TIP

Ask interviewers to send you their first interview so that you can listen to it and provide feedback before they go on to do more. This way, if you spot any bad habits or inconsistencies you can address them, rather than discovering them at the end when nothing can be done.

If interviews have been conducted in different languages then quality checking will be particularly important. Chapter 11 discusses quality assurance in such circumstances.

6.4 Interview preparation

So far we have considered the qualities and skills that a cognitive interviewer needs and how to ensure consistency. In the rest of this chapter we look at the practicalities of conducting cognitive interviews, whoever is conducting them. We start with how to prepare for the interview.

Before an interview, revisit the research objectives and practice administering the test questions and asking the probes. The interview protocol is a guide – and not a script – so be completely familiar with it before conducting any interviews, so that you are able to respond to what the participant says and does during the interview. This reflexivity is a key feature of qualitative interviewing.

Immediately before the interview, check you have all of the necessary documents. These might include:

- test questionnaires and show cards (showing answer options);
- cognitive interview protocol (including scripted probes, if appropriate);
- participant incentives and receipts for incentives;
- recorder and spare batteries;
- ID card or some other proof that you are who you say you are (photographic ID is useful, preferably confirming an affiliation to the organisation carrying out the research);
- Copies of any letters sent to the participant about the study;
- Pens and a clip board for the interviewer/the participant to use, or a computer/tablet/ mobile device, if appropriate. It shouldn't be assumed that participants will have a pen, or that the interview will take place somewhere where there will be a hard, flat surface to write on;

- details of who is being interviewed (name, address, telephone number, and other useful information); and
- directions on how to get to the interview location.

We record our interviews and use audio recorders with a built-in microphone. However, you may be planning to video record the interviews and/or use equipment that has a separate microphone. Whatever equipment is being used, it is important that you familiarise yourself with the recorder and check that is working before each interview, i.e. making sure devices are fully charged/have new batteries and are recording properly.

It can be useful to label the test questionnaires and electronic files (audio sound files, interview notes) so that you can link them to individual participants. We do this by assigning a serial number to each participant, using the interviewer's initials and a numbering system (SM01, SM02, etc.), plus any other relevant information, and use this to label their test questionnaire, interview recording and so on. You should not use any information that could identify your participants, such as their name or address.

Finally, make sure you follow any organisational procedures, or those specified by the client or ethics board, such as using a safety phone system, before starting fieldwork. We keep an interviewer safety fieldwork log for each project, which lists details of each interview appointment, so that someone knows where you and any other interviewers are when you are out on fieldwork: see section 6.9 for further details.

6.4.1 Getting to the interview

You should allow plenty of time to get to the interview location (if you are going out visiting participants) to ensure that you arrive on time. Check out in advance how you will get to the interview location. If you are planning to drive, will you be able to park nearby and will there be any charges or time restrictions?

TOP TIP

Give participants a courtesy call or text message a few hours before the interview to remind them about the interview.

When planning when interviews will take place, think about how many interviews can realistically be carried out in any one day. If it is necessary to move between locations, you should allow plenty of time to get from place to place. Of course, for some projects interviews may have to be scheduled back-to-back because the window of opportunity is narrow. This is often the case when you are interviewing in an institutional setting such as a prison or school, for example. In such situations it is a good idea to bring refreshments with as you may have no opportunity to nip out to get any during the day.

6.4.2 Preparing the interview environment

You need to take control of the interview setting or environment. If you are interviewing in someone's home, for example, and other people are around who might distract or overhear the participant, you should try to negotiate conducting the interview somewhere quiet, away from other people.

The physical layout of the room that the interview takes place in is also important. Consider, before the start, where the participant should sit. Will participants be required to complete a paper, self-administered questionnaire? If so, they will need a hard surface to rest upon. Will you need to set up your laptop, if the test questionnaire has been programmed to be answered using a computer? If so, you will need to identify somewhere suitable for the laptop to be placed, possibly close to a power supply. Will you require the participant to sit close to you, for example, so that you can observe how they fill in a web questionnaire?

TOP TIP

Explain what the interview will involve, in broad terms and ask participants to suggest where they think the best place in their home would be to carry out the interview. Don't be afraid to suggest another option, to change the seating or to ask for a TV to be turned down because the noise will affect your sound recording.

6.5 Introductions and informed consent

Introductions are vital for the success of the cognitive interview. Prior to arriving at the interview location, the participant should already have been given a thorough explanation about the study: who it is for, what taking part involves and what the data will be used for. At the time of the interview, it will be necessary to gain verbal, informed consent. If others will be doing (some of) the interviews, train them to always gain informed consent at the start of every interview using a protocol to ensure consistency. We wouldn't usually require written consent but this may be required, depending on the population being interviewed and/or ethical/client requirements. It could be, for example, that the project involves interviewing vulnerable adults or children where written consent is necessary.

According to Masson, 'informed consent' implies that would-be participants have been fully informed about the research purpose, what taking part would involve and any other necessary information to make an informed decision. Without full information consent cannot be judged to be 'valid' (Masson, 2004). We discuss how this can be achieved in section 3.9.1; however at the time of the cognitive interview, it is important that interviewers re-emphasise the following.

- The nature and purpose of the research (e.g. who it is sponsored by, who is carrying it out and who will see the results).
- What participants will be asked to do and how the information they provide will be recorded and used.
- The extent to which the information participants give will remain confidential.
- The fact that participation is voluntary and that the participant's decision about participating in the research (or not) will not affect any services or welfare benefits they may be receiving.
- Participants' right to refuse to answer individual questions or to withdraw from the research altogether.

If the project involves interviewing children and young people under the age of 16, you will need to give particular consideration to how parental consent will be obtained in advance of the interview. Additionally, at the start of the cognitive interview, it will be important to provide the above points in a clear and understandable format, ensuring that young people understand what it is they are being asked to agree to.

Before interviews begin, you should run through a detailed introduction with the participant. This may take around five minutes and should be built into the overall interview length promised to participants. The introduction should state who you (the interviewer) are, who you are working for and who the client is. A clear explanation of the purpose of the cognitive interview should also be included (that we are interested in whether participants understand the questions and how they go about answering them, not so much in the answers people give to the test questions). You should stress the interview is a test of the questions, not the participant. Other things to cover in the introduction include confidentiality assurances and explanations around data security. An example introduction checklist can be found in Figure 6.3.

6.6 Data capture and recording cognitive interviews

We recommend that all cognitive interviews are recorded, with participant consent. The recording serves two purposes.

a) It allows the interviewer to be free from the task of having to make detailed notes *during* the interview. Instead the interviewer can fully engage in listening to the participant and responding with appropriate spontaneous, exploratory probes.

- Introduce yourself
- Thank respondent
- Explain who the organisation you work for is/where you are studying
- Provide a brief summary of the study/survey that the test questions will appear on and who the funder or sponsor of the research is
- Explain the purpose of the cognitive interviews
- Explain how the interview will work (e.g. ask the survey question, ask them to answer, thinking aloud as they do so, then you'll ask them about how they went about answering the questions).
- It's not a test – there are no right or wrong answers
- Allow criticism ('I didn't write these questions so if you find something confusing/difficult please tell me')
- Assure confidentiality
- Audio/visual recording OK with respondent?
- Check OK for time
- Any questions?
- Administer incentive; obtain signature of respondent to confirm receipt
- Train respondent in think aloud, if appropriate

Figure 6.3   Cognitive interview introduction checklist

b) The recording acts as a full record of everything the participant and interviewer said and did. The recording can then be transcribed or used to create a written summary after the interview, refer to section 7.5 for more detail on making notes.

TOP TIP

When audio recording, non-verbal cues need to vocalised by interviewer, so that they can be recorded. For example, 'I see you are pointing to the arrow next to the first answer category at question 6'. This will be essential *after* the interview when the interview is being written up or transcribed, as you won't remember what the participant was looking at.

We recommend you use an audio or video recorder that has a reasonably long battery life and large memory so that it can be used throughout the course of a day without you having to worry about re-charging it or running out of storage room. Data security is important too when thinking about which model of digital recorder to invest in. There are now digital recorders you can buy which are encrypted and password protected. Although more expensive, clients may require you to use such equipment so that you comply with their data security requirements. In our experience participants find it reassuring that we use such recorders, which keep their information safe.

Participants need to agree to being recorded. We have found that a clear explanation about the purpose of the recording is enough to reassure people. You must make sure that participants are told who will have access to their recording and where and how the recording itself will be stored. Example 6.1 illustrates what we typically say to participants, as part of the introduction.

Example 6.1   Explaining to the participant that the interview will be recorded

'I'm going to record the interview, if that's OK with you. It means that I can concentrate on what you are saying rather than me trying to write notes, and it provides an accurate record of what you said. Is this OK with you?'

6.7 During the interview

Once the introduction has been given, it is useful to start the interview with some background questions about the participant, such as asking for their age, who they live with and whether they are in work, training, etc. These questions serve two purposes: they provide information about the participant's circumstances, which may be useful at the analysis stage (see Chapter 8); and they start to 'warm up' the participant, getting them to talk about themselves.

Having collected some background information you will move on to administering the test questions and conduct any think aloud and/or probing, following the interview protocol. Figure 6.4 provides interviewing tips.

- Ask open questions (probes) which allow the respondent to freely elaborate
- Leave time for the respondent to think and respond: don't interject too early
- Be persistent in probing if something is unclear, but be careful not to labour a point
- Don't assume – ask!
- Don't pretend to understand – ask!
- Don't lead, direct or put words into the respondent's mouth
- Clarify if necessary, but when summarising make sure that you check with respondents that your summaries are correct; this avoids leading the respondent or incorrectly summarising
- Listen to what the respondent is saying and avoid making notes (especially if the interview is being recorded)
- Allow for mistakes by the respondent as these will often signal problems with the test questions (for example, where an instruction is unclear)
- Avoid helping, play questions back to respondent if they ask you for assistance ('What does it mean to you?')
- Give encouragement and acknowledge difficulty
- Watch for visual clues (e.g. frowning, pointing, smiling) and ensure these are captured ('I noticed you frowned when I asked you that question. Why was that?')
- Stay calm and at ease
- Be non-judgemental and adaptable
- Cover all of the material in the interview test protocol and tick areas off once they have been covered, time permitting

Figure 6.4   Cognitive interviewing tips

It will be important to pace the interview well to ensure that you are able to cover all of the material within the cognitive interview test protocol. During the interview you can check that the participant is OK for time and, as you reach the end, let the participant know that you are nearly finished. Don't tell participants they are nearing the end too soon: this can cause irritation.

Participants may ask questions throughout the interview: either related to the interview process more generally, or to the questions that are being tested:

- *General questions*: Make sure you allow time, either before, during or after the interview, to answer the participants' questions. It may be that they have queries (for example what the purpose of the interview is), concerns (how their personal details and data will be stored) or want to confirm something (the interview length for example).
- *Question-specific questions*: Avoid helping the participant if they appear to be struggling to understand what they are being asked, or how they should answer. Play their questions back to them and explain that we want to try out the questions as they are, to check whether they are clear. Emphasise that it is not your job to help them in answering, but that you will come back and explore the issues afterwards in the probing.

TOP TIP

When participants request your help by asking how they should answer one of the test questions, or asks you to explain what a question is getting at, respond by saying something along the lines of 'answer how you think you should answer', or 'answer based on your understanding of the question'.

6.7.1 Difficult situations to watch out for

Before starting the interviewing, when the interview protocol is being developed, it is important to think about what issues may arise during the interview and how these will be dealt with. This may form part of your ethics application, as you will need to ensure that any risks of harm to the participant are minimised, refer to section 3.9.

Firstly, you should try to anticipate the kinds of issues and reactions that the test question may spark and think about how these should be handled in the interview. If you are testing questions which ask about the amount of debt people are in, for example, and you are interviewing participants who are likely to be experiencing financial hardship, they may well find the questions sensitive and probing may reveal some intense emotions. Be prepared when you are discussing such potentially sensitive issues, ensuring that you and or any other interviewers remain professional, calm and do not offer topic-specific advice or comment about participants' situations. Offer participants the opportunity to move on, or to skip areas they are not comfortable discussing. It can be useful to leave an information leaflet with participants at the end of the interview. This might list organisations that provide advice and support to people, for example, in financial difficulties. However, any information that is given to participants should be agreed with the sponsor beforehand.

You may find that the cognitive interview experience can anger or frustrate certain participants. This could be because they feel that the questions are too personal, or that the cognitive interviewing experience (i.e. being asked probe questions about how they have gone about answering questions) irritates the individual. If you feel that the participant has become angered or frustrated, you should acknowledge this and reaffirm the purpose of the interview. If you think it will help, stress the value of their contribution and offer them the opportunity to move on if they wish to. If the participant is frustrated with the cognitive interviewing technique, you will need to explain what you are trying to do (i.e. understand what is going on in their mind when they attempt to answer the survey question). A different probing approach may be required.

Testing survey questions can make people feel embarrassed, anxious or reticent. Again, it is the interviewer's job to reassure participants, provide encouragement and acknowledge any difficulty. Equally if you sense that a participant is becoming distressed, you should acknowledge this and check whether he or she wants to continue, take a break or terminate the interview.

6.8 Ending the interview

It is important to end the interview on a positive note. You should allow time for participants to 'come out' of the interview, especially if they have been discussing sensitive or personal issues. Before leaving, you should ensure that you have answered any questions participants have and thank them for their time and help. There are no rules around whether incentives are best given at the start, or the end, of an interview – interviewer preference usually dictates this, however make sure that you remember to administer this, if you are using one.

It is good practice to leave participants with an information leaflet, detailing the purpose of the cognitive interview and how their data will be used, as well as listing who to contact should they have any queries after the interview. You might also want to provide a list of support organisations or groups to contact if the interview has raised anything the participant wishes to follow up. It could be, for example, that you have been testing questions about people's finances where it could be an idea to refer them to organisations that provide advice on money management and budgeting.

6.9 Interviewer safety

When conducting a cognitive interviewing project (or any research project involving contact with members of the public) it is important to consider interviewer safety and support. In our experience it is exceptionally rare for things to go wrong but you should have procedures in place to protect yourself and anyone else conducting interviews. Think about the population group and/or area you will be interviewing (in) and decide whether a 'paired' interview approach is needed, where you are accompanied by another person during fieldwork.

To keep yourself safe it is good practice to always tell someone that you are going to be doing an interview so that if anything goes wrong people know where to start looking for you. Whether you are conducting research by yourself (for example as a lone practitioner or a student researcher) or as part of a team you should decide who you are going to tell: it could be another member of the research team, a friend or family member. You should provide them with details of the interview location and when you expect it to finish. When you have finished the interview you should also let someone know that you are now on your way home and then confirm when you have arrived home/back at work. This could be managed either through a phone call before the interview and one afterwards or by sending a series of text messages.

If at any point during the interview you are made to feel physically threatened you should leave as quickly as possible.

Depending on the context in which you conduct your research you may be able to anticipate that your interviews could touch on sensitive or personal subjects. In such cases you need to plan for how you can make the interview as comfortable as possible for the participant. Support for interviewers is also important when interviews touch on sensitive topics. In our experience even if you are testing something that appears innocuous it is not always possible to predict when participants will share personal issues. Therefore prior to conducting any interviews you need to have a plan about what you (or other interviewers working on the project) should do if you are told something that is upsetting or distressing.

On an individual project, all interviewers should be told who they are to go to should they need to talk to someone about any personal issues the assignment is raising. If you are working on your own then think about who you could go to, to talk though an issue: a friend, colleague, student supervisor, family member? If informal support networks are unavailable to you, we would suggest that you might make use of the support organisations that you are directing participants to (see section 6.8). You should also develop and follow procedures that set out what should happen if you or any other interviewer experiences anything in the field, when interviewing participants, which you find distressing or disturbing.

6.10 Chapter summary

- Good cognitive interviewers are good listeners, non-judgemental, friendly, neutral, professional, inquisitive and patient.
- Written protocols, interviewer training and quality checks on first interviews can help ensure consistency across interviewers.
- Prepare for your cognitive interviews carefully:
  - Know the interview protocol inside out;
  - Practice administering the test question and asking the probes;
  - Check you have all of the necessary documents you need before you head off to do an interview;
  - Test the recording equipment to make sure it works, before the interview;
  - Follow any procedures specified by ethics committees, gatekeepers or funders.
- Allow sufficient time to get to the interview location and take control of the interview environment.
- Spend time introducing the study, explaining what participation involves and obtaining informed consent.
- We recommend that interviews are recorded, with participant consent.
- Ask open questions, allow time for participants to think and respond, don't assume – ask, don't lead or put words in the participant's mouth, give encouragement and allow the participant to make mistakes.
- Keep an eye out for difficult situations and have a prepared plan of action to deal with them.
- Think about your own safety and put procedures in place to ensure it.
- End the interview on a positive note, answer the participant's questions and thank them for taking part.

References

DeMaio, T.J. and Landreth, A. (2004) 'Do different cognitive interview techniques produce different results?', in S. Presser, J.M. Rothgeb, M.P. Couper, J.T. Lessler, E. Martin, J. Martin and E. Singer (eds), *Methods for Testing and Evaluating Survey Questionnaires*. Hoboken, NJ: Wiley. pp. 89–108.

Masson, J. (2004) 'The legal context', in S. Fraser, V. Lewis, S. Ding, M. Kellett and C. Robinson (eds), *Doing Research with Children and Young People*. London: Sage in association with the Open University. pp. 43–58.

Willis, G. and Beatty, P. (2007) 'Research synthesis: the practice of cognitive interviewing', *Public Opinion Quarterly*, 71(2): 287–311.

SEVEN

DATA MANAGEMENT
JO D'ARDENNE AND DEBBIE COLLINS

7.1 Introduction

The aim of this chapter is to provide you with a strategy for managing your cognitive interview data. Data management is the first step in the analysis process. In this chapter we:

- Present an overview of the different approaches to analysis of cognitive interview data
- Provide a summary of the analysis approach we favour, called Framework, and describe where data management fits into this approach
- Look at the types of 'raw' data collected during cognitive interviews and at the practices that should be adopted to ensure that data are stored in an orderly fashion
- Set out the process by which your cognitive data can be reduced, classified and ordered to facilitate subsequent analysis.

Throughout this chapter will give practical examples of how to use Framework using two different software systems, Excel and NVivo. Finally, we describe data management strategies you can use to ensure the information you have collected remains secure. Chapter 8 describes how to analyse your data once it has been summarised, reduced, classified and organised.

7.2 Different approaches to analysis

There are a number of different analysis methods that one can use to analyse cognitive interview data: both qualitative and quantitative. In this section we summarise these methods.

7.2.1 Quantitative methods

Quantitative methods involve the use of standardised coding schemes to analyse cognitive interview data, for example Presser and Blair (1994), Conrad et al. (1999) and Willis et al. (1999). These coding systems reflect the 'dominant' question and answer model, identifying problems with: comprehension (communication); recall or computation tasks; bias or sensitivity (judgement issues); and response categories. They may also include some elements of behaviour coding, such as identifying problems interviewers have in reading the question or recording the answer (see section 2.2.8). In addition, they can cover what Willis et al. (1999) call 'logical issues' – that is items that cannot easily be conceptualised due to problems in the cognitive processing chain (i.e. an 'other' category for problems that cannot be classified according to the question and answer model). Studies that have utilised such coding systems have tended to be those that have sought to evaluate the validity and reliability of cognitive interviewing methods (see e.g., DeMaio and Landreth, 2004; Rothgeb et al., 2001) rather than test survey questions per se, although more rudimentary schema are used by researchers working in National Statistical Institutes in, for example, Germany and the Netherlands. The coding scheme lends itself to the interview data being abstracted to a count or quasi-qualitative indication of the number of times a particular problem type is found. Coding can be time-consuming although with developments in computing power, Blair and Brick (2010) suggest that they are becoming less so. If you decide to use such a scheme and involve several people in the coding then it is a good idea to measure intercoder reliability, which measures the extent to which coders agree on the coding of items. Proponents of these methods argue that the use of standardised coding and the calculation of inter-coder reliability improve the validity of cognitive interviewing results.

7.2.2 Qualitative methods

Gerber (1999) highlighted the value of ethnographic approaches to cognitive interviewing in sampling and recruitment, interviewing, analysis and interpretation, and particularly in understanding cultural differences. The use of qualitative methods to analyse cognitive interview data are particularly notable in this area although qualitative approaches are used by several national statistical agencies, including the Office for National Statistics in the UK and the National Centre for Health Research in the US. One approach used is the Constant Comparative Method (CCM) of analysis – also known as Grounded Theory – which has been used, for example, by Ridolfo and Schoua-Glusberg (2011) to understand how different cultural groups went about answering two survey questions on race and ethnicity. Focusing solely on response error can be dangerous, as problems with the validity of answers to survey questions can be missed. Using a method such as CCM, analysts generate an analytical and theoretical framework from the data. This allows the analyst to understand the role of context (of the survey and that of the participant) in shaping participants' understanding of the survey question and their responses to it (Miller et al., 2014).

7.3 The analytical process

Our approach to data analysis is qualitative and based on the Framework method developed by Ritchie and Spencer (1994). This is an interpretive, sociological approach that is concerned with identifying substantive findings and addressing specific, often policy-related research objectives. The name Framework comes from the thematic framework that is central to the method. A thematic framework (matrix) is used to classify and organise data according to key themes, concepts and emergent categories. Main themes are identified and subdivided into a series of related sub-topics that evolve and are refined through familiarisation with the raw data and cross-sectional labelling or coding of the data. Once judged comprehensive, each main theme is charted in its own matrix, where every participant is allocated a row and each column denotes a separate subtopic. Data from each case are then synthesised with the appropriate parts of the thematic framework.

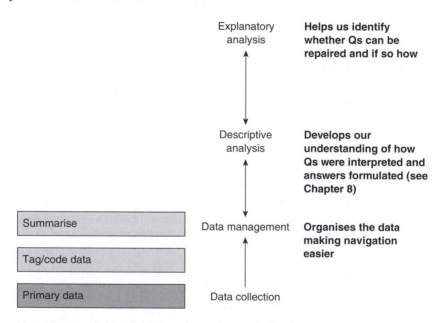

Figure 7.1   Steps involved in the analysis of cognitive interview data
Modified from 'The Analytical Hierarchy', Box 8.1, Spencer et al. (2003: 212)

Figure 7.1 describes the steps involved in the analysis process. Reading from the bottom up, you start with primary data (sound/visual recordings, transcripts, and so on) that have been collected during the cognitive interview. These are reduced to a more manageable form that can be navigated more easily through a process of data management. This chapter is concerned with this stage of the process. The link to the original data is clear and the voice of the participant is visible. Once this process has been completed the formal process of analysis can begin, and we describe the subsequent steps in Chapter 8.

7.4 Sources of primary data

There are numerous types of raw data collected during the course of a cognitive interviewing project. We refer to these data as 'primary data' or 'raw data' in that the information has not been simplified, reduced, combined or classified in any way. Types of raw data collected include:

- **Participant details**, e.g. completed screening questionnaires, see Chapter 6.
- **Recordings of interviews** or **transcripts of recordings**.
- **Completed test questionnaires**. This can either be self-completion forms or survey answers recorded in an interview protocol as part of testing face-to-face survey questions.
- **Interviewer observations** recorded in the interview protocol – see section 5.6.

The most detailed data will be the interview recordings (or interview transcriptions) as these will show what the participant said and did during think loud and probing. These data can be combined with interviewer observations (for example, it may have been noted that a participant changed their answer to a certain question) and completed questionnaires to build up a complete record of what happened in the interview.

Even a relatively small cognitive interviewing project will generate numerous hours of audio recordings (equivalent to hundreds of pages of interview transcripts) along with an abundance of other materials, including interviewer observations and completed test questionnaires. Without an approach for reducing and organising your data you will not be able to review it systematically. If you cannot systematically review your data there is a danger you will get lost in the details of some areas without gaining full oversight of the overall picture across all interviews.

7.5 Data reduction and organisation

Start by classifying and organising information under consistent themes, removing any extraneous or irrelevant material. This process involves two stages:

1. Organising the data for each interview.
2. Combining organised data from multiple interviews.

We will discuss each of these stages in turn.

7.5.1 Organisation of data for each interview

The first step in data management is to produce, for each participant, a document that summarises all relevant information collected within the interview. These documents are referred to as 'interview notes' or 'interview summaries'.

Interview notes can be written up using a template. The purpose of the template is to ensure that, for each interview, relevant data from all sources (e.g. audio recordings, observations, completed questionnaires) are contained within a single document. Having a template ensures that all interviews are written up in a consistent way, with all findings being described in the same order and with a similar degree of detail. This is useful for all cognitive interviewing projects but is particularly important if multiple people are carrying out the interviews as it helps ensure consistency. If you require multiple interviewers to produce notes you should provide information about this at the briefing. You need to inform interviewers about how notes should be structured and what level of detail is appropriate. Ensuring consistency in practice when writing up interview notes will make comparing interview findings across cases more straightforward.

The notes template will typically start with some details about the participant, including the demographic classification variables collected during the recruitment stage (see section 4.3). This background section may also contain a brief description of the interview situation and context, for example where the interview was held, whether anyone one else was present and a general opinion on how the interview went (e.g. how well the participant took to thinking aloud and whether there were any language barriers). This background helps to set the scene for the analyst not present in the interview and reminds those who were of the context in which the interview took place.

The notes template (Figure 7.2) will also contain a number of sections detailing the findings for each question tested. Notes templates should always include:

- the participant's survey answer to each question tested;
- any findings from think aloud for each question tested;
- any findings from the scripted probes for each question tested;
- any additional findings about a question that were not pre-empted by the scripted probes.

We recommend that the template should, as far as possible, follow the order and content of the interview protocol. For example, if all probing was conducted retrospectively (i.e. after all questions had been asked) the notes should contain all the survey answers first followed by all the findings from probes. It will be

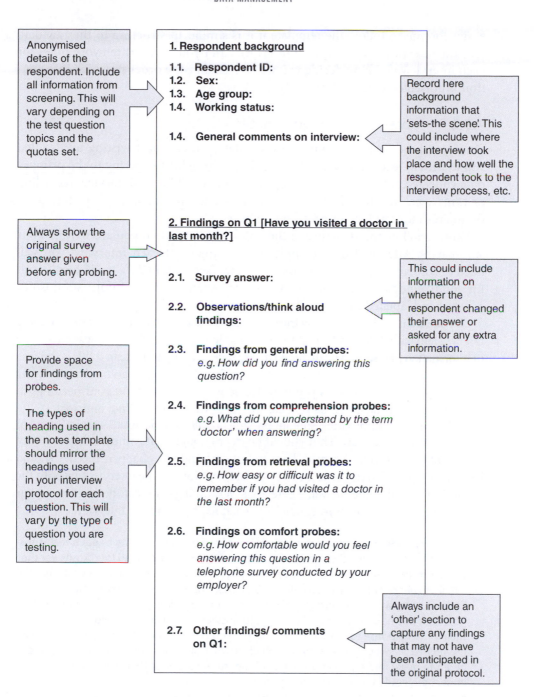

Anonymised details of the respondent. Include all information from screening. This will vary depending on the test question topics and the quotas set.

1. Respondent background

1.1. **Respondent ID:**
1.2. **Sex:**
1.3. **Age group:**
1.4. **Working status:**

1.4. **General comments on interview:**

Record here background information that 'sets-the scene'. This could include where the interview took place and how well the respondent took to the interview process, etc.

Always show the original survey answer given before any probing.

2. Findings on Q1 [Have you visited a doctor in last month?]

2.1. **Survey answer:**

2.2. **Observations/think aloud findings:**

This could include information on whether the respondent changed their answer or asked for any extra information.

Provide space for findings from probes.

The types of heading used in the notes template should mirror the headings used in your interview protocol for each question. This will vary by the type of question you are testing.

2.3. **Findings from general probes:**
   e.g. How did you find answering this question?

2.4. **Findings from comprehension probes:**
   e.g. What did you understand by the term 'doctor' when answering?

2.5. **Findings from retrieval probes:**
   e.g. How easy or difficult was it to remember if you had visited a doctor in the last month?

2.6. **Findings on comfort probes:**
   e.g. How comfortable would you feel answering this question in a telephone survey conducted by your employer?

2.7. **Other findings/ comments on Q1:**

Always include an 'other' section to capture any findings that may not have been anticipated in the original protocol.

Figure 7.2 Example of an interview notes template

easier for you to follow the template if it is similar in structure to the raw data (e.g. the interview recording or transcript). After you have written your notes for each interview you may decide you want to change the order in which information is presented (see section 7.5.2).

7.5.2 Principles of writing good notes

Once you have designed your notes template you can start writing up detailed summaries for each interview. You should do this whilst referring to the primary data collected. The main source of primary data will be the interview recording or transcript. Additional sources of primary data include any completed questionnaires or interview observations collected.

Always follow the structure of the notes template when you are writing your summaries. After you have completed a summary of each interview you will need to combine summaries across interviews (see section 7.6). It will be difficult for you to compare and contrast findings across interviews if information is not ordered and labelled in a consistent fashion.

If you find it difficult to follow the structure of the template this suggests that there is a problem with it. It may be that there are too few or too many headings or the type of information that should be included under each heading is unclear. If this is the case the best thing to do is to revise the template. Template design can be iterative: after writing up a few sets of notes you may decide you need to amend your headings to accommodate repeated themes that are emerging which you did not anticipate.

All interview summaries should provide a full and accurate record of what occurred in the interview. They should be clear enough that someone who was not present at the interview can read them and understand what happened. They should be concise and accurately reflect what was said and done in the interview, by both the participant and the interviewer. There are several things you can do to ensure your summaries are accurate representations of what happened in the interview.

a) **Always provide the original survey answer given by participants to each test question.** This is the answer they gave when the question was first asked (or the answer they wrote down in a self-completion questionnaire). It may be that probing reveals that the initial answer provided is inaccurate. In some cases participants may become aware that their initial answer is not correct and offer a revised response: you would want to make a note that this happened and of the revised answer. However, it is useful to know what their initial response to the survey was so that you can compare this initial response with the revised answer. By comparing original survey responses with 'real' answers you can begin to make inferences about types of measurement error that may occur and what impact this could have on survey estimates.

b) **Describe both positive and negative findings.** Obviously it is important to fully describe any problems the participant encountered when answering the questions. However, it is also important to describe events that indicate that a question was performing well, so that a full picture is presented.

c) **Always provide a clear distinction between participant-driven findings and interviewer-driven findings.** As noted in section 5.8.2, findings that are participant-driven (e.g. from think aloud or from respondent-driven probes) are less likely to elicit artefact findings. Therefore your notes should differentiate between findings from think aloud, findings from general probes such as 'How did you find that?' and more specific theory-driven probes.

d) **Back findings up with evidence.** It is not sufficient to simply say *'the participant understood X...'* or *'the participant could not remember Y...'* when writing up your notes. Use examples and quotes to illustrate and ground your summary in the data.

e) **Make it clear when you are quoting directly and when you are summarising.** Your notes are meant to be a detailed summary of what happened in the interview. You do *not* need to write out everything the participant said verbatim. However, using direct quotes can be helpful to illustrate key points or to explain an issue in the participant's own words. When writing your notes it should be clear to the reader whether something is a direct quote or your summary. You may wish to set up your own formatting conventions so that you can identify verbatim quotes from other types of information. For example, you may choose to always use quotation marks around quotes and display the text in italics.

f) **Stick to the facts.** It may be that when you are reviewing the primary data you find that some areas have not been explored sufficiently for you to get a complete picture of what the participant was thinking. When this occurs *don't* make assumptions about what the participant was trying to get across or make guesses regarding what the problem *might* have been. Describe the findings using as much detail as is available and then state that the area was not covered further. If an area of interest was not covered at all this should also be explicitly stated in the notes. You will need to differentiate your observations on the interview from those of the participant. You can do this by using a different font.

An example of a section of a completed set of notes is shown in Figure 7.3. Making interview summaries in the manner we have described is relatively time-consuming. From our experience, writing up a summary of a single, hour-long cognitive interview can take several hours, depending on the extent of probing and the complexity of the test questions. Allow sufficient time for this task at the project planning stage (see Chapter 3).

TOP TIP

Try to write up your notes as soon as you can after each interview. Even with a recording/transcription it is easier to write notes while the interview is still fresh in your mind. By listening to the recordings you can also review how well you performed in the interview. For example, you can review whether you successfully covered all the material in the protocol and how well you formulated any spontaneous probes. By doing this you can learn how to improve your technique before the next interview.

---

1. Respondent background

1.1. Respondent ID:	JD01
1.2. Sex:	Male
1.3. Age group:	18–30
1.4. Working status:	Employed part-time

1.4. General comments on interview:
The participant was a full-time student and was employed part-time in the evening in a local bar. The interview took place in the participants' hall of residence in a kitchen area. We were the only people present throughout the interview. The participant appeared relaxed throughout the interview and seemed comfortable thinking aloud.

2. Findings on Q1 [Have you visited a doctor in last month?]

2.1. Survey answer: No.

2.2. Observations/ think aloud findings: During the think aloud the participant described how he has recently moved into new student accommodation and as a result of the move had to register with a new doctor. He decided not to include this when answering. *'I did not actually see the doctor. I just had to fill in a form and leave it at the reception.'*

2.3. Findings from *general* probes: *e.g. How did you find answering this question?*

The participant felt this question was *'pretty easy'.* They did not elaborate further.

2.4. Findings from *comprehension* probes: *e.g. What did you understand by the term 'doctor' when answering?*

The participant thought the question was asking whether or not he had visited a GP (general practitioner) about a health problem.

2.5. Findings from *retrieval* probes: *e.g. How easy or difficult was it to remember if you had visited a doctor in the last month?* The respondent described how the last time he had spoken to a doctor was over a year ago. This was: *'Definitely not within the last month!'* This was an easy question to remember the answer to.

2.6. Findings on *comfort* probes: *e.g. How comfortable would you feel answering this question in a telephone survey conducted by your employer?*

The participant stated he was comfortable answering this question but he was *'puzzled'* why it would be included in a survey conducted by his employer. He thought some people might want an explanation about why this question is being asked.

2.7. Other findings/comments on Q1: The participant described how he had visited the student medical centre to show his ID card and hand in some paperwork but he had only spoken to a receptionist. He had not seen a doctor or made an appointment.

Figure 7.3 Example of a completed notes template

7.5.3 Making summaries: audio recordings or transcripts?

You can choose to make interview summaries either by:

a) reviewing the audio recordings of the interviews and making summaries based on these; or

b) getting your recordings transcribed and basing your summaries on the transcriptions.

There are advantages and disadvantages to both approaches. If you choose to make interview summaries based on reviewing the audio recordings the data management process is quicker (as you don't have to go through the extra work of getting the recordings transcribed). In addition, it can sometimes be easier to follow the thread of the conversation whilst listening to a recording compared to reading a transcript. This is because listening to a recording you can pick up on aural clues such as pauses, tone and inflection.

Producing and reviewing transcripts is more time-consuming than producing summaries from the audio recordings alone. However, some people find it easier to review written transcripts as opposed to audio recordings. For example, you may find it helpful to highlight and annotate sections of a transcript as a precursor to producing your interview summary.

A final advantage of using transcripts is that it is easier to back-check notes against transcripts than it is to back-check them against audio recordings. For example, when writing your summaries you may want to include page and line references to where findings come from in the transcript. This means that there is greater transparency as to how your summaries relate to the raw interview data collected. It should be noted time references can be used when writing summaries for audio recordings (saying how many minutes/seconds into an interview an event occurred). However, the process of back-checking time references is more time-consuming than checking against line references.

Your decision on whether to make your summaries directly from recordings or from transcripts will ultimately be based on how much time you have, whether you need to share raw (anonymised) interview data, in the form of transcripts, with any additional parties, and the extent to which quality checks on notes or transcripts will be conducted.

7.6 Combining findings from different interviews: the Framework approach

Once you have produced written summaries of all the cognitive interviews the next stage of data management is to amalgamate the summaries from **all interviews** into a single data-set ready for analysis. To do this we advocate the Framework method, first described by Miles and Huberman (1994) and then expounded in more detail in Spencer et al. (2003). Framework is a matrix-based approach for managing qualitative data. Summaries of each interview are entered into a series of grids; each row representing a single participant and each column representing an area of investigation. Data within the grids can then be read horizontally as a complete case summary for each participant, or vertically by areas of investigation, looking across summaries for all participants. This allows the data collected to be systematically reviewed.

The following sections describe how to design these matrices and how to populate them. Different software options for producing these matrices are also discussed.

7.6.1 Designing Framework matrices

The first stage in designing Framework matrices is deciding what information should be included under each column heading in each matrix. Unlike some forms of qualitative interviews cognitive interviews are highly structured and this makes the process of deciding how to organise your data relatively straightforward. It is useful to have a summary of each participant's background details in the first column of each matrix. After this a good starting point is to base your column headings on the subheadings used in your note templates. As described in section 7.5.1 these headings are generally based on:

- the participant's survey answer, clearly indicating which was the initial answer, if appropriate;
- any findings from think aloud;
- any findings on each area probed on (e.g. comprehension, retrieval, judgement response); and
- any additional findings not anticipated by the scripted probes.

An example of an unpopulated matrix with the column headings is shown in Figure 7.4.

It is useful to familiarise yourself with all the notes (particularly if you have not conducted any interviews yourself) before designing the matrices. By doing this you can establish whether there are any issues that were raised in the interview that were not originally anticipated by the probe sheet. If the same issue has been raised by multiple participants you may wish to include an additional column in your matrix regarding this issue.

You can choose to set up one matrix for each question tested. Alternatively, you may choose to put blocks of similar questions together into a single matrix, depending on what your research aims are. For example, if one of your research aims is to test two question formats (let's call them QA and QB) to see if participants find it easier to recall information using one format compared to another, it would make sense to set up a matrix that contains all information on recall from both QA and QB. This will make it easier to interrogate the data to address this research question.

7.6.2 Populating the framework matrices

Once you have set up your matrices the next stage is to populate them with the summarised data based on the notes for each interview. An example of a partially

1. Resp. details (ID, Sex, Age)	Findings on Q1: [Have you visited a doctor in last month?]						
	2.1 Survey answer	2.2 Observation/ think aloud findings	2.3. Findings from *general* probes	2.4 Findings from *comprehension* probes	2.5. Findings from *retrieval* probes	2.6. Findings from *comfort* probes:	2.7. Other findings

Figure 7.4   Example of column headings in an unpopulated matrix

		Findings on Q1: [Have you visited a doctor in last month?]				
1. Resp. details (ID, Sex, Age)	**2.1 Survey answer**	**2.2 Observation/ think aloud findings**	**2.3. Findings from *general* probes**	**2.4 Findings from *comprehension* probes**	**2.5. Findings from *retrieval* probes**	**2.6. Findings from *comfort* probes:**	**2.7. Other findings**
JD01 Male 18–30	No	R described how he recently had to register with a new doctor. He decided not to include this. '*I did not actually see the doctor. I just had to fill in a form and leave it at the reception.*'	The participant felt this question was '*pretty easy*'. They did not elaborate further.	The participant thought the question was asking whether or not he had visited a GP (general practitioner) about a health problem.	R described how the last time he had spoken to a doctor was over a year ago. This was: '*Definitely not within the last month!*' This was an easy question to remember the answer to.	R stated he was comfortable but he was '*puzzled*' why it would be included in a survey conducted by his employer. He thought some people might want an explanation about why this question is being asked.	R described how he had visited the student medical centre to hand in some paperwork but he only spoke to a receptionist. He had not seen a doctor.

Figure 7.5   Example of a partially populated matrix (one case charted)

populated matrix (with one case charted) is shown in Figure 7.5. The process of transferring summaries from each interview into the matrices is referred to as 'charting'. This process can be as simple as copying and pasting the relevant section of each set of notes into the relevant cell of each matrix. The process of charting your data provides a secondary opportunity to reduce the data collected. For example, upon transferring material into your matrix you may find that some superfluous or irrelevant material has been included in the interview notes.

It is useful to chart a few sets of notes into the matrices before you make final decisions as to what your column headings should be. By reviewing your interim chart you may make the decision to introduce new column headings based on emerging patterns in the data. Once you have charted a few cases you might find that some columns are over-populated and contain information that is related to different areas or themes. For example, you may find that there are several different types of comprehension problem associated with a single question. In this case you may wish to alter your matrix for this question so, instead of having a single column on comprehension you have 'Comprehension of term X', 'Comprehension of term Y', and 'Comprehension of term Z' columns, for example. Once you have finalised the design of your matrix you need to enter the information from all remaining sets of notes.

It should be noted that the purpose of charting is twofold. The primary purpose is to collate and reduce information from multiple interviews into a coherent structure from which you can do the analysis. However, the secondary purpose is that charting is a way of quality-checking the notes. When charting, you will be able to see if any information on the research aims is missing as this will result in empty cells in your matrices. If you are charting notes written by other interviewers you will also be able to sense-check these to see if the narrative is clear, and the amount of information provided is adequate. If, when charting, you feel that the initial summaries are too brief or vague you should return to the primary data (audio recording or transcript) to find the missing information and to clarify any points that are unclear. This may also highlight an interviewer training issue.

7.7 Software options

You do not require any specialist software in order to produce your Framework matrices, although some specialist packages are available. In this section we discuss the different software options for producing your matrices.

7.7.1 Non-specialist software

It is easy to produce matrices using non-specialist software packages that you are likely to already have installed on your computer. You may choose to produce your matrices either in a standard word document or in a spreadsheet (e.g. Excel or similar). Of these two options we recommend that spreadsheets are more suitable for charting cognitive interviews than word processing packages. When producing matrices in a word processing package (even if the orientation is set to landscape) you will be more restricted in terms of the number of columns and rows that will fit on a single page, particularly once the cells are populated with text.

In contrast, spreadsheets are designed for matrix-based data entry and are relatively easy to set up. We recommend that when using spreadsheets that you set the 'cell format' to 'text' and that you adjust the column widths so they are wide enough to accommodate at least seven words per line. You can produce multiple matrices within a single Excel file by having each matrix on a separate worksheet.

The main advantage of using spreadsheets for charting is that they are quick and easy to set up and they don't require any specialist software.

An example of a matrix produced in Excel is shown in Figure 7.6.

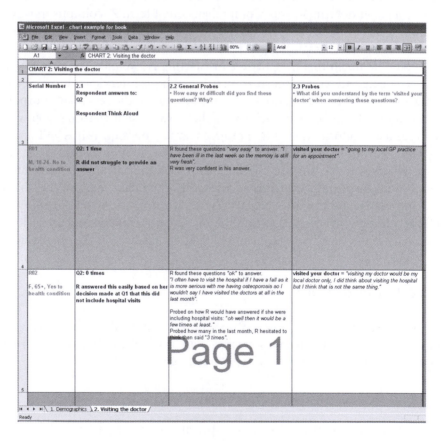

Figure 7.6 Example matrix produced in Excel

━━━━━━━━━━━━━━━━━━━━━ **TOP TIP** ━━━━━━━━━━━━━━━━━━━━━

In Excel you may wish to include additional columns for each of your sampling criteria (refer to section 4.2.4). For example, you could have one additional column for sex, one additional column for age group, etc. By doing this it will be easier for sort your cases by whatever criterion you may be interested in. For example, you could use the 'Data' then 'Sort' menus to arrange your cases so all your males are displayed first and then all your females. This function is useful if you wish to explore whether there are any patterns in problems encountered between different groups.

7.7.2 Qualitative data management software

An alternative to using spreadsheets packages is to use specialist software for managing qualitative data. The software we use is NVivo. Since 2011 NVivo has included a Framework functionality developed by qualitative researchers NatCen Social Research (Spencer et al., 2014). The main advantages of using NVivo over non-specialised spreadsheets are:

1. You can import primary data (e.g. transcripts) into the programme and create links between these and the interview summaries. In practice this means you can click on any summary cell in your matrix and drill down to the more detailed data on which the summary is based. In addition, you can import other forms of data into the software (such as audio or video files, scanned copies of questionnaires, and so on) and link these to the information that is entered in the matrix. All these procedures allow for greater transparency and cross-checking during the analysis process.
2. You can easily run new 'queries' to generate bespoke matrices after your initial matrices have been set up. For example, you can run queries where you produce new matrices refined by participant characteristics (e.g. only show females aged 60+) and by area of interest (e.g. only show findings related to the concept of 'comfort' for Q1–6). This means it easy to interrogate your data in ways that facilitate deeper analysis.

An example of a matrix produced in NVivo is shown in Figure 7.7. Note that by clicking on the cells you can be redirected back to the data sources it refers to (e.g. transcripts, interviewer notes or any other documents that have been imported).

7.8 Data security

So far we have considered how to organise and summarise your data, ready for analysis. In this section we discuss information security and the issues you need to consider to ensure you keep your participants' data safe.

At the planning stage, discussed in Chapter 3, you will need to consider how you are going to store your cognitive interview data. You have a responsibility to

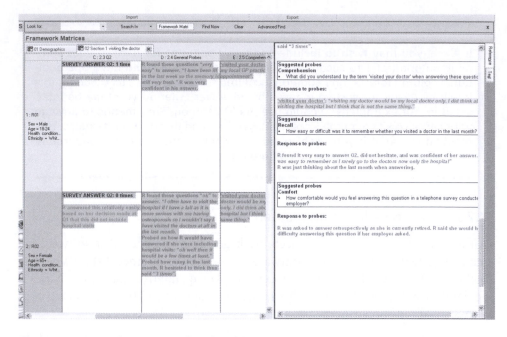

Figure 7.7 Example matrix produced in NVivo

make sure that participants information is only used for the agreed purposes and only viewed by the agreed parties (see section 3.9.4). This section looks at steps you can take to ensure your data are stored in a way that maintains participant confidentiality.

7.8.1 Storing data securely

The personal details of your participants such as their names, addresses, contact details and any other information kept as part of the recruitment process should be securely stored. Hard copies of documents containing these details should not be left in places where they could be overseen by people not involved in the project. Hard copies of these documents should be kept in a lockable drawer or cupboard when not in use.

Similarly, electronic files that contain personal details should not be viewable by people who are not involved in the project. This means electronic files should be password protected or saved in secure network folders that have access restricted to the appropriate people.

We recommend that participants' personal details are *not* included on any completed test questionnaires or on any interview transcripts. In order to keep track of who said what (and which completed questionnaire belonged to whom) you may wish to allocate a pseudonym or serial number to each participant.

Different organisations have different procedures for making sure that personal data are kept safe and secure. For example, certain organisations may request that personal details are transferred across a secure FTP server by email using some form of encryption. Check with your institution and with the research funder about any procedures they may have regarding the storage and transmission of personal data before embarking on a cognitive interviewing project.

7.8.2 Maintaining privacy when reviewing recordings

If you are listening to a recording of a cognitive interview make sure that there is no danger of someone inadvertently overhearing what was said. Using headphones will ensure that the interview is not accidentally overheard by others in the vicinity.

7.8.3 Anonymising raw data

When gaining participant consent to take part in a study you should always specify who is going to be able to access the information collected. It's good to be able to reassure participants that findings will be reported anonymously (i.e. their names and other identifiable information will not be revealed) and only the researcher (and the research team) will know who has taken part in the study.

That said it may be a requirement of the study that you share interview transcripts with a range of stakeholders. For example, it may be that you need to share transcripts with a sponsor, funder or project supervisor. It is also possible that someone may wish to review the transcripts for quality-checking purposes. In these circumstances transcripts may need to be anonymised to protect the identities of participants. By anonymised we mean the participant's name (and any names of other people mentioned by the participant) should be removed from the transcript. Similarly, any other potential identifiers should also be removed. This could include specific places referred to by the participant, their job title and employer details or any other details that could inadvertently reveal who they are. Anonymising transcripts can be a time-consuming process.

Unlike transcripts, audio recordings or videos cannot be easily anonymised. It is possible that someone may be identified by the sound of their voice. Therefore, audio recordings should not be shared with people outside of the research team unless the participant has explicitly given their consent for this to happen.

7.9 Chapter summary

Cognitive interview data can be analysed quantitatively or qualitatively. Both approaches involve moving from participants' verbal reports to codes that classify the data.

The method we use is called Framework and is a qualitative approach. A thematic framework (matrix) is used to classify and organise data according to key themes, concepts and emergent categories. Data management is the first step in the analysis process.

Our recommended data management strategy involves the following two steps.

a) Reducing unrefined data into summarised data. In practice this means making a set of notes on each interview describing the relevant findings from the interview.

b) Combining summaries into a series of matrices. Summarised data can then be read horizontally as a complete case summary for each participant or vertically by area of investigation. This approach makes it possible to systematically review the data collected.

The production of the matrices can be done using non-specialist software (such as an Excel spreadsheet) or can involve specialist, qualitative data analysis software (such as NVivo).

It is important to consider data security as part of the data management process. You will need to take steps to ensure that participants' personal details can only be viewed by the appropriate people.

References

Blair, J. and Brick, P.D. (2010) 'Methods for analysis of cognitive interviews', *Proceedings of the Survey Research Methods Section. American Statistical Association,* pp. 3739–48 [online]. Available at www.amstat.org/sections/srms/proceedings/y2010f.html

Conrad, F., Blair, J. and Tracy, E. (1999) 'Verbal reports are data! A theoretical approach to cognitive interviews', *Federal Committee on Statistical Methodology Conference Proceedings.* Available at: www.fcsm.gov/99papers/conrad1.pdf

De Maio, T.J. and Landreth, A. (2004) 'Do different cognitive interview techniques produce different results?', in S. Presser, J.M. Rothgeb, M.P. Couper, J.T. Lessler, E. Martin, J. Martin and E. Singer (eds), *Methods for Testing and Evaluating Survey Questions.* Chichester: Wiley. pp. 89–108.

Gerber, E.R. (1999) 'The view from anthropology: ethnography and the cognitive interview', in M.G. Sirken, D.J. Herrmann, S. Schechter, N. Schwarz, J.M. Tanur and R. Tourangeau (eds), *Cognition and Survey Research.* New York; Willey. pp. 217–34.

Miles, M.B. and Huberman, A.M. (1994) *Qualitative Data Analysis: An Expanded Sourcebook.* London: Sage Publications.

Miller, K., Willson, S., Chepp, V. and Padilla, J.L. (eds) (2014) *Cognitive Interviewing Methodology.* Hoboken, NJ: Wiley.

Presser, S. and Blair, J. (1994) 'Survey pretesting: do different methods produce different results?', in P. Marsden (ed.), *Sociological Methodology*. San Francisco, CA: Jossey-Bass. pp. 73–104.

Ridolfo, H. and Schoua-Glusberg, A. (2011) 'Analyzing cognitive interview data using the Constant Comparative Method of analysis to understand cross-cultural patterns in survey data', *Field Methods*, 23(4): 420–38.

Ritchie, J. and Spencer, L. (1994) 'Qualitative data analysis for applied policy research', in A. Bryman and R.G. Burgess (eds), *Analyzing Qualitative Data*. London: Routledge. pp. 173–94.

Rothgeb, J., Willis, G. and Forsyth, B. (2001) 'Questionnaire pretesting methods: Do different techniques and different organisations produce similar results?', *Proceedings of the ASA Section on Survey Research Methods*. Alexandria, VA: American Statistical Association. Available online at www.amstat.org/sections/srms/proceedings/

Spencer, L., Ritchie, J. and O'Connor, W. (2003) 'Analysis: practices, principles and processes', in J. Ritchie and J. Lewis (eds), *Qualitative Research Practice* (1st edition). London: Sage Publications. pp. 199–218.

Spencer, L., Ritchie, J., O'Connor, W., Morrell., G. and Ormston, R. (2014) 'Analysis in practice', in J. Ritchie, J. Lewis, C. McNaughton Nicholls and R. Ormston (eds), *Qualitative Research Practice* (2nd edition). London: Sage Publications. pp. 295–345.

Willis, G.B., Schechter, S. and Whitaker, K. (1999) 'A comparison of cognitive interviewing, expert review, and behaviour coding: What do they tell us?' *Proceedings of the Section on Survey Research Methods*. Alexandria, VA: American Statistical Association. pp. 28–37.

EIGHT

ANALYSIS AND INTERPRETATION
DEBBIE COLLINS

8.1 Introduction

The aim of this chapter is to set out the steps involved in the analysis and interpretation of cognitive interview data using the Framework approach (see Spencer et al., 2003). The analysis of cognitive interview data has until fairly recently been a rather neglected area of discussion and documentation, yet it is arguably the most important phase (Blair and Brick, 2010; Collins, 2007; Knafl et al., 2007; Ridolfo and Schoua-Glusberg, 2011). Being conscious of your decisions at this stage, and documenting them, helps to ensure the process is transparent, open to scrutiny, and will help your findings gain credibility.

In this chapter we discuss:

- The importance of being clear about the aims of your analysis
- The analytical process and the distinction between descriptive and explanatory analysis
- The steps involved in descriptive and explanatory analysis
- The importance of understanding context
- The use of theory in your analysis
- Dealing with unique or odd cases
- Considering the implications of your findings for the survey.

We use examples from our own work to illustrate the analytical steps.

8.2 Aims of analysis

At a general level the aim of analysis is to answer the research questions that the pretest has been designed to address. These aims will vary: sometimes you may be interested in understanding mechanisms – how participants go about answering questions, the decisions they make along the way and the factors that can influence the response process. In other cases you may be interested in evaluating whether the question or series of questions is working in the way intended – do participants understand key concepts in a consistent way and in the way the researcher intended, are participants thinking about the specified reference period, are participants' answers sufficiently accurate and reliable to meet the measurement aims of the survey? Your analysis may therefore produce different outputs: descriptions; explanations; suggestions for further research or investigation; proposals or recommendations for changes to the test questions that might include deletion or revision (see Chapter 9). Whatever the aims and objective are, the analytical process will involve many common steps. In the rest of this chapter we walk through these steps and illustrate them using data from some of our published studies.

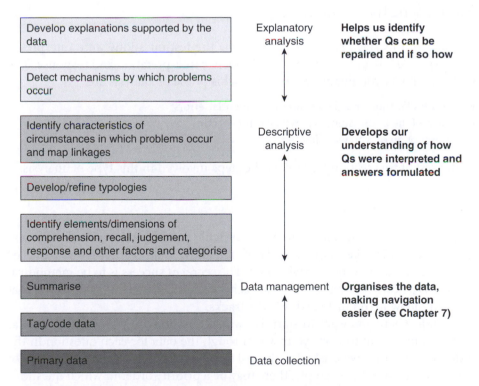

Figure 8.1   Steps involved in the analysis of cognitive interview data
Modified from 'The Analytical Hierarchy', Box 8.1, Spencer et al. (2003: 212).

8.3 The analysis process

In section 7.3 we described in broad terms the analytical process, paying particular attention to the data management and summarisation stage. Once this has been completed the formal process of analysis can begin, see Figure 8.1. Formal analysis involves two stages: description and interpretation. Description involves identifying and classifying problems and characterising the circumstances in which they occur. This stage helps us understand how questions are being interpreted and how answers are formulated. The second stage of analysis involves the identification of the mechanisms by which problems occur and the search for explanations for these. This process helps us to understand why and how problems occur, which in turn helps us think about what we might be able to do to resolve or ameliorate its impact, see Chapter 9.

This analysis process is iterative and it can be time-consuming. However, the time and effort you invest will be reflected in the depth of your understanding and cogence of your case for action. Let's start by looking in more detail at the descriptive phase of analysis, and walking through the steps involved.

8.4 Descriptive analysis

The aim of this stage is to understand *how* the test questions were interpreted and responded to and the factors that influence interpretation and response. The sorts of outputs you might produce from this phase of analysis are:

- the identification and classification of 'potential' errors;
- a map of the circumstances in which errors occur;
- a description of who was affected.

In the rest of this section we look at the steps involved in this type of analysis.

8.4.1 Getting started

Getting started can be one of the most difficult things to do, particularly if you have never undertaken any analysis of qualitative data before. Don't panic or allow yourself to become overwhelmed. The secret of success is to be methodical and to keep notes on what you find at each step, and what ideas occur to you that you can follow up on further down the tracks.

Decide where you want to start, i.e. which question are you going to look at first. You may want to work your way through the data for each question in the order in which they were asked in the test questionnaire. However, this might not always be the case. For example, there may be a priority order in which questions need to be reviewed, which is related to the timetable for production of the final questionnaire. Alternatively, if analysis is being undertaken by a team, you will need to decide who looks at which questions. If you are going to undertake analysis of questions in a different sequence to the test sequence, consider whether you need to look at questions in chunks and identify what those should be. For example, it might be sensible to analyse all the questions in a particular section of the test questionnaire or on a particular topic in one chunk because understanding what the participant was considering when answering earlier questions can influence how they answer subsequent ones.

8.4.2 Familiarisation

Immerse yourself in the data by reading the matrices (refer to section 7.6) and, if time allows, listen to some of the interview recordings. If you have been involved in the interviewing and summarisation process then you will have already begun this process. Even though you may be focusing on specific questions it is useful to read through the entire summary case-by-case, as this can provide valuable clues as to how the participant went about the task and the factors that may shape what they did and thought about when answering a particular question.

Note the range of interpretations, recall strategies, response and decision-making behaviours for each question and list these.

TOP TIP

It can be useful to look at each stage of the question and answer process separately at this stage. You may have decided to split each of these stages out in your matrix (see section 7.6).

8.4.3 Categorise

Having familiarised yourself with the data and noted the range of interpretations and response behaviours, the next step is to begin to group these together into types or categories. The process of categorisation has two components:

- identifying different interpretations, answer strategies, views on the acceptability of a question, and so forth; and
- identifying problems.

Identifying differences

Participants may have interpreted the test questions in different ways or used different answer strategies. You need to identify the dimensions that differentiate between these. Ask yourself: is this the same as that, or is it something different? Start to build a picture and group pieces of information together. In this way you begin to reduce your data further, which makes it easier to spot patterns. Let's consider Example 8.1.

Example 8.1   Classification of answer strategies

We tested the following question, which is asked as part of a face-to-face survey that collects detailed information on household finances.

Roughly how much money was left in the (first) [bank/savings] account at the end of last (month/pay period)?

This question followed questions about the types of bank and savings accounts participants held.

We identified a number of different answer strategies, which can be grouped into one of three types.

Recall	Estimation	Documentation
• Of what is left over at the end of the month • Of the balance based on last time the participant looked at/discussed the account balance	• Guessed what is in the account • Of what the participant likes to think is the minimum balance the account ever drops to	• Answer can only be provided with reference to documentation

Note that the estimation strategies used involved the participant making a judgement about how much is in the account: the information was not readily available in memory and documentation (i.e. a bank statement) was not referred to. See Betts et al. (2003) for more details.

TOP TIP

You may find that using a colour coding scheme (or another way of identifying data which share characteristics) helps you at this stage. You can use such a scheme as you work your way through the data, labelling and grouping findings into the categories you have developed.

Identify problems

To identify any problems or errors you need to refer to the original measurement aims of the test question and compare these to the range of interpretations, recall strategies, response and decision-making behaviours identified, noting where 'errors' or mistakes occur. We can't emphasise enough the importance of being fully informed, during this stage of the analysis process, of the measurement aims and the boundaries of the concepts your questions are attempting to measure. For example, to identify problems with a question about hours worked you would need to know the intended definition of work. Does it include both paid and unpaid work or just paid work? Knowing this will help you assess the evidence from your cognitive interviews and decide whether participants including hours worked volunteering is a problem or not. Being familiar with the boundaries of the concepts being measured and the precise measurement aims is undoubtedly easier if you have designed the questions, or at least been involved in their design. If you are unsure of the measurement aims of the test question then your problem identification will be more circumspect and be couched in terms of 'depending on the measurement aims this might be a problem'.

Let's consider Example 8.1 again. When testing this question we identified two sources of error: overestimation by couples and documentation being out of date.

8.4.4 Understanding context

Whilst the main focus of the cognitive interview is on the question and answer process this doesn't happen in vacuum (Miller, 2011). Participants bring with them their past experiences, emotions, cultural references, habits, preferences, and so forth. These factors can shape the way in which people understand the question task, their willingness to engage in the process of providing an answer, and the responses they provide. As part of the cognitive interview you may have captured this information, in which case you will want to make use of it in your analysis. For example, you might want to develop a typology that classifies participants in terms of their comfort with being asked the test questions. You might use this information when looking for patterns in the data, at the explanatory stage. For example, you could then use this typology to explore whether comfort levels had any impact on response behaviour.

Another form of contextual information to consider is how the findings arose: was it something that the participant mentioned spontaneously or was it something that only came to light during probing? For example, you may have been testing an income question to explore, among other things, acceptability. You might want to differentiate between those participants who immediately expressed a dislike of the question on first being asked it and refused to answer it from those who provided an answer but on probing said that they didn't like being asked about their income.

8.5 Explanatory analysis

The aim of explanatory analysis is to understand how 'potential' problems and the patterns in the problems observed have come about. Outputs from this stage are often:

- reasons why a problem occurs; and
- the implications of problems identified for the main survey.

The evidence you unearth at this stage of the analysis will inform decisions about what change(s), if any, are needed to the questions, see Chapter 9.

Combining evidence from cognitive interviews with that from other sources, such as survey (pilot) data, anecdotal evidence from interviewers or coders, or objective measures such as eye movements or mouse clicks, can add to the strength of the conclusions you draw about the performance of the test question and any changes that are required (refer to section 2.3). In the rest of this section we look at the steps involved in explanatory analysis.

8.5.1 Identify patterns

Look for patterns in your data, as these will help you identify mechanisms by which problems occur; for example, the way in which the test question was understood relates to the selection of a response option or how participants' circumstances relate to problems found. Let's consider Example 8.2.

> ### Example 8.2   Testing questions about receipt of welfare benefits
>
> We tested a set of questions concerned with collecting information on receipt of welfare benefits and tax credits. These questions were asked in an existing, long-running survey that collected information on the household finances of the general population as part of a face-to-face interview.
>
> Participants are asked whether they received a number of welfare benefits. These were listed on a series of five show cards. Participants experienced difficulties identifying the benefits and tax credits they received because:
>
> - they did not know the actual name of the benefit or tax credit;
> - the way benefits were grouped together on each of the cards did not seem logical to participants because benefits of a similar type, such as health or retirement, were split across several cards;
> - the name(s) participants knew their benefit(s) by or the name of the benefit on their benefit letter(s) did not correspond with the name(s) listed on the card.

In Example 8.2 the types of difficulties experienced were identified by looking for patterns in the data.

Map the links between comprehension, recall, judgement, response and the characteristics of test participants. Do you see different patterns in say, comprehension and answer selection across different subgroups? Let's consider Example 8.2 again. In this study we found that participants aged 80 and over had particular difficulty in accurately reporting the benefits they were getting and how much they were receiving for each one.

Note that you may find no evidence to suggest the question was problematic. This is an important finding. Alternatively, you might find that the question was problematic in certain circumstances. It is important here to understand why problems occur in some circumstances and not others.

If you can't find any patterns then this may suggest that you have not conducted enough interviews or that your interviews have not been conducted in a consistent way. You may need to stop at this point, review your study design and consider whether further cognitive interviews are needed, perhaps with a sharper focus of enquiry and a more consistent approach. Alternatively you may need to go back and review the findings from your descriptive analysis. Are your categories sufficiently differentiating between different types of problem or behaviour? Have you considered contextual factors sufficiently?

8.5.2 Develop explanations

The next step is to develop explanations of the patterns you have found. These may be based directly on participants' own accounts (that were captured in the cognitive interviews) or indirectly, where you make inferences from the interviews informed by findings from other empirical studies or from theory to develop an explanation (see section 8.5.3). Don't be afraid to make inferences: the important thing is to test these out and explore whether your data support them. This is an iterative process, whereby you refine your explanations through a process of questioning and interrogating the data.

One way to approach the development of explanations is to review the patterns and linkages you have identified. For example, your analysis shows that the term used in the question to describe the concept being measured is being misunderstood. You now need to look for evidence that may explain why this term is being misunderstood. This involves asking questions of the data. For example, is the term unfamiliar to participants? Is it being confused with something else? Do the preceding questions influence the participant's interpretation and if so, how?

Let's consider our two examples again. In relation to Example 8.1 we found that couples could over-report the amount in a bank or savings account when this was a jointly held account. The explanation for this problem centres on the definition used in the survey. The survey asks for individual shares of jointly held assets. However, this concept of individual shares does not exist for some older married couples, who viewed their finances as a joint resource: 'what's his is mine and what's mine is his'.

In relation to Example 8.2, we found that those aged 80 and over had particular difficulties recalling the benefits and tax credits they received and their value. The cognitive interviews revealed that this was typically because someone else managed their finances, or because they received multiple benefits, the value of each component not being known/recalled without reference to documentation. Infirmity meant that these participants were reluctant or unwilling to consult documents, though in some cases there was evidence to suggest that the cognitive interviewer was also reluctant to request to see documentation.

The questions you ask will be influenced by what you know already – for example from similar studies, the wider literature or other evidence sources. In the case of Example 8.2, an analysis of the survey data for previous years revealed that the quality of data of those over 80 was not as good as for other survey participants (see Balarajan and Collins, 2013).

8.5.3 Using theory

It can be useful to use theory to help you in your analysis. You can use theory to explain your test findings. For example, you might test a question that asks about how many times the participant's child was admitted to hospital during the past 12 months. You find that in some cases participants are reporting admissions that took place outside the reference period: they are reporting hospital admissions that are up to three months beyond the 12-month reference period. (This over-reporting is discovered during probing.) You note that this happens in cases where this is the only hospital admission the child has had. This behaviour is known in the survey methodology literature as telescoping and it can affect the validity of self-reported frequency of events (see Ziniel, 2008). Alternatively, your cognitive interview findings might reveal that participants are engaging in satisficing behaviours, such as skim-reading instructions (see Oppenheimer et al., 2009) or always picking the same, often positive point, on an answer scale irrespective of the question, known as acquiescence bias. Satisficing occurs, in part, when participants do not invest sufficient effort in each stage of the question and answer process or omit certain stages, encouraged by features of the survey questions (Krosnick et al., 1996).

You can also use theory to generate hypotheses that you can explore and test. This is known as a deductive research approach. Let's consider how this might work in practice. You might have tested a revised version of a travel dairy (see McGee et al., 2006). In redesigning the travel diary you adopt some specific design features that, according to theory, should make the diary easier to navigate and therefore reduce errors (see Jenkins and Dillman, 1997). In the analysis you want to explore whether there is any evidence to suggest that the revisions have improved navigation, encouraging participants to read instructions; follow sign-posting; and apply definitions correctly? You might develop a coding schema that identifies particular types of problems so that you can map where errors occur in the diary. For example, is there still a problem with particular columns being left blank, resulting in missing data? Are instructions being used when participants get stuck? If you tested the original diary using cognitive interviewing methods then you could compare your data for the two versions. Even better would be to have data on the performance of the old and new diaries from a range of sources, which you could compare. This would allow you to triangulate your findings and form a more robust view of the performance of each version, which might allow you to determine which version was 'better' in terms of improving data quality. This is what we did on this study, testing the travel diary.

8.6 Dealing with cases that are unique, odd or don't fit the typology

As part of your analysis you may identify cases that are unique, seem odd or don't fit with your typology or explanation of the process. When this happens you need to examine these cases and your analytical approach and decide what to do.

You may identify a unique case. What are the features that make it unique? It may be that because of the small size of your sample you have only captured one example of a particular set of circumstances. For example, you may only have had one participant in your sample who was self-employed. The difficulties this participant may have had answering a question about their job, hours worked and income may relate to their circumstances – being self-employed. You might want to include this case in your analysis because you believe it illustrates the sorts of problems other participants might have in these circumstances.

Sometimes you may come across cases where the participant's response to a probe seems a little odd. For example, you might have asked a participant what he understood by a particular term and he may have given what appears to be an illogical answer. Don't ignore these apparently random cases. In this situation you will need to review the case fully. Is there a pattern throughout the interview of the participant providing 'off-the-wall' responses? Is there anything about his circumstances that might explain this, for example is he on medication? You should also reflect on what happened in the interview. Was the participant effusive, spontaneously describing what he was thinking about at each question or did the interviewer have to ask a lot of probing questions to elicit information on his thought processes? In short, do you think the participant was engaged in the cognitive interview process or was the participant distracted or uninterested? Reflecting on these issues will help you decide how to treat this case and what weight you should attach to it.

In other cases you may have developed a typology, see section 8.4.3, and in the process of trying to apply it to your data you discover that some cases don't seem to fit. In this situation you will need to go back and review your typology in light of these cases. The typology may need to be refined or discarded. What you must not do is try to force the data to fit the typology.

8.7 Considering implications

The final step in your analysis is to consider the implications of the problems and explanation you have identified. Do you think the problem is something that will compromise the quality of the survey data? The more you know about the aims of the survey and how the data will be used the better placed you will be to assess the potential impact of the problem. If you are able to draw on other data – from other pretests (see Chapter 2) or if you are testing questions from an existing survey, look at the data for those questions – then this will help you be more confident in suggesting implications.

Let's consider Example 8.1 again. In this example we found that there was a problem with couples providing a joint balance rather that a share of a joint balance for a bank or savings account. The implication of this finding is that the value of the asset is likely to be overestimated when couples both give joint balances rather than their share. This type of error would not necessarily be picked up during a 'real' survey interview unless the interviewer specifically checked whether the answer given was a total balance for a joint account or the participant's share of it.

Figure 8.2 illustrates the implications of certain kinds of problems you might find.

Problem	Implication
• Concepts or terms are not understood in a consistent way • Concepts or terms are not understood in the way intended	→ The validity of survey responses could be affected
• The reference period cited in the question is not used – participants either report events outside the reference period or don't think back far enough	→ This could result in over-reporting or under-reporting, respectively
• Errors occur in recalling events because participants cannot recall the information required at all or in the detail required	→ This could result in under-reporting
• Items are omitted because participants misinterpret the question, use their own definition or cannot recall the information required	→ This could result in under-reporting
• Calculations are avoided: participants estimate or use other short cuts	→ This could result in under- or over-reporting
• Answer options are not clearly labelled or do not use language participants are familiar with	→ This could result in over- or under-reporting or missing data
• Respondents are unhappy about providing the information being sought	→ This could result in missing data
• A numeric answer scale is not understood or is used incorrectly	→ This could result in missing data or incorrect data being collected

Figure 8.2 Problems and their potential implications

8.8 Chapter summary

- Analysis involves two stages: description and interpretation. The analysis process is often iterative and you should allow sufficient time for it.
- You can use contextual information in your analysis, for example to explore the validity of participants' survey answers.
- It can be useful to use theory to help explain your findings or to guide your analysis.
- The final step in analysis is considering the implications of your findings. How might they affect survey estimates?
- Analysis planning should infuse all parts of the design and implementation of your cognitive interview study.
- We recommend that you refer to the measurement aims of your test questions when carrying out your analysis.

References

Balarajan, M. and Collins, D. (2013) *A Review of Questions asked about State Benefits on the Family Resources Survey*. Working Paper No. 115. London: Department for Work and Pensions. Available at: http://socialwelfare.bl.uk/subject-areas/services-activity/poverty-benefits/departmentforworkandpensions/family131.aspx

Betts, P., Breman, R. and Collins, D. (2003) *Comparing Strategies for Collecting Information on Personal Assets*. Department for Work and Pensions Research Working Paper 9. London: HMSO.

Blair, J. and Brick, P.D. (2010) 'Methods for analysis of cognitive interviews', *Proceedings of the Survey Research Methods Section. American Statistical Association* 3739–48 [online]. Available online at www.amstat.org/sections/srms/proceedings/y2010f.html

Collins, D. (2007) 'Analysing and interpreting cognitive interview data: a qualitative approach'. Paper given at the Questionnaire Evaluation Standards Workshop, Ottawa, Canada [available online].

Jenkins, C.R. and Dillman, D.A. (1997) 'Towards a theory of self-administered questionnaire design', in L. Lyberg, P. Biemer, M. Collins, E. de Leeuw, C. Dippo, N. Schwarz and D. Trewin (eds), *Survey Measurement and Process Quality*. New York: John Wiley & Sons. pp. 165–96.

Knafl, K., Deatrick, J., Gallo, A., Holcombe, G., Bakitas, M., Dixon, J. and Grey, M. (2007) 'The analysis and interpretation of cognitive interviews for instrument development', *Research in Nursing & Health*, 30: 224–34.

Krosnick, J.A., Narayan, S. and Smith, W.R. (1996) 'Satisficing in surveys: initial evidence', *New Directions for Evaluation*, 70: 29–44. doi: 10.1002/ev.1033.

McGee, A., Gray, M., Andrews, F., Legard, R., Wood, N. and Collins, D. (2006) *NTS Travel Record Review Stage 2*. London: Department of Transport. Available at: http://webarchive.nationalarchives.gov.uk/+/http://www.dft.gov.uk/pgr/

statistics/datatablespublications/personal/methodology/ntsrecords/
ntstravelrecord2.pdf

Miller, K. (2011) 'Cognitive interviewing', in J. Maddens, K. Miller, A. Maitland and
G. Willis (eds), *Question Evaluation Methods: Contributing to the Science of Data
Quality*. Hoboken, NJ: John Wiley & Sons Inc. pp. 51–75.

Oppenheimer, D.M, Meyvis, T. and Davidenko, N. (2009) 'Instructional
manipulation checks: detecting satisficing to increase statistical power', *Journal of
Experimental Social Psychology*, 45: 867–72.

Ridolfo, H. and Schoua-Glusberg, A. (2011) 'Analyzing cognitive interview data
using the constant comparative method of analysis to understand cross-cultural
patterns in survey data', *Field Methods*, 23(4): 420–38.

Spencer, L., Ritchie, J. and O'Connor, W. (2003) 'Analysis: practices, principles and
processes', in J. Ritchie and J. Lewis (eds), *Qualitative Research Practice*. London:
Sage. pp. 199–218.

Ziniel, S. (2008) 'Telescoping', in P. Lavrakas (ed.), *Encylopedia of Survey Research
Methods*. Sage Research Methods. Available at: http://dx.doi.
org/10.4135/9781412963947

NINE

APPLICATION OF FINDINGS

JO D'ARDENNE, DEBBIE COLLINS AND MARGARET BLAKE

9.1 Introduction

The aim of this chapter is to help you consider what changes, if any, you will make to your survey questions based on your cognitive interview findings. Whatever the composition of your questionnaire development and testing phase – whether it has involved multiple rounds of cognitive or multiple pretesting methods – it is likely that you will want to review the findings from an individual round of cognitive interviews and make some decisions about the next steps in the design and testing process based on these.

In this chapter we look at:

- How to decide if a question requires change
- The type(s) of changes or actions you may want to propose:
  - changes to wording of questions and answer options;
  - dropping questions;
  - changes to question layouts (for self-administered surveys);
  - alternative forms of data collection;
  - additional testing; or
  - that no changes are made. .
- How to present findings.

We illustrate this process with examples from our own work.

9.2 Deciding whether changes are needed

Having undertaken analysis of your cognitive interview data (see Chapter 8) you should now have some evidence about how well the question is performing. You now need to consider what action needs to be taken, based on this evidence. There are a number of steps in making this judgement.

Aims

- Review the measurement aims of the question and compare them with the aims of the cognitive interview. Which measurement aims did the cognitive interviews attempt to evaluate?

Evidence

- Review the evidence for each of these measurement aims. What does the cognitive interview data tell you about the performance of the question?
- Is the evidence clear, for example does it tell you why (some) people had difficulties or made mistakes when attempting to answer the question?
- Is the evidence consistent, for example is it consistent with theory and/or findings from other studies?
- Did you test the question with a wide range of people? Were they the right people? Is your sample sufficiently diverse to support your conclusions?
- Do you have any other data that support or add to your cognitive interview data, for example eye-tracking data?

Context and constraints

- What do you know about the main survey?
- Where do the test questions fit within the main questionnaire?
- Are there likely to be any constraints on what you can propose, for example due to mode, time series, or interview length?

Having reviewed the measurement aims, the evidence on question performance and the constraints you should be in a position to form a view about whether you need to make any changes to the questions. This is a matter of judgement: you have to weigh up the evidence and decide what the next step should be.

9.3 Types of recommendations

There are a number of potential recommendations that you might make, based on the evidence available to you from your cognitive interviews (Czaja and Blair, 1996; Willis, 2005). Your recommendation might be to:

- change the question wording or instructions;
- change the answer options;
- change the question order or filtering rules;
- change the way the information being sought is collected, e.g. change the mode of data collection, use a diary rather than ask questions;
- drop the question altogether;
- add in additional instructions for interviewers or improve interviewer training;
- do nothing until the measurement objectives have been reviewed, clarified or amended; or
- do nothing and leave the test question unchanged.

In deciding what action to recommend you should think about the following issues.

- What are the measurement aims of the question?
  - o Are they already clear or do they need to be clarified?
- How will the questions be used in the survey?
  - o What mode will be used?
  - o Is questionnaire length or respondent burden an issue?
  - o Will the problems found in the cognitive interviews be found in the survey, and if so how commonplace or significant might they be?
- How will the survey data for this question be analysed?
  - o What level of accuracy or differentiation is required?
- How will the survey findings be used?
  - o Is comparison over time or between surveys important?
  - o Will the findings be used to measure specific policy objectives or targets?
- What other evidence do you have about how the question may work?
  - o Findings for other questions in the same questionnaire
  - o Experience from other projects
  - o Literature about questionnaire design practice
  - o Knowledge of policy or social changes.
- What further options are there for testing?
  - o Is a second round of cognitive testing planned?
  - o Will a field pilot offer a further opportunity for testing?

In some cases there may be several potential remedies to the same problem. You will have to decide which one is the most appropriate for your survey. You may also find that a question or set of questions has multiple problems, which would suggest conflicting remedies. The rest of this section will provide more detail on how to make different types of recommendations and provides case studies describing recommendations we have made based on findings from cognitive interviews.

9.3.1 Wording changes

Your findings may indicate that a particular term used in the question is misunderstood (by some people). In deciding how to deal with this you need to make sure that you understand why it is being misunderstood: is the term unfamiliar; is it being confused with something else? Knowing why will help you decide what the remedy should be. For example, if it's unfamiliar then the remedy may be to use a more familiar term or to provide a definition.

The cognitive interview data may provide you with evidence on the language participants use to describe a particular concept. You may find that there is a particular term or number of terms that are consistently used to describe a concept and that using these would aid comprehension (see Example 9.1 below).

Example 9.1   Wording is unfamiliar

Aims

We carried out a series of cognitive interviews to test new questions that were to be included in a telephone survey of people who claim Employment and Support Allowance (a welfare benefit offered to people who are unable to work due to a health condition or disability). One set of questions tested asked about the types of services, if any, that had been offered to participants by their former employer before they stopped working due to their health. One measurement aim was to capture what proportion of claimants had previously had access to an Employee Assistance Programme. The question we tested is shown below.

Q: Did you have access to an Employee Assistance Programme through your employer? [*READ OUT IF NECESSARY: this is an independent counselling or advice service.*]

1. Yes
2. No
3. Don't know

Evidence

Only one participant who took part in the cognitive interviews had heard of the term 'Employee Assistance Programme'. All other participants incorrectly thought that this phrase referred to financial assistance provided by employers, a sick pay scheme, or assistance from the government to help people return to work. An interviewer clarification was provided at this question but it was not always read out as the instruction to the interviewer stated 'read out if necessary' and participants did not always express any confusion.

Recommendations

As a result of the testing we recommended that the name of the programme was dropped, as this was not well known, and replaced with a description of it. The revised question is shown below.

> **Q:** Did you have access to an independent counselling or advice service through your employer?
>
> 1. Yes
> 2. No
> 3. Don't know

Words that are too technical are not the only source of problematic terminology in question wording. Often commonplace words are ambiguous or have multiple meanings. In these cases participants might understand the question's gist but in a way that varies from that of the question's intended purpose. It could be that participants are consistently excluding things which, according to the measurement aims, should be included. In these instances you may wish to amend the question to clarify its intended breadth. Example 9.2 illustrates this point.

Example 9.2   Wording is ambiguous

Aims

We were asked to test, using cognitive interviewing, a patient and carer experience questionnaire used to evaluate home nursing and hospice services. The questions were asked over the telephone. One of the questions tested aimed to measure satisfaction with pain relief.

Q: How would you rate the overall level of support given in the following areas by the [home nursing service/hospice] ... Relief of pain.

1. Poor
2. Fair
3. Good
4. Very good
5. Excellent
6. *[Not read out] Not applicable*

According to the question's measurement aims relief of pain was anything staff did to help relieve pain, be it medication, complementary therapies or other activities.

Evidence

Analysis of the cognitive interview data identified two different interpretations of the term 'relief of pain':

- a broad definition, including medication, massage, advice or anything that could 'make someone comfortable'; or
- a narrow definition, involving providing medication (e.g. morphine).

(Continued)

179

(Continued)

The broader interpretation was in line with the question's intended meaning. Participants who adopted the narrower definition were in situations where the nurse provided by the service had no involvement in administering medication – that was done by someone else. These participants felt the question was not applicable.

A similar question had been asked in previous surveys of home nursing and hospice services and it was found to have high levels of 'missing data' due to people answering 'Not applicable'. The survey sponsor wanted to address this problem, believing the question should be relevant to all their service users, even those who did not receive medication via the service.

Context and constraints

The question on pain relief had been included in other surveys with carers. Prior to making alterations we consulted with data users regarding how important it was for their patient and carer experience survey to be directly comparable with other experience surveys. They felt clarifying the question and making the question more appropriate to the services they offered was of a higher priority than being able to compare results to other surveys.

Recommendations

As a result of the cognitive interviewing and the consultation with data users we recommended that the question was rephrased to include more examples of pain relief. The revised question wording is shown below.

Q: How would you rate the support provided by the [home nursing service/ hospice] in the following areas…Relief of pain; this could be through medication, massage, complementary therapy, advice or anything else to relieve pain?

1. Poor
2. Fair
3. Good
4. Very good
5. Excellent
6. *[Not read out] Can't answer.*

As the client felt this question should be applicable to all their service users we also included an additional instruction for interviewers to record reasons why people were unable to provide an answer.

Wording problems may not be due to terminology at all but be due to how the question is constructed. The question structure, or syntax, may result in people misunderstanding the question. Rephrasing the question to make it clearer may be the solution in this situation.

The question may be too long: participants may lose sight of what information they are being asked to provide. This could be because the question includes a definition or explanation. You may decide that the question needs to be shortened: the definition should be dropped or simplified. In coming up with your recommendation you could draw on questionnaire design principles, such as avoiding double negatives or double-barrelled questions (see e.g., Willis and Lessler, 1999).

9.3.2 Answer option changes

The cognitive interview findings may reveal that there are problems with the answer options used in a question.

- The languages used in the answer options may be too technical or ambiguous.
- There may be a mismatch between the question and the answer options provided. For example, we tested the following question: 'I am now going to read out some statements about your community. For each one please choose a phrase from the card to say how much you agree or disagree … you feel you are part of a community (either in your local area, or some other community?'). The answer scale was a 5-point, agree/disagree scale. However, participants, in the main, wanted to respond with a 'yes or no' answer (Hales et al., 2000).
- The answer options may be incomplete, so not allowing participants or interviewers to record the participant's in-mind answer. For example, the question may ask the participant to list all sources of information on pregnancy but may be incomplete and may not include an 'other' option.
- The question may specify a response in a particular format but participants are unable to provide it in this format. For example, the question may require participants to record an exact amount but participants may only be able to provide an estimate within a specified range.
- The answer options may not be mutually exclusive when only one answer is allowed: the participant may tick more than one box but only one answer is required.

Again, if in your analysis you have been able to identify the mechanisms by which problems arise it will help you to propose ways to tackle them. In the case of overly technical language you may wish to substitute the words you use. If there is a mismatch between the question and the answer categories you may wish to revise the question stem. If answer categories are missing you may suggest adding these in. If answer categories overlap you may wish to refine the language you use or collapse two or more overlapping categories into a single code.

Example 9.3 provides an example of where we have changed answer categories as a result of cognitive interviewing.

Example 9.3   Amending answer options

Aims

We were asked to test, using cognitive interviewing, new questions to be included in the Welsh Health Survey (WHS). One of the questions tested aimed to measure whether participants visited the dentist, and if so how regularly. The question tested was as follows:

Q: In general, which of the following do you go to the dentist for?
Tick one only

1. A regular check-up (i.e. at least once a year)
2. An occasional check-up
3. Only when I am having trouble with my teeth
4. I don't ever go to the dentist

Evidence

Analysis of the cognitive interview data revealed that participants used different categories to indicate the same behaviour. For example, various participants described visiting the dentist due to toothache or bleeding gums. However, some of these participants coded this under option 2 (an occasional check-up) whereas others coded this under option 3 (only when I am having trouble with my teeth). Participants did not consider the answer codes to be mutually exclusive and the answer options were not reliably measuring real differences in participants' behaviour.

Recommendations

Based on these findings, we recommended that the second and third answer categories be collapsed into a single option as they were not conceptually distinct. The revised question wording is shown below:

Q: In general, which of the following do you go to the dentist for?
Tick one only

1. A regular check-up (i.e. at least once a year)
2. An occasional check-up or when I am having trouble with my teeth
3. I don't ever go to the dentist

For further details of this study please refer to Balarajan et al. (2011).

9.3.3 Dropping questions altogether

In some cases a recommendation resulting from cognitive interviewing could be to drop a question altogether. This decision could be made for several reasons. For example, it could be that:

- Participants are consistently unable to provide the information requested (the measurement aims are found to be unrealistic)
- Upon review the question is found to be superfluous to requirements.

Example 9.4 illustrates the process by which you might recommend dropping a question.

Example 9.4.   Dropping questions

Aims

The following question was asked in a large, continuous government survey that collects detailed financial information about families living in Great Britain. The survey collects information on savings and investments, among other things. This information, coupled with information on income, is used to identify entitled non-recipients of particular benefits and tax credits, and to provide estimates of the numbers of such entitled non-recipients (see Betts et al., 2003).

Q: Now there are some questions about accounts with banks, building societies, the post office, supermarkets, or other organisations. These could also be internet or telephone banking facilities. Do you have now, or have you had at any time in the past 12 months any accounts? This could be in your name only, or held jointly with someone else?

1. Yes
2. No.
3. *[Don't know/refused]*

This question acts as filter: if participants answer 'yes' then they are asked more detailed questions on what types of bank and savings accounts they have, the interest they receive on each type of account, and its value.

Evidence

The cognitive interviews revealed the following.

- The question was misinterpreted in some cases, with participants thinking about a narrower range of accounts than was intended.
- This led to participants initially answering 'no' to this question when in fact they had accounts, which in turn led to information not being collected on types of bank and savings accounts held, interest received and the accounts' value.

The implication of the cognitive interviewing was that if participants in the survey answer 'no' to this question in error then information on current and

(Continued)

(Continued)

savings accounts would be lost. This would result in the total value of assets held being underestimated. There was some evidence from prior waves of the survey that underestimation of savings and investments was already occurring.

Context and constraints

As this question was asked in a continuous survey we needed a clear rationale for proposing a change to the questionnaire, as this could affect the continuity of the time-series data.

We had to decide whether the problem identified by the cognitive interviews was likely to occur in the main survey and if so, what impact it might have on the survey data. In this case we already knew that underestimation of savings and investments was occurring; the aim of the cognitive interviews was to understand how this was happening. This question was one source of error. The rationale for dropping the question was as follows.

- We had evidence that it was being misinterpreted and that this led to missing data. Participants answered 'no' they didn't have any bank accounts, savings accounts or investments when actually they did. By answering 'no' to this filter question additional information on the value of these accounts was lost.
- The filter question was therefore not doing its job: people were answering 'no' when they should have been answering 'yes'.
- The filter question appeared to be superfluous: the next question in the sequence could be asked of everyone with the addition of a 'none of these' category.
- This was a straightforward change.
- The questionnaire was already long, so dropping a question may be a positive step.

Recommendation

Our recommendation was to drop the filter question and instead ask everyone the next question in the sequence: 'Which of these accounts do you have now, or have you had in the last 12 months?'

For this question participants are shown a card listing the different types of accounts: current account with a bank, building society, supermarket/store or other organisation; National Savings Bank (Post Office) – Ordinary Account; National Savings Bank (Post Office) – Investment Account; TESSA (Tax-Exempt Special Savings Account); ISA (Individual Savings Account); and/or savings account, investment account/bond, any other account with bank, building society, supermarket/store or other organisation. We recommended a 'none of these' answer option was added to the response options as the original filter question was no longer used.

In this example you could reasonably argue that the problem with the filter question is obvious. However, it's often the case that compromises are made in the design of survey questionnaires. In this example, it's possible that the filter question was introduced in an attempt to reduce respondent burden. Having evidence to show that (a) the filter question was problematic, and (b) how it resulted in problems was useful for the survey sponsor, who has to justify any change in the question wording to data users.

9.3.4 Layout changes

You may have been testing a self-administered questionnaire and your cognitive interviews may have identified some problems with the layout.

- Participants may not have followed routing instructions (on paper questionnaires).
- They may not have seen answer options in a second column.
- They may not have seen or read instructions.
- They may not have understood how to complete grids.

You may want to propose changes to the layout of the questionnaire, to the font used, the size and colour of text, or the graphics used to indicate navigation. A number of the cognitive interviewing reports we have written have included suggestions for amending the visual presentation of instructions (e.g. Balarajan et al., 2011; McGee and d'Ardenne, 2009; McGee et al., 2006a and b). Theory and empirical evidence can help you in making your recommendations to some extent (see section 8.5.3). However, additional testing is likely to be needed to assess how successful your proposed changes are. And there is likely to be a limit to how far you will be able to overcome all the problems you find. For example, not everyone reads instructions even if you take steps to make them more visually prominent or change their position.

9.3.5 Proposing alternative forms of data collection

Your analysis may indicate that the question is too complex and participants are unable or unwilling to provide the information being sought. In these circumstances a more radical change may be needed. An alternative means of obtaining the data may be required, for example using a diary, obtaining an objective measurement or using another source of information to collect the data required (such as administrative data). The alternatives you propose will be limited by practicalities such as whether or not an objective measurement is possible or whether administrative data are available and accessible for individual survey participants.

Example 9.5 describes a study where we have recommended a change in data collection methods as a result of cognitive interviewing.

Example 9.5   Changing data collection methods

Aims

We conducted cognitive interviews to test new questions for a telephone survey of people who claim Employment and Support Allowance (refer to Example 9.1 for further details). One of the questions tested was about the length of time the participant had been in receipt of this benefit. The question tested is shown below:

Q: When did you submit your claim for ESA? If you have applied more than once think about your most recent claim.

MONTH:
YEAR:

An aim of the cognitive interviews was to establish whether participants could recall the date they applied for ESA.

Evidence

Participants could not always recall with accuracy the date they claimed ESA. Confusion over the application date occurred for two main reasons:

- Participants did not always make the claim themselves – in some cases this was done by a key worker or family member.
- Participants had submitted claims on multiple occasions and were unsure which claim the question was referring to.

When participants gave inaccurate information on 'date of claim' this had negative implications later on in the questionnaire. This is because the date they gave was repeated as a reference period for a number of subsequent questions.

Context

Administrative records are held on people who receive ESA. It was planned that these administrative records would be used as the sample frame for the survey (e.g. people who claim ESA who had given their permission to be contacted would be approached to take part in the survey). These administrative records include information on claim dates.

Recommendations

We recommended that the administrative (benefit record) data on individuals' ESA claim data should be used rather than relying on respondent self-reports. We also recommended that participants be asked a question to check the accuracy of this information. The revised survey questions are shown below:

Q: Our records show that you submitted your [most recent] claim for ESA in [INSERT CLAIM DATE FROM ADMIN DATA]? Is that correct?

1. Yes
2. No

{If no}
Q. When did you submit your claim for ESA? We only need to know the month and year rather than the exact date. If you have applied more than once think about your most recent claim.

MONTH:
YEAR:

9.3.6 Proposing further testing

In answering the questions listed in section 9.2 you may decide that you do not have sufficient evidence to make firm recommendations. You may, for example, realise that your sample was deficient: perhaps you did not manage to interview people with certain characteristics or only a small number of people went down a particular route in the test questionnaire. You might want to carry out additional cognitive interviews before drawing conclusions and making any recommendations. Alternatively, the cognitive interview findings might be unclear and you may decide that further testing is required, perhaps with a revised cognitive interview protocol, to understand what is going on. Or you may feel that cognitive interviewing cannot answer some of your research questions, and that other kinds of evidence are required to help you decide what to do. In these circumstances you might recommend additional testing and specify what this might involve.

Example 9.6 provides an example of how we used further methods of testing prior to making a final recommendation on question wording.

Example 9.6   Proposing further testing

Aims

We conducted cognitive interviews to test some new questions to be included on the Health Survey for England (HSE). The new questions were designed to measure people's knowledge about social care funding and the cost of residential care. At the time the survey was fielded there was no cap on the total amount people might have to pay for social care, out of their own pocket, over the course of their lifetime. However, the UK government were considering

(Continued)

(Continued)

introducing a cap so people would not have to pay more than a certain amount out of their own funds. One of the questions we tested was on whether or not people were aware that this cap could be introduced in the future. The question tested is shown below:

Q: Are there any plans to limit the total amount that someone would have to pay for all their care over their lifetime?

1. Yes
2. No
3. Don't know

Evidence

Analysis revealed that participants varied as to whether they understood the question. Some participants were familiar with the planned reforms (as they had been discussed in the media) and understood the question as intended. However, other participants misunderstood the question, with some thinking it was asking about whether the government had plans to cap the amount they spent on social care per person, or whether there were plans to limit the amount residential care homes could charge.

Recommendations

As a result of this we recommended rephrasing the question so that it was more clearly asking about a limit on the *amount of money* people have to pay rather than the *amount of care* they can receive. Another solution discussed was directly referring to the policy of interest as part of the question. An alternative phrasing was produced:

Q: In the next few years the government will be introducing a new policy to limit the amount people will have to pay for their own care over their lifetime. Before today had you heard about this policy?

1. Yes
2. No
3. *[Spontaneous] Don't know*

Constraints

There was a concern that by explicitly mentioning there was a policy plan in this area people might say yes even if they had not heard of the policy. This could lead to survey results overestimating levels of awareness of this policy.

Final outcome

Before deciding on what the final question wording should be we conducted a split ballot test as part of the survey pilot. Half the pilot participants were assigned to the question that directly asked about the policy whereas the other half were asked a question that was more akin to the one tested in the cognitive interviews.

The rationale behind this was to collect more information on the impact of changing the question wording before deciding which question should be fielded in the main survey. Interviewers were briefed about the purpose of the test and were asked to provide feedback on how well the different questions worked at the pilot debriefing.

The pilot resulted in a clear finding about which question was better. The question which mentioned the policy was recommended for the main survey.

9.3.7 No change! Retain current question wording

In some cases, after reviewing the data collected from the question testing you may decide that no changes are required. This could be because no problems were detected with the question. Alternatively you may feel that the issues detected were not serious enough to warrant a change when weighed up against other factors.

Example 9.7 provides an example of an occasion when no action was taken on a cognitive interview finding and explains why the decision was made not to make any changes.

Example 9.7   Retain question wording

Aims

We conducted cognitive interviews to test questions on multiple topic areas to be used in Understanding Society, a longitudinal survey of people living in the UK, designed and managed by researchers at the Institute of Social and Economic Research (ISER) at the University of Essex and funded by the Economic and Social Research Council. One module of questions tested was on life satisfaction. The measurement objective of these questions was to capture participants' satisfaction with their health, their income and their life overall.

The questions tested are shown below.

Q: Next a few questions about how you feel about your life. On a scale from 0 to 10, where 0 means 'not at all satisfied' and 10 means 'completely satisfied', how dissatisfied or satisfied are you with the following aspects of your current situation?

(a)   ... Your health? (ENTER NUMBER FROM 0 TO 10)
(b)   ... The income of your household? (ENTER NUMBER FROM 0 TO 10)
(c)   ... Using the same scale of 0 to 10, how dissatisfied or satisfied are you with your life overall? (ENTER NUMBER FROM 0 TO 10)

(Continued)

(Continued)

One of the aims of testing was to investigate how appropriate the answer scale was.

Evidence

The cognitive interviewers observed that some participants would answer with a word (e.g. saying 'satisfied' or 'very satisfied') rather than giving a number. Participants sometimes had to ask for clarification about what the numbers referred to, for example, *'Does 10 mean completely satisfied?'*, or for the question to be repeated so they could hear the answer categories again. After these clarifications participants were able to provide a number. There was one exception to this: one participant had difficulties assigning a number to the concept of satisfaction and was repeatedly unable to do so until the cognitive interviewer drew the scale on a piece of paper for him. It is possible the nature of the task was entirely novel to this participant, hence the difficulty.

On probing, some participants said they would rather use descriptive words such as happy/unhappy or good/poor.

Recommendation

There is some literature to suggest that full verbal labelling, where every scale point is given a verbal label (rather than just a number), improves scale validity and reliability (e.g. Krosnick and Fabrigar, 1997). However, with longer scales (such as the one used in this example) it would be difficult to verbally label every point on the scale. Therefore, one option discussed was altering the scale so that it became a five-point fully labelled verbal scale, rather than using the 0–10 scale provided.

Context and constraints

The questions on life satisfaction had previously been included in the British Household Panel Survey (BHPS). There was an interest in retaining the 11-point scale so that Life Satisfaction could be compared over time without the confounding effect of a change in scale length/type.

Final outcome

The wording of the questions did not change as a result of the cognitive interviews.

In the cognitive interviews the questions were asked of participants in a face-to-face interview, the questions being read aloud. However, the survey team at ISER subsequently decided that these questions should actually be administered as part of a separate self-completion form, handed out during the interview. This was also the form of administration used in the BHPS survey. It was thought that seeing the questions written down would ameliorate most of the issues observed during the cognitive interviewing. For further details about this testing please refer to Gray et al. (2008).

In this example the importance of preserving the time-series outweighed the need to address the issues raised in the cognitive interviews. Although the cognitive participants sometimes asked for clarification, or voiced a preference for a different type of scale, they were mostly still able to provide an appropriate answer. Therefore their preferences were not having a noteworthy effect on the quality of the data being collected. The instance of one person who was unfamiliar with the 0–10 format was not, on balance, considered enough to justify a change to the answer scale wording.

This example also serves as an illustration as to why it is important to administer questions in the same mode in the cognitive interviews as they would be administered in the actual survey (see Chapter 10), as the mode of presentation can impact on the response process.

9.4 How to present the recommendations or changes

As we mentioned in section 9.1, it is often the case that cognitive interviews are carried out as part of the questionnaire development process and provide evidence on how well test questions are meeting their measurement aims. The evidence gleaned from these interviews is used, with other information, to make decisions about whether and how questions should be changed. If you are testing questions that were written by someone else then you will probably need to report on your findings and propose recommendations. Even if this is not the case, producing a written record of your findings and your rationale for what you did as a result is good practice (Boeije and Willis, 2013). Presenting your findings and recommendations in a clear, logical way will help decision-makers understand the key issues and how you reached your conclusions.

Your recommendation may serve several purposes:

- provide a logical argument, supported by the evidence for your recommendation, that will inform decisions about next steps;
- give clear guidance on what changes need to be made, particularly if these changes will be implemented by another team of researchers.

Below we set out suggestions for presenting your findings and recommendations.

- If you are producing a report for a funder, agree with them the content and structure in advance. Check whether they want you to follow certain conventions and how they would like you to present your recommendations.
- Present findings on understanding of the survey task, overall reactions to the survey questions, ease of completing the questionnaire etc. in a general findings section.
- Present findings for each question or series of questions separately. Include the test question wording in the text.

- Provide a short description of the measurement aims of the question and the aims of the cognitive testing.
- Present the findings from the cognitive interviews in a clear and concise way. You may want to use the four-stage question and answer mode (Tourangeau, 1984) to structure your findings, focusing on the stages that were explored in the cognitive interviews along with any other issues that emerged.
- Illustrate your findings, where appropriate, with the use of verbatim quotes, making this clear by using a different font and quotation marks. We always put verbatim quotes in italics.
- Don't just describe your findings: explain them (see section 8.5).
- Discuss the implications of your findings. Why might this be a problem? What impact would this have on survey estimates?
- Make recommendations and clearly label them as such.
- Provide a clear link between findings and recommendations. 'We found x. It is a problem because of y. We recommend z because.'
- Make your recommendations as specific as possible: set out as clearly as possible what action is required.
- If you are proposing changes to the question wording, response options, or question order then provide details, for example provide a redrafted question. Clearly indicate which parts of the question have been changed.
- It can be useful to provide an overall summary of findings and recommendations. We often present this as a table (see Table 2.1 in Balarajan and Collins, 2013, for example).
- Where questions have been removed or added, or additional instructions or changed formatting have been suggested it can also be useful to present the whole questionnaire in its revised form to aid researchers and study sponsors in gaining an overview of the proposed changes.

It is useful to add an additional section after the recommendations section, called 'final decisions on implementation' (see Gray et al., 2011 for an example). This allows the reader to understand what was eventually implemented on the main survey and is particularly helpful when the recommendations from the cognitive interviews include a number of options, or when, despite a recommendation, a final decision was made to make no change.

9.5 Chapter summary

- Making recommendations can be the main output from cognitive interviewing projects. You will need to allow time to do this once your analysis is complete.
- When making recommendations:
  o consider the measurement aims of the question;
  o review all the evidence available;
  o think about the different options and the pros and cons of each;
  o consider the wider survey context and what the data will be used for; and
  o have a clear rationale for your recommendations, which is supported by your cognitive interview data and an appreciation of the wider constraints.

- What you recommend will depend on a wide range of factors, some of which relate to information obtained during cognitive interviewing. But many of these factors relate to a broader understanding and knowledge of the survey in which the questions will be asked and an appreciation of the constraints on what changes can be made.
- Recommendations need to be presented in a way which makes them clear and easy to implement. Care should therefore be taken in how they are presented.

References

Balarajan, M. and Collins, D. (2013) *A Review of Questions Asked About State Benefits on the Family Resources Survey.* Working Paper No. 115. London: Department for Work and Pensions. Available at: http://socialwelfare.bl.uk/subject-areas/services-activity/poverty-benefits/departmentforworkandpensions/family131.aspx

Balarajan M., Gray, M. and Jessop, C. (2011) *Cognitive Testing of New Questions for the 2011 Welsh Health Survey.* Welsh Government. Available at: http://wales.gov.uk/docs/statistics/2011/110208healthcognitiveen.pdf

Betts, P., Breman, R. and Collins, D. (2003) *Comparing Strategies for Collecting Information on Personal Assets.* Department for Work and Pensions Research Working Paper 9. London: HMSO.

Boeije, H. and Willis, G. (2013) 'The Cognitive Interviewing Reporting Framework (CIRF): towards the harmonization of cognitive interviewing reports', *Methodology: European Journal of Research Methods for the Behavioral and Social Sciences,* 9(3): 87–95. doi: 10.1027/1614–2241/a000075.

Czaja, R. and Blair, J. (1996) *Designing Surveys: A Guide to Decisions and Procedures.* Thousand Oaks, CA: Pine Forge Press.

Gray, M., Constantine, R., Blake, M., d'Ardenne, J. and Uhrig, N. (2008) *Cognitive Testing of Understanding Society: The UK Household Longitudinal Study Questionnaire.* Understanding Society Working Paper Series No. 2008 – 04. Available at: https://www.understandingsociety.ac.uk/research/publications/working-paper/understanding-society/2008–04.pdf

Gray, M., d'Ardenne, J., Balarajan, M. and Uhrig, N. (2011) *Cognitive Testing of Wave 3 Understanding Society Questions.* Understanding Society Working Paper Series; No. 2011 – 03. Available at: https://www.understandingsociety.ac.uk/research/publications/working-paper/understanding-society/2011–03.pdf

Hales, J., Henderson, L., Collins, D. and Beecher, H. (2000) *2000 British Crime Survey Technical Report (England and Wales).* Appendix K – Question Development and Testing. National Centre for Social Research. Available at: www.esds.ac.uk/doc/4463/mrdoc/pdf/a4463uab.pdf

Krosnick, J. and Fabrigar, L. (1997) 'Designing rating scales for effective measurement in surveys', in L. Lyberg (ed.), *Survey Measurement and Process Quality.* New York: Wiley. pp. 141–64.

McGee, A. and d'Ardenne, J. (2009) 'Netting a Winner': Tackling Ways to Question Children Online. A Good Practice Guide to Asking Children and Young People about Sport and Physical Activity. Sports Council for Wales. Available at: www.sportwales.org.uk/media/351853/netting_a_winner_-_english.pdf

McGee, A., Gray, M., Andrews, F., Legard, R., Wood, N. and Collins, D. (2006a) NTS Travel Record Review Stage 2. London: Department of Transport. Available at: http://webarchive.nationalarchives.gov.uk/+/www.dft.gov.uk/pgr/statistics/datata blespublications/personal/methodology/ntsrecords/ntstravelrecord2.pdfhttps://www.google.co.uk/ - #

McGee, A., Gray, M. and Collins, D. (2006b) NTS Travel Record Review Stage 1. London: Department of Transport. Available at: http://webarchive.national-archives.gov.uk/+/www.dft.gov.uk/pgr/statistics/datatablespublications/personal/methodology/ntsrecords/ntstravelrecord1.pdf

Tourangeau, R. (1984) 'Cognitive science and survey methods', in T. Jabine, M. Straf, J. Tanur and R. Tourangeau (eds), Cognitive Aspects of Survey Methodology: Building a Bridge Between Discipline. Washington, DC: National Academy Press. pp. 73–100.

Willis, G. (2005) Cognitive Interviewing: A Tool for Improving Questionnaire Design. Thousand Oaks, CA: Sage.

Willis, G. and Lessler, J. (1999) Question Appraisal System QAS-99. Research Triangle Institute. Available at: http://appliedresearch.cancer.gov/areas/cognitive/qas99.pdf

PART III
COGNITIVE INTERVIEWING IN PRACTICE

TEN

SURVEY MODE AND ITS IMPLICATIONS FOR COGNITIVE INTERVIEWING

MICHELLE GRAY

10.1 Introduction

The aim of this chapter is to highlight the things you need to consider when designing and carrying out cognitive interviews to test survey questions for different modes – telephone and self-administered paper and web – and for mixed mode surveys. Specifically, this chapter considers:

- The mode in which the questions should be tested
- The role of the cognitive interviewer.

Advice around how best to take account of mode in cognitive interviewing is sparse. Some practitioners have attempted to replicate the survey mode within the cognitive interview, in some form or another (Gray et al., 2011; Rothgeb, 2007; Vernon, 2005), a practice which has been referred to as 'mode mimicking' (Beatty and Schechter, 1994). This chapter provides practical suggestions as to how to test survey questions for telephone, postal, web and mixed mode surveys.

The suggestions put forward in this chapter build on the literature and reflect and our own experience.

10.2 Survey mode

First, let's define what we mean by survey 'mode'. Survey mode refers to the medium through which survey responses are collected: by an interviewer – in person or by telephone; or self-administered – by mail/post or via the internet. In addition, survey questionnaires can take the form of paper documents or more commonly be computerised, see Figure 10.1 (de Leeuw, 2005).

The choice of survey mode is driven by three sets of factors:

- Survey administration and resource issues, such as cost, the length of time available for data collection and the geographical spread of the sample
- Questionnaire issues such as questionnaire length, complexity, question order, question form and content
- Data quality issues such as sample frame bias, response rates, response bias, participant selection issues, control of the response situation and the quality of recorded responses (Czaja and Blair, 1996).

Mixed mode surveys use a single questionnaire that is administered in different modes with the aim of collecting the 'same data' across all modes. The use of mixed mode surveys is increasing as they are seen as a way of cutting survey costs (Dex and Gummy, 2011).

	Face to Face		
Interviewer-driven modes	Paper questionnaire *Paper And Pencil Interviewing (PAPI)*	Computer questionnaire *Computer-Assisted Personal Interviewing (CAPI)*	
	Telephone		
	Paper questionnaire	Computer questionnaire *Computer-Assisted Telephone Interviewing (CATI)*	
Respondent-driven modes	Paper questionnaire received in the post or given to respondent	Web questionnaire *Computer-Assisted Web Interviewing (CAWI)*	Mobile phone questionnaire[a]

Figure 10.1 Survey modes and technical terminology

Note: [a] We are now seeing an increase in the use of mobile, 'on the go', means of surveying respondents using smartphones, Personal Digital Assistants (PDAs) and palmtop computers. Additionally, kiosk surveys can deliver real-time feedback from fixed locations such as hospital waiting rooms and visitor attractions.

10.3 Cognitive interviewing and mode

We know that survey responses may be affected by the mode in which the question is asked (Dillman and Mason, 1984; Krysan et al., 1994; Tarnai and Dillman, 1992), and it is likely this will be the case when testing survey questions using cognitive interviewing methods (Presser et al., 2004). Indeed, some have questioned whether researchers are at risk of drawing incorrect, or different, conclusions when the cognitive interviewing mode does not match the survey mode (Beaty and Schechter, 1994; Schechter et al., 1996), and there seems to be a consensus that at some point in the questionnaire development life-cycle, questions in need of testing should be presented to participants in the same mode as they will appear in the actual survey (Prüfer and Rexroth, 2005). For example, Pretesting Guideline number 4 of the Cross-Cultural Survey Guidelines (Survey Research Center, 2010) recommends that 'cognitive laboratory pretests should be conducted in the same mode as the final survey'.

In practice, your decision to simulate the survey mode or 'mode mimic' will be influenced by two factors.

- The purpose of the cognitive interviews.
- Whether you think the mode in which the test questions are presented to participants will affect the way in which they go about answering them.

Let's consider these two factors a little further.

10.3.1 The purpose of the cognitive interview

The purpose of your cognitive pretest, as discussed in Chapter 3, will influence your design and therefore whether you simulate the survey mode.

Simulate (mimic) mode	Mode simulation less important
To finalise the survey questions before the questionnaire is fielded	Explore understanding of terms and concepts
(For telephone) whether the lack of visual prompt material hinders respondents as they attempt to answer the questions	When questions are not yet ordered in a logical or systematic way
(For self-completion questionnaires) evaluate how respondents understand and process instructions and visual cues, such as routing instructions	When the survey mode has not yet been decided

Figure 10.2   When to simulate (mimic) mode

Based on information presented in Beatty, P. and Schechter, S. (1994), 'An examination of mode effects in cognitive laboratory research'. 1994 Proceedings of the Section on Survey Research Methods, American Statistical Association, 1275–80.

Schechter et al. (1996) conducted focus groups with 10 recognised experts in cognitive and/or survey research. Experts discussed the purpose of cognitive interviewing and the impact this will have on the choice of mode for presentation of the test questions. Figure 10.2 summarises the findings from their research, providing guidance on the situations in which mode simulation (mimicking) is useful and when simulation may not be necessary.

10.3.2 The role of mode in survey response

As we have already mentioned, the mode that your test questions will be presented in in the actual survey may affect the way in which participants go about trying to answer them. Figure 10.3 summarises the key features of each mode. You may want to undertake cognitive interviews to assess whether the mode, and its implementation, is helping or hindering participants from answering the questions as you intend. If this is the case you should consider simulating (mimicking) the mode.

Face-to-face	Telephone
• Question presentation can be both auditory and visual • Respondents see the interviewers and the impressions they form of them may influence their answers (social desirability) • Interviewers can use visual cues to help build rapport and to help respondents if they get stuck, for example if they see respondents looking puzzled they can re-read the question	• Question presentation is auditory only • If questions are too long respondents may only remember the last part of the question or the latter response options in the list (known as recency effects) • The interviewer has no visual cues, so building rapport can be more difficult
Paper self-completion	**Web**
• Question presentation is visual only • Respondents only have the information on the page to help them: there is no interviewer available to answer queries or read the questions to them if they find reading difficult • There is no interviewer present to provide encouragement to the respondent to sit down and fill in the form	• Question presentation is visual only • Similar issues to paper – in addition: • The speed of respondents' internet connection may vary and this can affect whether they are willing to complete the questionnaire and their perception of its length • Respondents' skill in using computers may vary and influence their willingness and ability to (continue to) complete it

Figure 10.3 Features of mode to consider for cognitive interviews

Let's take a closer look at telephone and self-completion modes.

Telephone surveys

In a telephone survey the questions are spoken aloud (orally) by the telephone interviewer and the participant has to respond to this auditory stimulus (he or she has to hear and process the spoken questions). There is no visual compo-nent to the questions: no visual display of the answer options or reminder of the question wording is available for example, as in other modes. You will need to consider whether the lack of visual stimulus may affect how participants go about answering your test questions, and if so then it may be appropriate to test these question over the telephone. For example, you might want to test ques-tions with long answer scales, that involve rating and ranking tasks, or that are quite long.

In addition, you may want to test your question over the telephone because you want to explore whether participants feel time pressured when answering the questions over the telephone and what affect this may have on how the ques-tions are interpreted, the effort given to the task (e.g. does the participant give 'top of mind' answers) and how the questions are subsequently answered.

Self-administered paper surveys

Self-administered questionnaires rely on visual stimuli completely. In paper self-administered questionnaires the order in which the participant answers the questions is not controlled, there are no interviewer explanations and the par-ticipant may be more likely to provide honest answers to sensitive questions (Beatty and Schechter, 1994).

Dillman and Redline (2004) argue that Tourangeau's (1984) four-stage ques-tion and answer model should be modified when applied to self-administered questionnaires, to include 'perception'; perception being participants' seeing and recognising of the questionnaire and the individual questions and subsequent reading of them (refer to section 1.2).

Participants are required to process up to four different forms of information when attempting to complete a self-administered questionnaire:

- narrative – to convey meaning;
- numerical – to convey the order of the questions and where to go next;
- symbolic – the arrows and tick boxes that represent the navigational path and the task; and
- graphical – features of the visual design such as colour, shading, and the location of the information.

These different forms of communication convey the form-filling task to the par-ticipant in the absence of an interviewer (Redline and Dillman, 2001, cited in Dillman and Redline, 2004).

The layout of the written information will also have an impact on how people navigate through it, following routing instructions and filling in their answers. For example, Wolfgang, Lewis and Vacca tested a self-administered paper questionnaire and found that a large gap between the end of the question stem text and the answer box caused some participants in their sample to choose the wrong box (1994, cited in Willis, 2005).

You may want to explore whether the design and layout of your test self-completion questionnaire helps or hinders participants' comprehension, retrieval, judgement and response to the questions, and how participants follow routing (filtering) and other instructions (DeMaio and Rothgeb, 1996; Jenkins and Dillman, 1997).

Does the layout of your test questionnaire matter? Yes: it is well documented that the visual presentation of self-completion questionnaires can influence how participants answer survey questions. For example, it has been demonstrated that visual presentation can influence:

a) how participants understand navigational instructions (Jenkins and Dillman, 1997);
b) how participants select answer categories (Toepoel and Van Soest, 2006; Tourangeau et al., 2004);
c) the quality of data collected (Mahon-haft & Dillman, 2010).

TOP TIP

Ensure that your test questionnaire is well laid out and resembles, as closely as possible, the final formatted instrument. This may mean you will need to get it professionally designed and printed.

If it is not formatted participants may inadvertently make errors as a result of the questionnaire format and not due to problems in question wording.

If you have to test an unformatted version of a self-completion questionnaire it is important to explain to participants that they are looking at an early mock-up and in the real survey the visual presentation will be different. Explain to participants you are only hoping to test the wording of the questions, otherwise participants may provide a lot of feedback about the general visual design of the instrument.

Figure 10.6, at the end of this chapter provides an example of an interview protocol for testing a paper self-completion questionnaire.

Web and computer-assisted self-administered interviewing (CASI)

Many of the design principles for paper self-administered questionnaires that we have just described apply to web and CASI questionnaires; however there are additional features that are unique to these modes.

- They involve interaction between the survey participant and a computer, tablet or mobile device.
- Navigation through the questionnaire can involve 'clicking' on a button to go to the next question, if the questionnaire uses a page-per-question format, or the use of the scroll bar.
- Responding to questions involves using a mouse, keys on a key pad, or touching a particular point on the screen to select an answer.
- Instructions may only become visible if the participant's behaviour triggers its appearance, for example by clicking on a link or hovering over an icon.
- Error messages may appear on the screen in response to something the participant does, for example if the participant enters an answer that seems unlikely or tries to move on without answering a question but where the program expects a response.

You may want to assess the 'usability' of the questionnaire as well as examining the four stages of the question-and-answer process, see sections 2.2.4 and 12.3 for further discussion of usability testing. If you want to assess 'usability' or visual design then you will need to test the questions in a computerised form.

10.4 Simulating the mode

In this section we discuss the things you need to consider when simulating the mode in a cognitive interview. By simulating (mimicking) the mode we mean attempting to replicate the main features of the eventual data collection mode during the administration of the test questions or questionnaire in the cognitive interview.

We say *attempting to replicate* because we do not think it is possible or desirable to exactly reproduce survey conditions in a cognitive interview. A cognitive interview is, as discussed in Chapter 6, a very different type of interaction to a survey interview. The goal is rather to try to ensure that the test questions are presented to participants in the same way that they would be presented in the survey itself. To achieve this, the interview protocol must clearly set out:

- what you, the interviewer, should say as part of your initial introduction of the task;
- how the test questions are to be presented to participants, for example should they be presented on paper or in electronic form;
- whether you, the interviewer, should be present during the administration of the questions; for example, should you be in a different room whilst the participant completes the self-administered questionnaire;
- how you, the interviewer, will deal with any questions or queries the participant has about the test material;
- the types of cognitive interviewing methods to use, for example think aloud or probing; and
- how any observations should be recorded.

As discussed in section 10.3.1, the aims of your test will guide your decisions to some extent but it is worth considering these practical implementation points, and we spend the rest of this section looking in more detail at each of the points above. Example 10.1 illustrates the way in which you might design a mode simulation.

Example 10.1 Mode simulation (mimicking) in cognitive interviews testing web survey questions with children

Study

The study tested questions for the Children's Sports and Physical Activity Participation Survey (a large-scale survey of primary school pupils, aged 7–11) and the Young People's Sports and Physical Activity Participation Survey (a large-scale survey of secondary school pupils, aged 11–16) (McGee and d'Ardenne, 2009).

Description of methods

- The test questions were programmed into a web questionnaire and interviewers instructed children to complete the web questionnaire as though they were alone.
- Interviewers were present during web completion and openly observed children completing the questionnaire. The questions were not felt to be sensitive and the risk of observation affecting the children's form-filling behaviour was therefore deemed to be fairly low.
- Interviewers were briefed to be able to offer help to children (especially the younger ones) if they asked for it whilst they were completing the web questionnaire. When this occurred it tended to be for help with navigation, for example how to move on to the next screen. These occasions were noted and fed back to the research team.
- Three different techniques were used during the cognitive testing of the web surveys:

  o **observation** – interviewers observed children as they completed the web questionnaires. Interviewers were required to take notes during the observation;
  o **concurrent think aloud** – participants were asked to think aloud as they went through the questionnaires, to give an insight into problems pupils experience in relation to navigating the tool and understanding the overall task;
  o **retrospective probing** – face-to-face – used to follow up with more direct questions (probes) about how the participant found the task of filling in the online questionnaire.

10.4.1 The introduction

At the start of the interview you want to build rapport and explain to the participant what the interview will entail. However, you need to think carefully about what is said in the introduction because you don't want to inadvertently influence the participant's behaviour during the test as this could distort your findings. This is particularly important when testing self-completion questionnaires, where you need to be careful that you don't (accidentally) encourage participants to read instructions or give them the impression that they need to spend time considering their answers (see Chapter 5).

TOP TIP

Write a script that will be read out at the start of the interview, immediately before the test questions are presented, so that the introduction is standardised across all interviews.

As part of the introduction you may wish to explain how survey participants would receive the questionnaire in a 'real-life' context. For example, you could explain that in real life you/an interviewer would not be there to help them. You could also explain *how* and *when* people will receive the questionnaire. Is it by post or email? Would they be handed it after completing a face-to-face interview? Or whilst they were waiting to see their GP? Would they get it at home or at work? These contextual factors are important as they could have an impact on how participants view the sensitivity of the questions.

10.4.2 Presentation of test questions

Your interview protocol should clearly set out exactly how the test questions should be presented to participants, for example whether answer options are to be read aloud. This will help ensure that the presentation is standardised across all interviews. If other people are carrying out interviews then you will need to ensure they are trained in how they should present the questions and, if appropriate, record the answers (see Chapter 6).

If the test questions will form part of a computerised questionnaire then you will need to decide whether you can test the questions in a computerised form or whether you will test them on paper.

Self-administered web or computer-assisted modes

Assuming you are in the later stages of questionnaire development and the purpose of the cognitive interview is to explore navigation, screen layout, visual design, etc, we would advise testing a web/computer-assisted version of the test questionnaire. This is especially the case if your web or self-administered computer questionnaire is complicated in terms of skip patterns, text fills, etc., and it would be difficult to translate this to a paper format. Although you may be able to replicate the visual presentation of individual questions on paper, you will undoubtedly find that it causes many problems during the pretesting that could otherwise have been avoided had you tested them in a computerised form. If test questionnaires need to be programmed, be sure to include in your budget and timetable the necessary computing time.

When testing web questionnaires you should provide instructions to the interviewer on whether they should log on themselves or ask the participant to log on. The latter option may be more appropriate if ease of accessing and logging on is one of the areas you hope to test.

Computer-assisted interviewing for interviewer-administered modes

Generally speaking, test questions designed for interviewer-administered modes that use computer-assisted interviewing can be tested on paper. This is because the delivery of the instrument should feel the same from the point of view of the participant (aurally presented questions with show cards where necessary). For computer-assisted telephone surveys where it is possible to substitute with paper test questionnaires, it is felt to be a better use of computing resources to programme the questions once the wording has been finalised, i.e. after the cognitive testing. There may be instances where cognitive interviews using the computer instrument are appropriate, however; for example for very complicated and heavily filtered questionnaires, or when the programme already exists, for example where the cognitive interviews are taking place in parallel with a pilot and the questionnaire has already been programmed. The benefits of testing interviewer-administered computerised questionnaires include the following.

- Data are easily captured – responses to the test questions can be collected via the program.
- You, as the interviewer, are not required to follow any routing instructions, or adhere to any rules, since these can be programmed, allowing you to focus more on the participants' cognitive processing.
- If your cognitive interviewers are also survey interviewers (see section 6.2.1) they can provide you with feedback on how the computerised instrument works in practice, in terms of ease of administration, for example.

- Time may be saved later in the survey questionnaire development timetable, since the structure of the questionnaire will already have been programmed. However, this time saving will depend on the amount of changes that are needed post cognitive testing.

If paper is a substitute for the computerised questionnaire, you need to allow sufficient time to format the questionnaire or questions prior to the cognitive test. Whatever the mode, it can be useful to include some socio-demographic questions that will provide some background, contextual information on the participant. Finally, you should consider whether you need to include other survey questions that would 'surround' the test questions, to mirror (as far as is possible) the context in which the questions will be asked within the actual survey. This may be important if, for example, you have concerns about question order effects regardless of mode.

10.4.3 Presence of the interviewer

If you are testing questions for a telephone survey, think about how this will be carried out. We have used two approaches.

- Within a face-to-face cognitive interview, the interviewer goes into a different room, calls the participant and asks him or her the test questions. Once the test questions (or a series) of them have been asked, the interviewer returns to the same room as the participant to carry out probing face-to-face.
- The entire interview, including the cognitive probing, is carried out by telephone (see section 10.5).

Figure 10.4 sets out the pros and cons of each approach.

Example 10.2 presents an approach used to simulate a telephone survey mode within a face-to-face cognitive interview.

Example 10.2   Testing telephone survey questions as part of a face-to-face cognitive interview

We mode mimicked as part of a methodological, grant-funded project, where the aim was to explore the ways in which the mode of data collection impacts on how participants go about answering questions (Gray et al., 2011). Since our practice is to (usually) visit participants at their homes, and this was the case for this project, interviewers and participants communicated from different rooms within the house using mobile phone (interviewer) to mobile phone or landline (participant). Other research organisations, such as Statistics Norway, have followed similar procedures.

	Advantages	Disadvantages
Simulating mode *within* face-to-face interview	• Helps interviewers build a rapport with respondents that may encourage more open and honest disclosure • Can use visual aids during probing • Use of visual cues during probing that might signify respondent problems • Less time-pressured. Incentives can also be given there and then	• Face-to-face interaction between interviewer and respondent, before and after test question administration, may impact on the findings • Despite the questions being tested over the phone, the whole experience (being in another room to the interviewer) may be somewhat different from the respondents' viewpoint to being interviewed entirely by phone
Simulating mode *entirely* by telephone	• Replicates conditions of a telephone survey interview (e.g. all communication taking place over the phone) • Reduced cost since no need to send interviewers out to respondents' homes	• Absence of visual cues and body language signifying potential issues with the questions that would otherwise be picked up on during face-to-face interaction between respondent and interviewer • Potentially a limit as to how much time you can spend on the telephone, affecting the quality and quantity of the data elicited

Figure 10.4   Pros and cons of different approaches to simulating telephone survey conditions

TOP TIP

- If you are going to test telephone survey questions over the phone in a participant's home, be sure to explain to your participant in advance that this is what you will need to do.
- If you are using a mobile, as in Example 10.2, you will need to check mobile phone coverage.
- You – as the interviewer – should call the participant, to save them the cost of a telephone call.

When testing self-administered surveys you may want to be present while the participant completes the form so that you can observe the process. If this is the case then you will need to think through what you say to participants about your presence and what you will be doing whilst they complete the test questionnaire. You might say something like this:

> I'd like you to fill in this form as though I am not here and in the way you would if you were at home. Please take whatever time you need. Let me know when you're done and then

we'll talk through it. You may see me scribbling; I'll be making a few notes on what you're doing so that we can talk about them afterwards.

Alternatively you may decide that it's not appropriate for you to be present whilst the participant completes the form. In this case you need to consider what information will be lost and whether this could be captured in some other way (refer to section 10.4.6).

10.4.4 Dealing with participants' questions

Participants may not understand the survey (question) task, for example that they have to fill in a diary, recording each 'stage' of each journey on a separate line. They may be confused about where to start recording or if they are supposed to read the instructions. You need to anticipate such questions and think through how you (and any other interviewers) will respond to them. As discussed in Chapter 6, a useful tactic is to throw the question back at the participant and ask 'What would you do if I wasn't here?'

In an interviewer-administered survey interview, interviewers will often try to help participants who are in difficulty by, for example, rephrasing the question (although they are not meant to do this). In a cognitive interview this type of help should not be provided. Clear guidance must be given to interviewers on what to say and what to record as the participant answers the question.

10.4.5 Selection of cognitive interviewing method

Consider whether it will be appropriate to interrupt the test question administration and response process. For example, you might not want to when:

- there is a desire to observe the participant during completion of the questionnaire, which might be the case when testing paper, web or other self-administered questionnaires;
- the cognitive technique(s) being used require the participant to articulate their thought processes during the time they are answering the test questions, either via concurrent think aloud and/or concurrent probing.

If you are testing a paper self-completion questionnaire you may find it easier to probe retrospectively, otherwise you will have to keep asking the participant to stop what they are doing. It is particularly important to avoid concurrent probing if you are investigating whether participants can follow navigation instructions on paper, as the probing will interrupt the flow of the questionnaire and thus make this task more difficult.

10.4.6 Observation

Consider what impact observation may have on your test findings. Is observation necessary? The answer to this question will depend on the aims of your test (refer to Examples 10.1 and 10.2).

If you are planning to collect observational data consider your options: will you, the interviewer carry out the observation, will it be collected by a separate observer, by videoing the participant completing the form, or via the use of eye-tracking or mouse-tracking software (if the questionnaire is computerised)? Will the observation take place in the participant's home or will you need to attend a special 'lab', perhaps with a two-way mirror to facilitate discreet observation. However, you will need to gain the participant's informed consent to these forms of observation, and even if discreet there is still a risk that the observation may change the participant's behaviour.

10.5 Telephone cognitive interviewing as a replacement for face-to-face cognitive interviewing

The option of conducting cognitive interviews over the phone may be appealing if the target population is quite geographically dispersed or would find a telephone interview more convenient, for example business managers. The costs of undertaking cognitive interviewing by telephone are also lower, as you don't have to pay for interviewers to travel. You may feel it is sensible to undertake the entire cognitive interview by telephone if you are testing telephone survey questions. However, you may also consider testing questions designed for other modes by telephone for the aforementioned reasons (cost, time, and so on). Bear in mind the points discussed in section 10.3.

If you decide to undertake the entire cognitive interview by telephone, it is important to think through the practicalities of this and ask yourself what will be feasible, for example the time you can expect someone to stay on the phone or the extent of probing that may be possible. Be aware that information can be lost in a telephone cognitive interview because the observation of non-verbal cues and the feedback mechanisms between interviewer and participant that are based on them, such as the participant seeing the interviewer is listening and interested in what she has to say and so continuing to elucidate, is not possible. It may be harder for you to establish and build rapport with the participant over the telephone and this could influence participant motivation and interest, which may affect the success of your interview (Beatty and Schecter, 1994).

10.6 Testing sensitive questions

Sensitive questions, for example that ask about a behaviour that may be deemed by society to be undesirable, are often asked in self-administered questionnaires to reduce social desirability bias and so encourage more honest reporting (Tourangeau et al., 2004). If you are testing sensitive questions, it is worth considering how you will do so. For example, will you allow participants to self-administer the questions in private (and therefore avoid concurrent cognitive interviewing techniques and observation all together)? Will you establish how the participant has answered the questions, or will you not require them to discuss their survey responses? Example 10.3 describes an approach we used to test sensitive questions on sexual behaviour.

Example10.3   Testing sensitive questions in CASI

Study

The National Survey of Sexual Attitudes and Lifestyles (Natsal – see www.natsal.ac.uk) is the largest study of sexual behaviour undertaken anywhere in the world, and has been conducted every 10 years since 1990. In 2010 cognitive interviewing took place to test proposed new questions, most of which had been designed for a computer-assisted self-administered interviewing (CASI) module. In the CASI mode, the participant answers the questions on the interviewer's laptop privately, but the interviewer is still present.

Description of methods

- A standalone, test version of the CASI questionnaire was produced for the cognitive interviewing.
- Participants completed the CASI questionnaire in private (i.e. without an interviewer observing them since the questions were highly sensitive and we felt that observation would not be appropriate and would affect the findings).
- Once the questionnaire was completed, interviewers conducted retrospective probing to explore how key terms had been understood.
- Instead of looking at the CASI program on the screen, which would have revealed the participants' answers, interviewers used cards with individual questions printed on them to revisit the test questions during probing. The participant was not required to reveal their survey responses at all, unless this information was volunteered as part of the discussion (see Gray and Nicholson, 2009).

10.7 Cognitive interviewing for mixed mode surveys

So far in this chapter we have considered the implications of survey mode for cognitive interviewing practice in relation to single mode surveys. In the remainder of this chapter we look at what modifications to cognitive interviewing practice are required when you are testing questions designed for mixed mode surveys. Specifically we look at the test design, sample design, whether to mode mimic, choice of probes and analysis issues.

Firstly, let's consider why you might want to test mixed mode questions using cognitive interviewing methods. Mixed mode surveys risk measurement error. Each data collection mode has its specific characteristics, and a change in mode may require changes in wording or changes in design in order to achieve measurement equivalence (Survey Research Center, 2010). However, the nature of the changes required to achieve measurement equivalence may not be immediately evident. There may be resistance to the idea that questions may need to be worded or designed differently for different modes even though 'considerable evidence now exists that the choice of survey mode affects participants' answers to survey questions that are worded the same' (Dillman and Christian, 2005, p.1).

Cognitive interviewing is one tool that can help you develop questions for use in mixed mode surveys to assess measurement equivalence. The design of such cognitive interviewing studies needs particular care and we highlight important design considerations in this section, with particular reference to an Economic and Social Research Council funded study we were involved in that explored the nature of mode effects (Gray et al., 2011).[1]

10.7.1 Test design

As we have already mentioned, it is important to consider the purpose of the cognitive interviews, and particularly whether an iterative approach to testing, involving a test–modification–retest method, is required. The following questions may be useful to consider.

- Is the purpose of your test to understand the mechanics of mode effects or to make practical suggestions on question wording and format that will be used in finalising the design of a mixed mode survey?
- Are you testing 'new' or existing questions?
- If you are testing existing questions, what mode were they designed for? Are they part of a time series? (The answer to this latter question will indicate the weight of evidence that may be required to make any changes to the questions.)
- Are other pretesting/experimental methods going to be used to assess the risk of measurement error?
- What sorts of evidence will the cognitive interviews be able to provide?

Cognitive interviewing is a qualitative technique and as such it will not provide evidence on the existence of mode effects. Rather it can describe the ways in which mode effects might arise.

---

[1]This study was supported by the UK Economic and Social Research Council [grant number RES-175-25-007] awarded to NatCen Social Research.

10.7.2 Sample design

Depending on the aims of your test you may need to consider how you will allocate participants to mode. You will probably want to be able to compare how questions work in the different modes, irrespective of the characteristics of the participants. It would make little sense to test the same questions in different modes with the same participants, since this would feel very repetitive and participants are likely to realise that they are being asked the same questions. Rather you could randomly allocate participants to mode; for example, if you are testing questions for a web/telephone, or CATI (Computer-Assisted Telephone Interviewing) survey you would randomly assign half your participants to the web questions and half to the telephone (CATI) questions. This type of design has been used in a number of studies (see e.g., Gray et al., 2014; Kovar et al., 2001). However, random allocation may not be sufficient, given that cognitive interviewing samples are usually fairly small (see Chapter 4). As an additional step you may want to match participants so that your mode groups (for example, web and CATI) contain people with similar characteristics, see Figure 10.5. The selection of sampling criteria to match on will be important as your experimental design will be more robust if you select criteria that affect responses to the test questions.

	Web		Telephone (CATI)	
	Men	Women	Men	Women
Aged 16–24	10	10	10	10
Aged 25–44	10	10	10	10

Figure 10.5 Illustration of sample matching

The risk, if you don't match, is that half of your sample (receiving one mode) may have very different characteristics to the other half (receiving the other mode). If you find any differences between modes in how a particular question was interpreted, for example, you will not know whether this is a real difference or an artefact resulting from differences in the characteristics of the people you interviewed in the two modes. For further advice on experimental designs see (Krosnick, 2011).

There are implications for splitting the sample by the number of modes included in the mixed mode study, however. You will need to conduct more interviews than you would if you were testing questions in a single mode and this will increase costs.

10.7.3 Conduct of the interviews

Depending on where you are in the questionnaire development life-cycle, and especially in relation to how close you are to having the questionnaire finalised, we would suggest that cognitive interviews for mixed mode surveys are conducted using some form of mode mimicking. In relation to the mixed mode example described in Figure 10.5 involving telephone and web, this would mean:

- asking the telephone survey questions over the telephone; and
- presenting the equivalent web survey questions in a web questionnaire.

The introduction of the questions and cognitive probing should be standardised, as should the cognitive interview protocol, see section 10.7.4.

10.7.4 Writing probes

We would suggest that the same comprehension, recall, judgement and response probes are used in all the cognitive interviews in *all* modes. The use of standardised probes will, in combination with protocols to ensure that probing is carried out in a consistent way across modes (e.g. always retrospectively), minimise differences in the way in which the cognitive interviews are conducted so as to ensure that any differences you observe between modes are real and not the result of differences in the way the cognitive interviews were carried out.

In addition to exploring the question and answer process, however, you will also want to probe on areas that relate specifically to the mode of data collection the questions have been presented in. So, considering our telephone/web mixed mode example again, you might have a set of probes for the telephone mode, which explore issues around ease or difficulty answering questions without visual prompts and aids and how participants found the lists of answer categories in terms of length, etc. Whereas for the web, probes might explore how participants found the screen layout, whether they read the instructions and how they navigated their way through the questionnaire.

Of equal importance will be the necessity to explore how (what are intended to be) functionally equivalent questions work in the different modes. For example, how an end labelled numerical answer scale works over the telephone, compared to in a web questionnaire.

10.7.5 Data analysis

In terms of how to analyse the data, you could follow the approach outlined in Chapter 8, however there will be additional steps that you will need to take to ensure that you have fully described any specific problems and their mechanisms.

Let's say that *comprehension* of a question, or a key term within it, is the focus of your test and therefore what you explore within the analysis. Below are some steps that you might work through when approaching analysis and interpretation.

a) First you would conduct an all-case analysis, for example reviewing all cases across *all* modes for the test question, exploring the data to see whether there was consistency in comprehension. If you found variation in comprehension of the question across modes then you would want to review the data to identify the mechanisms that affected understanding. It may be that the question, or a word within it, was poorly understood across all participants you interviewed, regardless of the mode they received the question in.

b) Next you would review the cases (participants interviewed) *within* mode, so, for example looking at how all of the telephone-assigned participants interpreted and answered the question. At this stage of your analysis, you will be looking for evidence of issues or problems that relate solely to the survey mode.

c) Finally you would compare modes, looking at how the telephone-assigned participants interpreted and answered the question compared to those participants who received the web version. You might find, for example, that comprehension of the question varied by mode and that features of the mode appeared to facilitate or hinder comprehension.

10.8 Chapter summary

When testing questions designed to be asked in different modes (face-to-face, telephone, paper and mail self-administered), consider:

- How you will present the questions to participants – whether, or not, you will mimic the intended data collection mode (for example, ask participants to self-complete a programmed web questionnaire when testing questions for a web survey); and
- whether or not the cognitive interviewer will be present, and if so whether they will be present throughout or only during the cognitive probing.
- In practice, the decision around whether or not to 'mode mimic' will be influenced by what the purpose of the cognitive interviews is and whether or not you think that the mode your test questions are presented in will affect the way the questions are answered.
- If a decision is made to mimic the survey mode, there are a number of things you will need to think about when planning your cognitive test:

  o how you will attempt to simulate the mode;
  o how you will introduce the interview and what the participant is required to do;
  o the presentation of the test questions;
  o the presence of the interviewer;
  o how you will deal with participant queries;
  o the selection of cognitive interviewing method(s);
  o observation.

- Cognitive interviews can be conducted entirely by telephone. Think carefully about this option and consider whether it will be appropriate, given the aims of your test.
- Cognitive interviewing can be used to test questions designed for mixed mode surveys. Sample design is important in this circumstance.

215

When testing self-completion questionnaires you will need to include instructions on how the questionnaire should be given to the respondent..

Placing the self-completion questionnaire

- *Explain to respondents that for the real survey they would receive a pack in the post. Hand the respondent the questionnaire and instruction sheet [the instruction sheet should be placed inside the first page of the questionnaire].*
- *Ask the respondent to fill in the questionnaire as though you were not present. Encourage respondent to **think aloud** for this part of the interview.*

Observation checklist

Provide a space for interviewers to record observations as respondents complete the questionnaire.

Observation	Q Number/Details
☐ Does R answer any Qs that do not apply?	
☐ Does R skip any Qs they should answer?	

Probing on navigation

In addition to probes on questions, for self-completion documents you may wish to include probes on the usability of the questionnaire.

Aims of testing:

- *To explore whether routing instructions are clear*

Suggested probes

- How easy or difficult did you find filling in this questionnaire? Why do you say that?
- How clear was it which sections you should fill in? Could this be made clearer?

Probing on Q1

Provide a list of aims and scripted probes for each question being tested. Again, interviewers are encouraged to add their own probes based on earlier observations.

Aims of testing Q1:

- To explore suitability of **answer categories,** do any additional options need to be added?
- To explore sensitivity and whether respondents are **comfortable** answering this question.

Suggested probes

General
- Now, let's go back and look at Q1. How easy or difficult did you find this question? Why?

Comprehension
- In your own words what do you think this question is trying to ask?

Figure 10.6 Example cognitive protocol for a self-completion questionnaire

References

Beatty, P. and Schechter, S. (1994) 'An examination of mode effects in cognitive laboratory research', *1994 Proceedings of the Section on Survey Research Methods*. Alexandria, VA: American Statistical Association, 1275–80.

Czaja, R. and Blair, J. (1996) *Designing Surveys: A Guide to Decisions and Procedures*. Thousand Oaks, CA: Pine Forge Press.

DeMaio, T.J. and Rothgeb, J. (1996) 'Cognitive interviewing techniques: in the lab and in the field', in S. Sudman and N. Schwarz (eds), *Answering Questions*. San Francisco, CA: Jossey-Bass. pp. 177–96.

de Leeuw, E.D. (2005) 'To mix or not to mix data collection modes in surveys', *The Journal of Official Statistics*, 21(2): 233–55.

Dex, S. and Gummy, J. (2011) *On the Experience and Evidence about Mixing Modes of Data Collection in Large-scale Surveys Where the Web is Used as One of the Modes in Data Collection*. Southampton: Nation Centre for Research Methods/Economic and Social Research Council. http://eprints.ncrm.ac.uk/2041/1/mixing_modes_of_data_collection_in_large_surveys.pdf

Dillman, D.A. and Christian, L.M. (2005) 'Survey mode as a source of instability in responses across surveys', *Field Methods*, 17: 30–52.

Dillman, D.A. and Mason, R.G. (1984) 'The Influence of survey method on question response'. Paper presented at the annual meeting of the American Association for Public opinion Research, Wisconsin.

Dillman, D.A. and Redline, C.D. (2004) 'Testing paper self-administered questionnaires: cognitive interview and field test comparisons', in S. Presser, J.M Rothgeb, M.P. Couper, J.T. Lessler, E. Martin, J. Martin and E. Singer (eds), *Methods for Testing and Evaluating Survey Questionnaires*. New York: Wiley-Interscience. pp. 299–317.

Gray, M. and Nicholson, S. (2009) *National Survey of Sexual Attitudes and Lifestyles 2010: Findings and Recommendations from Cognitive Question Testing*. Available at: www.natsal.ac.uk/media/822297/natsal%202010_cognitive%20pilot%20report%20-%20final.pdf

Gray, M., Blake, M. and Campanelli, P. (2011) 'The use of cognitive interviewing methods to evaluate mode effects in survey questions'. Paper presented at the fourth Conference of the European Survey Research Association (ESRA), July 18–22, Lausanne, Switzerland.

Gray, M., Blake, M. and Campanelli, P. (2014) 'The use of cognitive interviewing methods to evaluate mode effects in survey questions', *Field Methods*, 26(2): 156–71.

Jenkins, C.R. and Dillman, D.A. (1997) 'Towards a theory of self-administered questionnaire design', in L. Lyberg, P. Biemer, M. Collins, E. de Leeuw, C. Dippo, N. Schwarz and D. Trewin (eds), *Survey Measurement and Process Quality*. New York: John Wiley & Sons. pp. 165–96.

Kovar, M., Lee, L., Hess, M. and Arday, S. (2001) 'Cognitive testing of a questionnaire for a dual-mode survey of medicare beneficiaries', *Proceedings of the Annual Meeting of the American Statistical Association*. Available at www. amstat.org/sections/srms/Proceedings/y2001f.html

Krysan, M., Schuman, H., Scott, L.J. and Beatty, P. (1994). 'Response rates and response content in mail versus face-to-face surveys', *Public Opinion Quarterly*, 58: 382–99.

Krosnick, J.A. (2011) 'Experiments for evaluating survey questions', in J. Madans, K. Miller, A. Maitland and G. Willis (eds), *Question Evaluation Methods: Contributing to the Science of Data Quality*. Hoboken, NJ: Wiley. pp. 215–38.

Mahon-haft, T.A. and Dillman, D.A. (2010) 'Does visual appeal matter? Effects of web survey aesthetics on survey quality', *Survey Research Methods*, 4(1): 43–59.

McGee, A. and d'Ardenne, J. (2009) *'Netting a Winner': Tackling Ways to Question Children Online. A Good Practice Guide to Asking Children and Young People about Sport and Physical Activity*. Sports Council for Wales. Available at: www. sportwales.org.uk/media/351853/netting_a_winner_-_english.pdf

Presser, S., Couper, M.P., Lessler, J.T., Martin, E., Martin, J., Rothgeb, J.M. and Singer, E. (2004) 'Methods for testing and evaluating survey questions', *Public Opinion Quarterly*, 68(1): 109–30.

Prüfer, P. and Rexroth, M. (2005) 'Kognitive Interviews'. *ZUMA How-to*-Reihe,15. Available at: www.gesis.org/fileadmin/upload/forschung/publikationen/gesis_reihen/ howto/How_to15PP_MR.pdf

Rothgeb, J. (2007) *ACS Labor Force Questions: Results from Cognitive Interview Testing1*. Washington, DC: Center for Survey Methods Research/Statistical Research Division, U.S. Census Bureau.

Schechter, S., Blair, J. and Vande Hey, J. (1996) 'Conducting cognitive interviews to test self-administered and telephone surveys: which methods should we use?', University of Maryland Survey Research Center Working Paper. (Download from UMD Survey Research Center, http://www.amstat.org/sections/srms/ Proceedings/papers/1996_002.pdf).

Survey Research Center (2010) *Guidelines for Best Practice in Cross-Cultural Surveys*. Ann Arbor, MI: Survey Research Center, Institute for Social Research, University of Michigan. Available at: www.ccsg.isr.umich.edu (accessed January 2014).

Tarnai, J. and Dillman, D. (1992) 'Questionnaire context as a source of response differences in mail vs telephone surveys', in N. Schwarz, H.J. Hippler and S. Sudman (eds), *Order Effects in Social and Psychological Research*. New York: Springer-Verlag. pp. 115–129.

Toepoel, V., Das, M. and Van Soest, A. (2006) 'Design of web questionnaires: the effect of layout in rating scales', *Journal of Official Statistics*, 25(4): 509–28.

Tourangeau, R. (1984) 'Cognitive science and survey methods', in T. Jabine, M. Straf, J. Tanur and R. Tourangeau (eds), *Cognitive Aspects of Survey Methodology:*

Building a Bridge Between Discipline. Washington, DC: National Academy Press. pp. 73–100.

Tourangeau, R., Couper, M. and Conrad, F. (2004) 'Spacing position and order: interpretive heuristics for visual features of survey questions', *Public Opinion Quarterly*, 68(3): 368–93.

Vernon, M. (2005) *Pre-testing Sensitive Questions: Perceived Sensitivity, Comprehension, and Order Effects of Questions about Income and Weight.* Washington, DC: Bureau of Labor Statistics.

Willis, G.B. (2005) *Cognitive Interviewing: A Tool For Improving Questionnaire Design.* London: Sage.

ELEVEN

CROSS-NATIONAL, CROSS-CULTURAL AND MULTILINGUAL COGNITIVE INTERVIEWING

MICHELLE GRAY AND MARGARET BLAKE

11.1 Introduction

The aim of this chapter is to provide practical guidance on conducting cognitive interviews in cross-national, cross-cultural and multilingual settings. All survey research is essentially *comparative* (Harkness et al., 2010). However, in this chapter we use the term 'comparative' research to refer to cross-national, cross-cultural and multilingual research activities.

The chapter starts by setting the scene, discussing the importance of measurement equivalence in comparative research and providing an overview of the approaches to designing comparative survey questions. We then go on to discuss the issues to consider when planning and carrying out cognitive interviews as part of a comparative research project. Specifically, we provide guidance and highlight some considerations in relation to:

- Choosing the countries, cultures or languages to include within the cognitive test
- Phasing
- Developing the interview protocol
- Sample design and recruitment of participants
- Recruitment and training of interviewers
- Analysis and the interpretation of findings.

Finally, we discuss alternatives to cognitive interviewing for comparative research, such as expert review and questionnaire appraisal.

11.2 Background

In this book so far we have described cognitive interviewing and shown how it can be used to test questions, often as part of the questionnaire development stage of a survey. It can uncover problems with survey questions which, if left untreated, could result in measurement error.

When designing questionnaires, researchers face the challenge of ensuring that all members of the survey population understand the questions in both the intended way and in a way that is consistent between participants. This job is easier if your survey population is relatively homogenous, but becomes a more difficult when the population is more varied. In Chapter 4, we discussed the importance of ensuring that your cognitive interviewing sample reflects the range and diversity of participant characteristics within the survey population. In this chapter, we discuss the implications for cognitive interviewing when surveys involve:

- different countries (or nations);
- participants from different cultural backgrounds;
- participants whose first languages are different from the main (or source) language of the questionnaire.

It is important to recognise that different surveying situations can present different combinations of the above. For example, even within one country, survey participants can have very different *cultural backgrounds* and/or may need to complete the survey questionnaire in *languages* other than the main language of that country.

Cross-national research involves the conduct of the same survey in more than one country and it has become more commonplace over the last few decades, reflecting a growing interest in comparing the characteristics, behaviours and attitudes of different nations. Prominent examples in Europe include:

- The European Social Survey (ESS), an academically driven cross-national survey has been conducted every two years across Europe since 2001. The survey measures the attitudes, beliefs and behaviour patterns of people resident in more than thirty nations.
- The Survey of Health, Ageing and Retirement in Europe (SHARE), a longitudinal survey has been collecting data on the health, socio-economic status and social and family networks of individuals aged 50 years and over who are resident in 20 countries, since 2004.

11.2.1 The issue of equivalence in measurement

Let's now consider measurement equivalence and look at the role cognitive interviewing can play in helping you to establish it. If you are working on surveys involving different countries, cultures and languages you will be concerned about measurement issues, particularly the comparability, reliability and validity of the data. The questionnaire design phase needs particular attention and often requires the input of a wider group of people, for example those with country, culture and language expertise. The eventual goal is to achieve equivalence in measurement. In the comparative research literature, there are many different labels used in relation to equivalence: 'construct equivalence', 'direct equivalence' and 'functional equivalence' being three (Johnson, 1998). Essentially, the goal is always the same: in order to make meaningful comparisons, the data collection instruments must have similar measurement qualities across the various settings.

We know that concepts do not always translate well, however. Across countries and cultural groups, there may be concepts that will not work as intended, either because they do not exist or because they exist in different forms. A General Practitioner (GP) – the name used to describe a family doctor in the UK – for example, would not be the right descriptor to use in a question asked in other European countries, since this label is not used outside of the UK.

The lack of equivalent concepts can become most evident when you have to translate the questions into other languages, though this can also apply even when the same language is being used (e.g. UK and US English). For example, the word 'cooker' in British English is another commonly used term for an oven, though in American English the word refers to a person who cooks. Imagine you included the following question in a survey in both nations: 'Do you have a cooker?' Would the survey's findings be comparable?

There are three basic approaches to comparative survey question design that you can adopt.

a) **Asking the same questions** (ASQ), where the most common approach is to develop a source questionnaire in one language and then produce other target language versions, usually on the basis of translation or translation and adaptation.

b) **Asking different questions** (ADQ), involving researchers asking the most salient questions for each population on the given common constructs. The result is different questions and possibly even different indicators being used in each setting, though the questions are assumed to tap into a construct that is shared across all involved.

c) **A mix of approaches** that combines ASQ and ADQ (see Example 11.1).

See Survey Research Center (2011): www.ccsg.isr.umich.edu/ (accessed June 2014).

Example 11.1   Adapting a questionnaire to accommodate different populations

In 2004 the Health Survey for England had a special focus on ethnic minorities (Sproston and Mindell, 2006). Mostly the survey questions were translated into various Asian languages, or were offered in English to Black and minority ethnic participants. However, on the topic of tobacco consumption an additional question about smokeless tobacco use was asked for South Asian participants to capture this type of use, which was specific to this group.

For comparative research, it could be argued that there is an even greater need to pretest survey questions, within the different settings, than there is for a survey involving one country, culture and/or language.

Cognitive interviewing is increasingly being used in the development of cross-national, cross-cultural and multilingual questionnaires. However, undertaking comparative cognitive interviewing raises many challenges. In the next few sections we provide an overview of the main issues to consider when designing your cognitive interviewing pretest in these contexts. These are:

- the choice of countries, cultures and/or languages for testing;
- timing or phasing of the testing;
- interview protocol development;
- sampling and recruitment of participants;
- recruitment and training of interviewers;
- data analysis;
- interpretation of findings.

11.3 The choice of countries, cultures and/or languages

If you are planning to carry out a survey in different countries or cultures and in more than one language, you will need to decide if you can conduct cognitive interviewing in *all* settings. This decision will to a large extent be determined by the time and money available and the number of countries, cultures or language groups the survey will cover. If your survey is planned to be fielded in 26 countries and translated into over 20 languages, for example, then it is likely that testing will only be possible in a (small) subset of those. You will need to decide in which countries to test.

There are a number of factors, some quite practical, to consider that will help you make decisions about which countries, cultures and languages to include within your cognitive test.

- The composition of your research team in terms of their knowledge of the countries and cultures and their language proficiency. For example, if you are planning to undertake cognitive testing on a cross-national project covering Ireland, Spain and Germany does your team include members from each of those countries? Do you have the language proficiency and local knowledge to be able to develop protocols and recruitment materials, conduct the analysis and interpret the results?

- The availability of researchers or interviewers trained in cognitive interviewing in different countries, from different cultural backgrounds and who speak the different languages – to allow interviews to take place in different settings.
- (For cultures and languages) the prevalence of each culture and language within the settings. For example, consider whether some languages are more commonly spoken than others.
- The similarities and differences between countries, cultures and languages. For example, whether there are shared characteristics of particular countries, or commonalities between certain languages, meaning that not all need to be represented in your cognitive interviews.

In Example 11.2 the decision around whether the cognitive interviews are conducted in the source language only (British English) or in the source language *and* the other language (Welsh) is relatively straightforward.

Example 11.2   Deciding on the languages to test questions in

A survey is carried out in Wales, where the questionnaire is offered to participants in either British English or Welsh. You have been asked to test some new questions. You need to decide whether to only test the questions in English, which is the source language for the survey questionnaire, or whether to also carry out some cognitive interviews in Welsh, as the questionnaire will be translated into this language (Howarth, 2008).

However, in surveys where there are many more languages, the decision is clearly more difficult because there are more languages to choose from. Example 11.3 illustrates how you might choose countries for a cross-national cognitive test.

Example11.3   Choosing countries for a cross-national cognitive interviewing study

Study: The European Social Survey (ESS) is an academically driven, cross-national survey that has been conducted every two years across Europe since 2001. It varies, but usually around 30 countries participate, meaning the survey is conducted in various nations, with different countries and in multiple languages.

Who was included in the cognitive test for Round 7? Participants from the UK, Poland, Estonia and Spain were included.

The rationale behind the choice: A combination of substantive and practical reasons informed the choice. These were, in no particular order, as follows.

- A decision was made to test in the UK so that the questions could be tested in the language they had been designed in (the source language).
- There was a desire to test translated versions of the questions for cultural problems, however budgetary limitations meant that in addition to the UK, a maximum of three other countries could be included.
- Countries were chosen on the basis that they:

  o were likely to participate in Round 7 of the ESS;
  o differed in terms of levels of immigration (according to ESS data);
  o represented a geographical spread (from eastern, western and southern Europe); and,
  o were able to complete the testing within the required timetable (i.e. staff were available).[1]

11.4 Phasing of the testing

Assuming you have chosen the countries, cultures and/or languages to include within your cognitive test, you will next need to decide how to phase the cognitive interviews. By this we mean, whether you will choose to carry out the cognitive interviews:

a) *sequentially* – where you test the source questionnaire first (i.e. in one country, with participants from the same cultural background or in the source language only), before moving on – once you have made the necessary refinements and are happy with it – to test it in other countries, cultures and languages; or,

b) *in parallel* – where the source questionnaire is tested simultaneously in a number of different countries, cultures and/or languages.

---

[1]We would like to acknowledge the partners involved in this cross-national cognitive test. Rory Fitzgerald, Sally Widdop, Lizzy Gatrell and Yvette Prestage (all at City University, London) as well as Mare Ainsaar, Ave Roots and Laur Lilleoja (University of Tartu, Estonia); Mónica Méndez Lago and María Cuesta Azofra (both at Centro de Investigaciones Sociológicas – CIS, Spain) and Anna Pokorska, Piotr Binder, Hanna Bojar, Franciszek Sztabinski (all at the Institute of Philosophy and Sociology, Polish Academy of Sciences, Poland) and Hanna Uhl (at MillwardBrown Polska). The advance pretesting activities for Round 7 of the European Social Survey in the UK were supported by the UK Economic and Social Research Council [grant number RES-627-25-0003, awarded to the Centre for Comparative Social Surveys (CCSS) at City University London.

You would be carrying out sequential testing when your questionnaire has been designed in a source language and where adaptations to the instrument as a result of testing in other languages, and/or cultures, are unlikely to impact on the source questionnaire design. This may be the case when your questionnaire is being tested for use among minority populations. However, you should allow changes to the source questionnaire if, as a result of testing in other contexts or languages, you identify problems with the source questions. In other cases the source question will be fine, but what you need is an improved language translation or some additional clarification or questions for the minority groups.

If you are carrying out a cross-national survey, testing is more likely to happen in parallel. The source language may be English, to facilitate cross-national working, but the proportion of English speakers in the survey's target population may be similar to the proportions of people speaking other languages, in which case there is no need to test it in English first since this language will be no more important during fieldwork than any other. Parallel testing may also take place in countries or nations that have more than one official language. Returning to Example 11.2, a decision was made that the 2011 census should be developed and tested in parallel in Welsh and English, rather than developing and testing the English version first (Howarth, 2008).

11.5 Interview protocol development

The development of a protocol for a comparative cognitive interviewing study requires some planning. This is because the conduct of cognitive interviews in different countries, with different cultural groups and/or in more than one language presents added complications with regards to attempts to standardise the protocol.

If different countries (or organisations within these) are involved in the study, they may vary in terms of cognitive interviewing experience. It may be that your cognitive test will include different cultures that are known to react less well to certain kinds of cognitive techniques. Additionally, the interview protocol will need to be translated where different languages are present, meaning that you will need to plan how this is to be facilitated.

Ultimately, there are three main decisions you will need to make, which will inform how you develop your interview protocol.

- Which cognitive techniques you will use (think aloud and/or probing; other techniques).
- Whether you will use scripted or unscripted probing.
- How you will develop your protocol (or probe sheet).

In the rest of this section we consider these decisions in more detail.

11.5.1 The choice of cognitive techniques for comparative research

There has been a debate in the literature about the extent to which cognitive interviewing is culturally transferable. Studies have shown that some of the most widely accepted cognitive interviewing techniques can be problematic in certain cultures (e.g. Blumberg and Goerman, 2000; Coronado and Earle, 2002; Kissam, et al., 1993; Pan, 2004).

Some studies have found that certain kinds of probes (paraphrasing, for example) may not be appropriate in certain languages (Pan et al., 2010). This highlights the importance of:

- familiarity with the non-source languages when developing your probes (for example, by involving language experts where they are available, or by referring to evidence in the literature); and
- considering the types of probes chosen in relation to how they are likely to work in all languages.

The consensus when writing probe questions for cross-national, cross-cultural or multilingual cognitive interviewing, seems to be:

- Include an introduction that fully explains the purpose of, and what is involved in, a cognitive interview for the benefit of cultures which might otherwise be less open to the process. One idea could be to include example exercises to make the ideas more concrete (Levin et al., 2009).
- Write probes that are focused, direct and related to the test question so that you reduce the risk of vagueness or limited responses to them.
- Provide alternative probes if the initial ones fail, i.e. if the participant does not understand the content of the probe.
- Use think aloud as an additional approach where possible but do not rely on this as the only method used.

The other technique widely used in cognitive interviewing is 'think aloud'. The advantage of this approach, in comparative cognitive interviewing, is that the method is flexible and allows people to use the language and meaning appropriate to their culture. However, some cultures are more comfortable with 'thinking aloud' than others and the extent to which people are comfortable in 'justifying' their survey answers will vary (Agans et al., 2006; Willis and Zahnd, 2007; Willis et al., 2005). In planning cognitive interviewing, particularly across countries, it is important to bear this in mind and to develop a protocol that is flexible enough to allow for some tailoring to the cultural norms of a particular setting but standardised enough to allow comparison of the findings.

11.5.2 Scripted vs. unscripted probes

You also need to decide whether the probes will be *scripted* – read out exactly as worded in all countries, cultures and (most importantly) languages (see Miller, 2008), or *unscripted*, where interviewers are told to cover a list of areas but are able to do so using their own judgement around which probe questions to ask (Fitzgerald et al., 2011; Goerman and Caspar, 2010; Miller et al., 2011). Figure 11.1 outlines some of the advantages and disadvantages associated with each approach.

We would argue that standardising the coverage of the probing areas, at the very least, is necessary in order to facilitate a comparative data analysis as it will ensure that the same issues are asked about in all interviews. The use of standardised probes can also be helpful for new interviewers who have not yet gained experience in using their own form of words to explore the areas of interest. In addition, we advise that even when interviewers are told to use scripted probes, they should not be discouraged from asking additional probes to explore unanticipated issues. In carrying out research across countries it is worth bearing in mind that the skills and experience of those carrying out the interviews may vary according to how well established cognitive interviewing is in each country and the organisations that make up your team. Furthermore, the style of cognitive interviewing in different countries and organisations can vary. For example, some organisations tend to use specially trained field interviewers, whilst others use researchers to conduct the interviews, and different interviewing conventions may be used by each type of interviewer. In a cross-national project attention

	Advantages	Disadvantages
Scripted probes	• An identical approach to cognitive interview data collection can be applied, across counties, cultures and languages, meaning comparisons of the data can be made. • Even where probing is scripted, flexibility can still be encouraged whereby interviewers are able to ask additional probes (see Lee, 2012).	• One of the features of the cognitive interviewing method is the interviewer's ability to diverge from the script. Interviewers can be discouraged from using flexibility when scripted probes are used, meaning that unanticipated issues or problems that should ideally be explored further can be missed.
Unscripted probes	• Interviewers can use the list of areas to explore as a basis for formulating their probe questions, but are not fixed to precise wording around how to ask them.	• Less experienced interviewers might struggle to formulate balanced and neutrally worded probe questions during the interview.

Figure 11.1 Advantages and disadvantages of scripted and unscripted probing in comparative cognitive interviewing

needs to be given to ensuring researchers and interviewers are trained to use a standard protocol in a consistent way, even if it is not the style they are used to.

11.5.3 The development of the cognitive interview protocol

A cognitive interview protocol, particularly the probing method, must work in all target countries, cultures and languages but how should this be developed? There are two schools of thought:

- simultaneous development of the probes in different settings or languages, for example (Goerman and Caspar, 2010); and
- development of probes in the source language, which are then translated into the non-source target languages (Fitzgerald et al., 2009).

There is no right or wrong way to develop a protocol, it is about thinking through what resources are available to you in terms of people in your team with the necessary language skills (see section 11.3). Your decision here is also likely to be informed by the time available for the development of the protocol and how this fits in with the individuals who need to be involved.

11.6 Sampling and recruitment of participants

Sampling and recruitment for cognitive interviewing is covered in Chapter 4. In this section we highlight the considerations specific to comparative research. The key points are:

- the importance of consistency in the sample design for different countries and cultures within the same cognitive interview project;
- consideration of whether to include monolingual or bilingual speakers of the languages being tested; and
- the importance of including language subgroups in the sample so that the questions are tested with people who speak different dialects or with regional variations in language.

11.6.1 Sample design

Where possible, the sample design for comparative cognitive interviewing should be consistent between settings. Across the countries, cultures or language groups, the same overall demographic criteria for sampling should be used (e.g. gender, age, employment, education). There may need to be additional sampling criteria included in certain countries or cultures if it is felt to be important for the overall aims of the testing. Additionally, for some groups it may not be possible to apply the criteria in exactly the same way. For example, when conducting cognitive interviewing in minority languages in the UK, the age and education profile of those responding in languages other than English may be different from those who choose to respond in English (tending to be older and less educated). You and your team will also need to agree how to ensure your sampling criteria are consistent across settings. For example, screening questions about education would need to be worded differently in different countries but should identify broadly consistent groups so that you can make valid comparisons between those with higher and lower levels of education.

11.6.2 The recruitment of participants and language considerations

When recruiting participants in a multilingual cognitive test, you may need to decide whether participants should be monolingual or bilingual. Goerman and Caspar (2010) suggest that participants should be recruited to represent how they would be interviewed in the survey (i.e. recruited as monolingual if they can only speak one of the languages being offered in the survey and recruited as bilingual if there are two or more languages being offered in the survey which they could speak). They highlight the importance of well-worded screening questions, used in the recruitment phase, to identify the participant's main language. The inclusion of monolingual and bilingual participants may be important because people who are bilingual (including in the source language) may find it easier to understand the questions translated from the source language, being more familiar with common concepts and ways of expressing things than people who cannot speak the source language. This is something you might want to explore in your analysis.

The importance of screening for monolingual or bilingual speakers may vary according to whether your research is being conducted in countries with two or more national languages (e.g. Switzerland or Canada) or those where there is a single predominant language (e.g. English in England) but where migrant groups have introduced minority languages (e.g. Bengali, Urdu, Polish in England). In multilingual countries with multiple national or established languages, all languages would be offered in a survey. In this case there is a genuine choice to be made between languages and there may be no single predominant language. In the English context, the standard offer is an interview in English and people would usually only choose another language if they could not speak English well enough. Therefore, people choosing languages other than the source language in England are unlikely to be bilingual (unless they are bilingual in two languages other than English). This will affect sampling criteria, screening questions and how the languages are offered. Within the UK as a whole, when research is conducted in Wales, bilingual Welsh and English speakers will choose between Welsh and English.

Where there are known differences in one language, reflecting different dialects or regional differences in vocabulary, the aim should be to try to recruit participants from a variety of areas to ensure regional variations of the language are included in the testing (Levin et al., 2009). These could be regional variations in the country where the survey is being carried out, or regional variations in the country of origin when testing questions in languages spoken by migrant populations.

An additional complication is that the languages or dialects that minority groups speak may not have a consistent written form, or people may not be literate in that language. For example, most migrants to the UK from Bangladesh come from an area called Sylhet and speak an unwritten dialect, meaning standard written Bengali is not accessible to this group. This particularly affects self-administered surveys, but also face-to-face instruments with show cards. It is important that the cognitive interviewing sample includes people who speak such dialects and come from different regional and educational backgrounds to test whether the target population can read the survey questions or documents being proposed.

It is also important to consider the skills of those interviewing and recruiting participants who speak multiple languages. For example, your recruiters need to be able to speak the relevant languages and be culturally competent as well as experienced in the local areas (Sha et al., 2010). Where this is not possible in all cases, a multilingual screening sheet can be used, followed up by contact from an interviewer or researcher who speaks the language. Interviewers need to speak the dialects or languages predominant among the target population for the research.

11.7 Selection and training of interviewers

Cognitive interviewers need to possess a number of specific skills, which we review in Chapter 6. If you are conducting a comparative cognitive test (and especially one that involves more than one language) there will be additional skills that interviewers require. This section has been designed to help you think about these additional skills, and covers:

- who will conduct the interviews; and
- how you will train the interviewers.

11.7.1 Who will conduct the interviews

For cross-cultural and multilingual cognitive interviewing, it may be that you do not need to look any further than the research team for your interviewers. However, as we discussed earlier in section 11.3, your research team may lack certain cultural or language skills and you may need to recruit cognitive interviewers to carry out the interviews for you. Essentially the same principles apply as were covered in Chapter 6.

In the context of cross-cultural interviewing within a country, you will need (within your interviewing team) to be able to speak, read and write in the target languages. Interviewers will need to be able to read survey questions that have been translated. For example, if interviewers are interviewing in Welsh they will need to administer the test question in Welsh.

As mentioned in section 11.3, when conducting cross-national research, it should be borne in mind that countries and organisations may vary in their cognitive interviewing traditions, particularly in how well established they are, whether researchers or interviewers tend to do the cognitive interviewing, and on whether structured probing, spontaneous probing or think aloud tends to be the predominant technique. It is essential that early on in the project these differences are discussed, agreement reached on the approach to be used, and any resulting training needs identified.

11.7.2 Interviewer training for comparative cognitive interviewing

Training of interviewers for comparative cognitive interviewing (especially that which is multilingual) should be well thought out. The training should cover the cognitive interviewing method and the language/cultural issues specific to your project. Goerman and Caspar (2010) recommend a four-stage training programme, over two days, covering: (1) training in the basics of cognitive interviewing; (2) training on the project specifics; (3) training on linguistic or cultural sensitivity issues that should be considered when interviewing; and finally (4) practice interviews in the target languages. At NatCen we have used the first three stages when briefing interviewers for a project that explored the way in which people of Bangladeshi and Pakistani origin answered questions about their satisfaction with social care services. As we only trained one interviewer for each language and the research team were not familiar with the languages being used we could not conduct practice interviews in the target languages during the briefing, although all interviewers carried out practice interviews in English.

It is essential that the new interviewers conduct some initial interviews in the source language used by the research team so that their interviewing skills can be evaluated (which we did on the aforementioned social care project). If you have a team of interviewers working on the study, it may be beneficial to appoint a 'lead' interviewer. This person can keep track of how the other interviewers are doing, communicating any problems that arise in the interviewing process to researchers (Levin et al., 2009), or they can accompany less experienced interviewers on their first interview and provide feedback. It is also necessary to get the recordings of early interviews in the target language transcribed and translated into English so that the research team can evaluate them and provide feedback before further interviews are carried out.

11.8 Data analysis

The analysis of cross-national, cross-cultural and multilingual cognitive interview data follows the same principles set out in Chapters 7 and 8. There are a few additional considerations however, especially where interviews have been conducted in multiple languages:

- whether the notes or transcripts of each interview will be written up into the target language, or the source language; and
- who will conduct the analysis?

11.8.1 The language to use for interview note and transcripts

Essentially, the language skills within the research team will prescribe the language to be used for interview notes and transcripts. If members of the research team only speak and read the source language, summaries of the interviews or transcripts (even though they were carried out in 'other' languages) must be accessible to all members of the research team. This will mean that notes or transcripts from the 'other' language interviews will either need to be written in: (a) the source language, so that the research team can read them; or, (b) 'other' languages and then translated, word-for-word, into the source language.

Where interview summaries have been produced in the source language (even where the interviews were conducted in 'other' languages), it is essential that a link can be made back to the original data. For example, it might be wise to include the actual words chosen for the translation in the other language, so that the research team has the raw data to hand when they need it. Additionally, the link to the original data can be facilitated by having the interviewers involved in any discussion of the findings. In the cross-national cognitive interviewing projects we have been involved in, we have invited the interviewers representing the countries (and therefore languages) involved, to a joint analysis meeting (Widdop et al., 2011).

11.8.2 Who will conduct the analysis?

You will need to decide, especially when you have included multiple languages within your cognitive test, who will carry out the data analysis. If you are working from notes, or summaries within a framework, it may be wise to include all country/culture/language representatives in an initial discussion of the findings. Some cross-national cognitive interviewing projects reported in the literature have used a 'joint analysis' approach (Miller, 2008), involving a face-to-face meeting where those involved work through each test question and report on what was found in their country, culture or language. It has been argued that this method allows for consistency in analysis across countries (Miller et al., 2011).

In the cross-national cognitive interviewing for the European Social Survey that we have been involved in, joint analysis meetings have been held over two days. The co-ordinators took the different countries through the test protocol, question-by-question, asking for reports of the problems found and the reasons for these. For each issue that was aired (misunderstanding of a key concept for example), the co-ordinators checked whether the same (or different) findings were found across countries.

Even where there is a joint analysis meeting, it may be necessary for one person or one team to check the summaries to ensure that all cases from all countries are considered. This is only possible where the notes or transcripts are in a language which a single researcher (or team) can understand. In cross-national research involving many countries it is likely that notes and transcripts will be in the target language for each country and so analysis will have to be done in each country separately but drawn together at the analysis meeting or in another way using country summaries.

In organising the findings across countries, cultures and languages, we advocate the use of an error source typology that will allow you to classify errors found, so making the question-revision stage easier to facilitate. This also helps to rationalise and manage the vast amounts of data that result from cognitive interviewing in multiple settings and ensures that the issues raised by the cognitive interviews are considered in a consistent and standard manner.

An example of an error source typology that has been used in cross-national cognitive interviewing settings, is the Cross National Error Source Typology (or CNEST) (Fitzgerald et al., 2011). This typology attempts to assist questionnaire designers by providing a 'clear basis on which to reduce and avoid measurement error by basing remedial action on the underlying cause of the error found or produced during the design phase' (p. 1). The components of CNEST are as follows.

a) **Poor source question design** – either all or parts of the question have been badly designed, meaning measurement error is introduced.

b) **Translation problems:**
   i. resulting from translation error – human error in the translation process, for example the translator choosing an inappropriate, or less than ideal, word
   ii. resulting from source question design – source question features, such as the use of vague qualifiers in a response scale, that are difficult or even impossible to translate in a way that achieves functional equivalence.

c) **Cultural portability** – the concept that the question aims to measure does not exist in all countries/cultures, or it exists but in a way that does not permit the proposed measurement approach.

This is not the only error source typology in the literature. There are others (see Carrasco, 2003; Goerman and Caspar, 2007; Levin et al., 2009; Schoua-Glusberg, 2006; Willis et al., 2007), and they all share common features with CNEST.

11.9 Interpretation of findings

Having carried out the analysis of the cognitive interview data, the final stage is to make decisions around what changes may need to be made to the questions or survey administration. This topic is covered in detail in Chapter 9. In this section we focus on issues specific to comparative research. In all cognitive research, you may need to consider the re-phrasing of certain questions or response options for example, and in some cases you may even feel it is necessary to drop questions altogether, if enough evidence was found to suggest that they did not work across the settings.

These kinds of decisions will be much harder when the questions have been tested in different countries, cultures and languages. What will you do, for example, if a question works well in one culture but not another? The response to this problem will depend on various factors including whether the question has not worked well because:

- the concept does not exist in every culture;
- the concept exists but the way the question is worded does not transfer well;
- the problem lies in the language translation, rather than as a result of cultural differences; and/or
- the question is problematic even in the source language and context and cross-cultural testing has highlighted this.

Depending on these factors, solutions include:

- no change to the question because it works well for all other groups and contexts and to change it would result in poorer data for the majority, or because, although not totally equivalent, it is still a useful question;
- improve the target language translation, for example by offering annotations to translators to guide the process;
- make a slight tweak to the wording of the question or add a definition or explanation for all participants, or just for certain countries or groups;
- change the source question substantially because it does not work for the intended comparisons;
- leave the source question unchanged but ask different questions in different contexts.

11.10 Alternatives or additions to comparative cognitive interviewing

As we have already mentioned, budget and time constraints mean using cognitive interviewing to test questions in all cultural groups, in every country and target language is unlikely to be possible on most projects. In this section we discuss some strategies you can use when full, comparative cognitive interviewing is not possible. However, these methods can also be carried out in addition to cognitive interviewing, where budgets allow.

11.10.1 Focus groups in questionnaire development

Focus groups, which tend to be cheaper and quicker than cognitive interviews, can be used prior to deciding on the source questions. We discuss the use of focus groups early on in the questionnaire design phase in Chapter 2. People from the cultural groups of interest, including some who may be bilingual, can be asked about the concepts to be included in the questions in order that the design of the source questions reflects an understanding of how the research topic needs to be approached with different groups (see Agans et al., 2006). We do not recommend testing question wording in focus groups (see section 2.2.1).

11.10.2 Involving language experts

It can be useful to involve 'language representatives' in the questionnaire development, particularly if you are unable to undertake any cognitive interviews. We would advise that language representatives are bought in to comment on the translated questionnaires, checking for equivalence with the source language and between target languages, either before or after translation. This approach is also advocated by Goerman and Caspar (2010). Example 11.4 illustrates the use of this approach on a cross-cultural study.

Example 11.4   Testing questions with Muslim respondents

In this study we were testing questions for which the views of Muslims were of particular interest, although they were intended for a general population survey. It was essential that the questions were understood by Muslim participants from a range of cultural backgrounds, including those who would need interviews in minority languages. Cognitive interviewing in the minority languages was not feasible. Instead we conducted focus groups with people from a range of backgrounds, prior to designing the questions in English. After cognitive interviewing in English among the communities of interest, we held a round-table discussion in which language experts and translators from two translation agencies participated, to discuss the source (English) questions and their suitability for translation into various target languages. The idea was to ensure the English language source questions contained concepts, structure and wording that could readily be translated, before they were finalised.

Particularly when dealing with migrant minority languages, in selecting people to evaluate translated questions in a desk-based exercise, it is essential that they are from the same specific cultural or language groups as will be included in the survey, or at least that they understand those groups. Translators tend to come from urban areas, are often well-educated professionals and may not use the same style of language as those who will need the translations. It is not uncommon for agencies to provide translations that have been checked internally and edited to make them appear more 'professional' by using more sophisticated language, for example. This practice often makes them unsuitable for use among survey participants. Using 'local' bilingual survey interviewers to check the translations can be effective as they often have a good sense of where documents need to be pitched to make them accessible to the target population.

11.10.3 Desk-based appraisal for comparative research

There are some systematic desk-based appraisal tools, or checklists available that can help with problem identification, *without* involving participants or language experts – both of which inevitably come at a cost (see section 2.2.2). Dean et al. (2007) have put forward a revised version of the Question Appraisal System, or QAS-99 (Willis and Lessler, 1999), that accommodates steps to assess cross-cultural and language problems. Their enhanced version of the QAS (QAS-04) offers a low-cost and practical way to reduce measurement error in comparative research. QAS-04 incorporates two additional steps, in addition to the original six steps within QAS-99. These include a step with seven cross-cultural sub-codes such as 'measuring unit' and 'politeness' and a step with eight translation-related sub-codes (see Example 11.5).

Example 11.5   Extract from the QAS-04

> ▶ **STEP 8 – CROSS-CULTURAL CONSIDERATIONS: Assess questions for inappropriate or ineffective cross-cultural references.**
>
> **8a. REFERENCE PERIODS**: The reference period uses seasons, American MM/DD/YYYY format, or may be otherwise ambiguous or unusual in other cultures.
>
> **8b. KNOWLEDGE** may not exist: Respondent is unlikely to know the answer to a factual question because he/she not familiar with the American culture. Example: health insurance.
>
> (*Continued*)

(Continued)

8c. MEASURING UNITS: Measuring units are from English system. If surveying Latin Americans or Western European populations, the metric system should be used.

8d. ASSUMPTIONS: The question includes culturally inappropriate assumptions or graphics. All statements related to sports, drugs, foods, drinks, activities, meal time, music, family ties, holidays, religion, books, magazines, school system, health system, and history should be evaluated.

8e. RESPONSE CATEGORIES: There is no equivalent concept or rating scale in foreign language. Avoid rating scales with more than 5 categories.

8f. NAME FORMAT: Response categories lack a space for other types of names. Spanish speakers use maternal last name as well as paternal last name, and other cultures list the family name as the first name.

8g. POLITENESS: Courtesy and politeness can differ in other cultures. Consider adding a 'Please' before commands like, 'Do not include ...', 'Mark every ...', 'List all ...'. Consider using 'could' instead of 'should' if possible. Some commands or instructions might be perceived as rude, and respondents could change their attitude towards participating.

▶ STEP 9 – POTENTIAL TRANSLATION PROBLEMS: Identify problematic question characteristics.

9a. DOUBLE NEGATIVES: This type of construction is hard to translate and can easily cause misunderstandings in other languages.

9b. IDIOMS: Many idioms do not have an equivalent in other languages.

9c. ACRONYMS: The acronyms have no meaning in other languages. Consider providing an explanation with the acronym.

9d. UNCLEAR USE OF THE TERM 'YOU': 'You' not defined as plural, singular, feminine, masculine, formal, informal – a necessary step for translation.

9e. TIME ADVERBS: Question or response categories use adverbs to describe time, such as recently, lately, usually. Consider specifying time frame with number of days, weeks, etc.

9f. NO EQUIVALENT TERM OR CONCEPT in foreign language. Text may require an additional explanation.

9g. REFERENCES APPLICABLE ONLY TO ENGLISH: Toll free numbers, Web sites, contact information, books and other references are only available in the source language. Consider verifying which services or references are available in the target language. Also consider using numbers instead of letter on phone numbers.

> **9h. ADJECTIVES MODIFYING OTHER ADJECTIVES:** Using adjectives to modify other adjectives (e.g. 'house warming party', which must be literally translated as 'A party in celebration of the purchase of a home in which guests take presents for the new home owner') is an uncommon grammatical usage in languages other than English. Consider paraphrasing and clearly define each term.
>
> Reproduced from Dean et al. (2007)

11.11 Chapter summary

- Achieving measurement equivalence is particularly important in cross-national, cross-cultural and multilingual (comparative) research.
- Cognitive interviewing can be a useful tool in the development of comparative research questionnaires.
- When using cognitive interviewing to test comparative survey questions you will need to pay particular attention to:
    - o your choice of countries, cultures and languages to include;
    - o the phasing of the cognitive interviews;
    - o the development of your cognitive interview protocol;
    - o the design and implementation of your sample design and recruitment strategy;
    - o the recruitment and training of your cognitive interviewers; and
    - o the analysis and interpretation of your findings.
- Consider whether your choice of cognitive interviewing techniques will be culturally appropriate. In some cultural settings think aloud is not appropriate. Certain kinds of probes may not be appropriate in certain languages.
- When recruiting participants in a multilingual cognitive test, you may want to include monolingual and multilingual participants as they may have different levels of language competence.
- Develop strategies to ensure consistency in approaches to interviewing and analysis across countries. Interviewer training is important and it is essential that the quality of interviews is assessed and feedback provided early on so that any problems are dealt with.
- An analysis meeting which involves all the interviewers is one way in which you can try to ensure that findings from each country or cultural setting are being correctly interpreted and that findings from individual interviews are not be being overlooked.
- Focus groups and desk-based questionnaire evaluation methods can be useful as an alternative, or addition to cognitive interviews.

References

Agans, R.P., Deeb-Sossa, N. and Kalsbeek, W.D. (2006) 'Mexican immigrants and the use of cognitive assessment techniques in questionnaire development', *Hispanic Journal of Behavioral Sciences*, 28: 209–30.

Blumberg, R.L. and Goerman, P.L. (2000) *Family Complexity Among Latino Immigrants in Virginia: An Ethnographic Study of their Households Aimed at Improving Census Categories. Report submitted to the United States Census Bureau.*

Carrasco, L. (2003) *The American Community Survey (ACS) en Español: Using Cognitive Interviews to Test the Functional Equivalence of Questionnaire Translations.* Washington, DC: Statistical Research Division, U.S. Census Bureau.

Coronado, I. and Earle, D. (2002) *Effectiveness of the American Community Survey of the U.S. Census in a Borderlands Colonial Setting. Draft Report Submitted to the U.S. Census Bureau*, 19 March 2002.

Dean, E., Caspar, R., McAvinchey, G., Reed, L. and Quiroz, R. (2007) 'Developing a low-cost technique for parallel cross-cultural instrument development: the question appraisal system (QAS-04)', *International Journal of Social Research Methodology*, 10(3): 227–41.

Fitzgerald, R., Widdop, S., Gray, M. and Collins, D. (2009) 'Testing for equivalence using cross-national cognitive interviewing', Center for Comparative Social Surveys Working Paper Series. Available at http://pop.mjr.uw.edu.pl/DataBases/ESS2010/CCSS%20Working%20Paper%20No%2001.pdf

Fitzgerald, R., Widdop, S., Gray, M. and Collins, D. (2011) 'Identifying sources of error in cross-national questionnaires: application of an error source typology to cognitive interview data', *Journal of Official Statistics*, 27(4): 569–99.

Goerman, P.L. and Caspar, R. (2007) 'A new methodology for the cognitive testing of translated materials: testing the source version as a basis for comparison'. Paper presented at the American Association for Public Opinion Research Conference, 17–20 May, Anaheim, CA and submitted to 2007 JSM Proceedings, Statistical Computing Section [CD-ROM], Alexandria, VA: American Statistical Association, 3949–56.

Goerman, P. and Caspar, R. (2010) 'Managing the cognitive pretesting of multilingual survey instruments: a case study of pretesting of the U.S. Census Bureau bilingual Spanish/English questionnaire', in J.A. Harkness, M. Braun, B. Edwards, T.P. Johnson, L. Lyberg, P. Mohler, B.-E. Pennel and T.W. Smith (eds), *Survey Methods in Multinational, Multiregional, and Multicultural Contexts.* Hoboken, NJ: Wiley. pp. 75–90.

Harkness, J. A., Braun, M., Edwards, B., Johnson, T., Lijberg, L., Mohler, P., Pennell, B. and Smith, T. (2010) *Survey Methods in Multinational, Multiregional, and Multicultural Contexts.* Hoboken, NJ: Wiley.

Howarth, S. (2008) *Preparations for the 2011 Census.* Paper number: 08/037. National Assembly for Wales Commission.

Johnson, T.P. (1998) 'Approaches to equivalence in cross-cultural and cross-national survey research', *ZUMA-Nachrichten spezial*, 3: 1–40.

Kissam, E., Herrera, E. and Nakamoto, J.M. (1993) *Hispanic Response to Census Enumeration Forms and Procedures. Contract Report submitted to the U.S. Census Bureau*, March, 1993.

Lee, J. (2012) 'Conducting Cognitive Interviews in Cross National Settings', *Assessment*, published online 11 Febraury 2012. DOI:10.1177/1073191112436671, available at http://asm.sagepub.com/content/early/2012/02/08/1073191112436671

Levin, K., Willis, G., Forsyth, B.H., Norbery, A., Kudela, M.S., Stark, D. and Thompson, F.E. (2009) 'Using cognitive interviews to evaluate the Spanish-language translation of a dietary questionnaire', *Survey Research Methods*, 3(1): 13–25.

Miller, K. (2008) *Results of the Comparative cognitive Test Workgroup Budapest Initiative Module*. Available at: http://wwwn.cdc.gov/QBANK/report/Miller_NCHS_2008BudapestReport.pdf

Miller, K., Fitzgerald, R., Padilla, J., Wilson, S., Widdop, S., Caspar, R., Dimov, M., Gray, M., Nunes, C., Prufer, P. and Schoua-Glusberg, A. (2011) 'Design and analysis of cognitive interviews for comparative cross-national testing', *Field Methods*, 23(4): 379–96. doi: 10.1177/1525822X11414802.

Pan, Y. (2004). 'Cognitive interviews in languages other than English: methodological and research issues', in *Proceedings of the American Statistical Association, Section on Survey Research Methods*, May. Available at www.amstat.org/sections/srms/Proceedings/y2004/files/Jsm2004-000512.pdf

Pan, Y. et al. (2010) 'Cognitive interviewing in non-English languages: a cross-cultural perspective', in J.A. Harkness, M. Braun, B. Edwards, T.P. Johnson, L. Lyberg, P. Mohler, B.-E. Pennel and T.W. Smith (eds), *Survey Methods in Multinational, Multiregional and Multicultural Contexts*. Hoboken, NJ: Wiley. pp. 91–116.

Schoua-Glusberg, A. (2006) 'Eliciting education level in Spanish interviews'. Paper presented to the American Association of Public Opinion Research, Montreal, Canada.

Sha, M., McAvinchey, G., Reed, L.M., Rodriguez, S.M. and Carter, G. (2010) 'Participant recruitment, interviewing, and training: lessons learned from a Spanish language cognitive interviewing project'. Paper presented at AAPOR, May.

Sproston, K. and Mindell, J. (eds) (2006) *Health Survey for England 2004*. London: The Information Centre.

Survey Research Center (2010) *Guidelines for Best Practice in Cross-Cultural Surveys*. Ann Arbor, MI: Survey Research Center, Institute for Social Research, University of Michigan. Available at: www.ccsg.isr.umich.edu/

Widdop, S., Fitzgerald, R. and Gatrell, L. (2011) *European Social Survey Round 6 Cognitive Pre-testing Report*. London: Centre for Comparative Social Surveys.

Willis, G.B. and Lessler, J.T. (1999) *Question Appraisal System QAS-99*. National Cancer Institute.

Willis, G. and Zahnd, E. (2007) 'Questionnaire design from a cross-cultural perspective: an empirical investigation of Koreans and non-Koreans', *Journal of Health Care for the Poor and Underserved*, 18(6): 197–217.

Willis, G.B., Lawrence, D., Hartman, A., Kudela, M.S., Levin, K. and Forsyth, B. (2007) 'Translation of a tobacco survey into Spanish and Asian languages: The Tobacco Use Supplement to the Current Population Survey', *Nicotine & Tobacco Research*, 10(6): 1075–84.

Willis, G., Lawrence, D., Thompson, F., Kudela, M., Levin, K. and Miller, K. (2005). 'The use of cognitive interviewing to evaluate translated survey questions: lessons learned', in *Proceedings of the Federal Committee on Statistical Methodology Research Conference*, Arlington, VA, November. Available at https://fcsm.sites.usa.gov/files/2014/05/2005FCSM_Willis_Lawrence_etal_VIIIB.pdf

TWELVE

WIDER APPLICATIONS OF COGNITIVE INTERVIEWING

JO D'ARDENNE, MICHELLE GRAY AND DEBBIE COLLINS

12.1 Introduction

The aim of this chapter is to demonstrate some of the wider applications of cognitive interviewing. Cognitive interviews can be used to test a range of other documents, not just survey questionnaires. For example, cognitive interviewing has been used in administrative contexts to assess and improve voter registration forms (e.g. Chan et al., 2013) and ballot papers (e.g. Martin et al., 2012). In this chapter we discuss:

- The use of cognitive interviewing to test other types of documents, specifically:
  - o survey materials such as advance letters and information leaflets;
  - o web questionnaires; and
  - o public health information.
- The use of cognitive interviewing to explore the behaviour of players of gaming machines.

We will do this through a series of case studies, each demonstrating how cognitive interviewing has been adopted for a different purpose. The case studies provide background information on the study and on how the methods were adapted to meet the study's aims. We also describe the limitations of cognitive interviewing methods in the different contexts.

12.2 Testing survey materials

Cognitive interviews have been used to test a range of materials used in surveys other than survey questions themselves. Cognitive interviews have been used to test survey advance letters, information leaflets, requests for data linkage, requests for future contact and survey consent forms (Balarajan et al., 2012; d'Ardenne and Collins, 2013; Gray et al., 2008: Pan et al., 2010; Willis, 2006). The testing of survey materials can be conducted alongside the testing of survey questions or as a standalone activity.

The rationale for testing survey documents is to establish whether participants *understand* the information provided in the intended way and whether people are *willing* to act on the information. For example, the purpose of an advance letter is to provide information about a survey and to request that the reader takes part. Therefore the aims of cognitive interviewing could be:

a) establish whether participants understand the letter's content; and
b) to explore whether participants would consent to the request made and, if not, what factors could encourage them to do so.

It is worth noting that the second objective will rely on you asking *hypothetical probes* of your participant to explore areas you are not able to observe or probe on directly. These hypothetical probes could include:

• Would you open a letter like this if it arrived on your doorstep? Why/why not?
• Based on this letter, do you think you would take part in the survey? Why/why not?

Hypothetical probes are arguably more of a qualitative interviewing method than a cognitive interviewing technique. This is because instead of trying to access and understand participants' current thought processes you are trying to elicit reflections on potential or future events. It is important to note that participants' responses to hypothetical probes may not be an accurate reflection of what they would actually do in practice. Participants may assume they would be willing to take part based on factors associated with the cognitive interview that would not be mimicked in the actual survey context (e.g. rapport built with the cognitive interviewer). For this reason it is important to explain the context under which the survey documents would be received as part of the interview process (see also section 5.5).

Even when you carefully explain the context in which people will receive the documents participants may still make inaccurate assessments on whether they would respond. People's self-reports of what they intend to do, across a whole range of behaviours, are relatively poor predictors of what they actually go on to do in practice (Sheeran, 2002). This phenomenon is sometimes referred to as the 'intention-behaviour gap'. Therefore, if you are designing a new survey and you wish to establish the likely response rate you should conduct a pilot, rather than explore general levels of willingness in qualitative interviews (refer to section 2.2.5). Similarly, if you wish to establish whether different versions of an advance letter achieve different response rates you should consider conducting a split ballot experiment (see section 2.2.10). Cognitive interviews can be used to identify features of a letter people may find off-putting (e.g. visual design, language used, missing information) and to suggest alternatives. Hypothetical probes should be used as a starting point to examine these issues rather than as way of trying to predict survey response rates.

The following case study provides an example of a project where we included the testing of survey advance materials alongside the testing of new survey questions.

Example 12.1 Using cognitive interviews to test advance materials for the National Study of Health and Wellbeing

Background

Cognitive interviewing was conducted as part of the development for the 2014 National Study of Health and Wellbeing. This is the fourth in a series of surveys of mental health, the first of which was conducted in 1993. This study is carried out on behalf of the Health and Social Care Information Centre, with funds from the Department of Health. The information collected is used to provide prevalence information on both treated and untreated psychiatric disorders. The survey is conducted with adults aged 16 or over living in private households in England. Data are collected face-to-face in randomly selected households. Prior to interviewers visiting selected addresses a number of advance materials are sent. The aim of these advance materials is to encourage participation in the survey.

Alongside testing new questions for the 2014 survey, cognitive interviews assessed respondents' reactions to the proposed advance materials. These materials included a postcard, an advance letter and an information leaflet. It was important to evaluate these materials as they are the first point of contact between the survey organisation and the potential survey respondents. We wanted to ensure the materials were understood correctly. We also wanted to check that the materials did not, inadvertently, include things that could discourage people from taking part in the survey.

Methodology

Protocol design

Both survey questions and advanced materials were tested during the cognitive interviews. The testing of the advance materials came first, before the new survey questions were asked. Interviewers were briefed to present the advance materials in the order in which respondents would receive them in the actual survey. First the participants were presented with two versions of

(Continued)

(Continued)

a postcard designed to raise awareness and inform respondents that a letter would be arriving soon that would tell them more about the survey. The two versions of the postcard varied in terms of their tagline and colour scheme. Participants were asked whether they had a preference for either of the two cards and, if so, which they preferred and why.

Interviewers were then instructed to show respondents the advance letter and leaflet, which would come together. Interviewers were told not to give instructions or clarifications to respondents about how to read the documents. Probes were used to explore respondents' reactions to the advance documents:

- **Comprehension probes** were used to explore participants' understanding of the survey process based on what they had read, e.g. '*If you received this letter what do you think would happen next?*' Probes were also used to establish whether participants felt the letter provided sufficient information on what taking part involves, e.g. '*Is there any information you would want that is missing from the letter?*'
- **Hypothetical probes** were used to ascertain what the participant thought they would do if they received the advance materials in the real-life survey context, e.g. '*Do you think you would read this if it came through your door? Why do you say that?*'

Sampling and recruitment

A total of 14 interviews were conducted. Interviewers recruited participants via doorstep screening. Quotas were set to ensure participants varied in terms of their age, sex, employment status and health.

Fieldwork

Interviews were conducted face-to-face, in the participant's home and were audio recorded. Interviews lasted approximately one hour. The testing of the advance materials look approximately 15–20 minutes, with the rest of the interview being dedicated to testing new survey questions.

Analysis and reporting

Interviewers made detailed notes on each interview and summaries of these notes were subsequently entered into a framework for analysis. Researchers conducted a within and across case analysis, following the approach to analysis described in Chapters 7 and 8.

Key findings

Two survey names were tested and of these it was found that the existing survey name was favoured by participants. For this reason it was recommended that the existing survey name be retained. Views on the postcard taglines varied, with each receiving both positive and negative comments. We identified one tagline that had more extreme negative feedback and recommended that this tagline be dropped.

Testing of the advance letter and leaflet revealed that respondents thought several key pieces of information were missing, such as a contact number and information on what to do if they did not wish to take part. The advance letter tested was double-sided and some participants were unaware that information was provided on the back. This led to these participants missing all the information provided on the reverse side of the letter. It was recommended that an instruction was added to the front of the letter informing respondents to turn it over.

Some respondents had difficulty reading some of the text due the colour scheme chosen (black text on a turquoise background). We therefore recommended that the palette be changed to improve ease of reading.

12.3 Combining cognitive interviews with eye tracking

Usability testing (or user-testing) aims to capture information on ease of using a product from the perspective of that product's target audience. Usability testing is often discussed in relation to the development of websites and computer hardware, software and mobile applications. However, usability testing is also used to test a wide range of non-computer products, such as instructions for tools, games and medicines.

Like cognitive interviews, usability tests involve participants being asked to complete a task in a realistic setting. The tasks set will vary depending on the product being tested. For example, usability testing of a website could involve participants being set the task of finding specific information, which is displayed on different pages. Usability testing of an online reservation system may involve participants being set the task of 'making a booking' using criteria provided by the researcher.

There is a commonality between the methods used in cognitive interviews and usability testing. For example, like cognitive interviews, usability testing can involve:

a) *observations* of people completing a particular task;
b) asking people to *think aloud* whilst completing a particular task;
c) asking additional questions to elicit information on how people found the task. This could be via completing a 'task experience' questionnaire or via the administration of more qualitative questions or *probes*.

Given this commonality it is possible to conduct interviews that combine cognitive and usability testing. For example, we investigated usability issues as part of a cognitive interviewing project looking at how children attempted to complete an online questionnaire on sport and physical activity (McGee and d'Ardenne, 2009: see Example 2.2 in section 2.2.4 for a case study). The main purpose of the cognitive interviews was to establish whether participants understood the questions on physical activity, for example whether they could recall the information requested and whether they would feel comfortable providing this information in a classroom setting. In addition, we explored the usability of the web instruments. As a result of testing we made recommendations on certain design features such as the location of information and the size answer buttons. Some authors argue that combining cognitive interviewing with usability testing is more efficient as it means the cognitive and the usability aspects can be reviewed in tandem (Romano Bergstrom et al., 2013).

A range of other techniques are used in the usability testing of online materials. These methods include eye tracking (see section 2.2.4) and the analysis of paradata (see section 2.2.9) to look at how long people spend on each page, what links are clicked on, and so forth. Eye trackers can be used to measure precise details of what people look at and for how long, giving insight into what information people attend to and what is overlooked. Whilst eye-tracking technology has been around for a number of decades recent advances mean that eye-tracking equipment is becoming less obtrusive for respondents, less expensive, more accurate and more portable.

As with other usability testing techniques, it is possible to incorporate eye tracking into a cognitive interview. There are two reasons why this approach is beneficial. Firstly, eye tracking increases the *accuracy* and *specificity* of interviewer observations. Observations are a key part of cognitive interviews but in practice it is not always easy to make accurate observations of what participants are looking at. Does a quick glance indicate the participant failed to read all the information provided? Or does it merely indicate the participant is a fast reader? Therefore eye trackers allow researchers to make more detailed observations on what information is looked at and what is not. Secondly, the increased specificity of observations can provide useful information for interviewers generating spontaneous probes (see section 5.8). For example, eye tracking may reveal that a participant read certain words, phrases or answer categories multiple times. This could indicate that a participant finds the text unfamiliar or unclear. Interviewers can use this information to generate follow-up probes about the questionable text.

There is some evidence to suggest that hybrid interviews (combining eye tracking with standard cognitive interviewing techniques) increase the efficiency of cognitive pretesting by revealing problems that would have otherwise gone undetected. Neuert and Lenzner (2013) conducted an experiment whereby participants were allocated to either a standard cognitive interview or a hybrid interview condition. The number of questions found to be problematic was higher in the hybrid interview condition compared to the cognitive interview condition. The additional problems detected in the hybrid interviews were unearthed by interviewers who observed peculiar reading patterns as a result of the eye tracking.

The following case study provides an example of a project where we have combined cognitive interviewing methods with eye tracking to test questions for a web survey.

Example 12.2   Combining cognitive interviews and eye tracking to test web questions for Understanding Society

Background

Understanding Society is a large-scale longitudinal survey that collects information on a variety of topics (Buck and McFall, 2012). It is funded by the Economic and Social Research Council. In addition to the main survey, Understanding Society includes an 'Innovation Panel' that is used to trial new survey questions and new methods of data collection. The fifth wave of the Innovation Panel survey (IP5) included a mixed-mode approach to data collection (Burton, 2013). This involved a single questionnaire administered either face-to-face or via the internet.

We conducted cognitive interviews with eye tracking to inform the visual design of the web questionnaires. The aim of testing was to collect qualitative information on how user-friendly the web questionnaire was. We wanted to collect evidence on whether respondents are able to navigate the web screens, input data and find help if required. In particular we wanted to:

1. establish how easy or difficult respondents found logging in to the online survey;
2. check that respondents knew how to move from page to page;
3. observe whether respondents noticed and used the 'help' function;
4. examine whether layout and spacing influenced whether text was read or overlooked;
5. establish whether participants understood how to input information at different types of question; and
6. observe whether respondents encountered any error messages (as a result of skipping questions) or automated checks (as a result of inputting inconsistent information) and observe whether respondents knew how to 'move on' in these situations.

Methodology

Questionnaire design

It was not possible to test the whole web questionnaire due to its length. The questionnaire was reviewed to identify different 'types' of screen format. A test questionnaire was developed that included the following types of screens.

(Continued)

(Continued)

1. Log-on screen
2. A grid-based question format
3. A check all that apply format
4. A drop-down menu format
5. A number plus reference period question format (for income questions)
6. Date and time question formats
7. An open question format
8. A question with pictorial definitions.

Protocol design

We used a combination of eye tracking, think aloud and retrospective probing. The structure of the interview was as follows:

1. **Introduction and set-up.** This involved introducing the study, gaining consent to use the eye tracker and calibrating the eye-tracking equipment for each participant.
2. **Completing the web questionnaire and set tasks.** Participants were asked to complete the test questionnaire whilst thinking aloud. First, participants were asked to log on using a password contained in an advance letter (to mimic an approach used in the actual survey). Next, participants were shown the test questionnaire. Whilst filling this in participants were assigned set tasks. For example, participants were instructed to try and skip a question to see if they noticed the hidden 'prefer not to answer' categories that popped up.
3. **General probes on usability.** After completing the web questionnaire and tasks participants were asked some overview probes on how they found the instrument in terms of usability (e.g. *'Was the web questionnaire easy or difficult to use?'*), visual presentation (e.g. *'What did you think of the way the web questionnaire looked?'*) and navigation (e.g. *'How easy or difficult did you find it moving from one page to the next?'*).
4. **Review of 'gaze-replay' videos and specific probes.** After probing, interviewers showed participants a gaze-replay video. This video showed what participants were looking at, in real time, for each of the web screens. After viewing the gaze-replay for a screen the video was paused and scripted probes were used to collect more information about the question displayed. Interviewers were instructed to use spontaneous probes to find out more about issues revealed by the eye tracking. For example, interviewers were asked to follow up on why participants looked at text multiple times or if text was not looked at, if these practices occurred. Videos could be replayed and slowed down to help direct the spontaneous probing.

Sampling and recruitment

Participants were recruited using a combination of advertising and door-step screening (see sections 4.3.1 and 4.3.3 for further details on these recruitment methods). Quotas were set to ensure participants varied in terms of their age, highest qualification and self-rated confidence using computers. In total eight interviews were conducted. The eye-tracking element of the interview was explained to participants at the point of recruitment, and was described in an information leaflet provided to all recruits.

Fieldwork

Interviews were conducted at a Human–Computer Interaction Lab at City University, London. The eye-tracker model used was a remote Tobii X50. This form of eye tracker is unobtrusive (it is a small bar that sits underneath the computer monitor) and uses near-infrared beams to measure eye movements. Two interviewers were present at each session, one to conduct the interview and the other to monitor the eye-tracking equipment. All participants gave consent for their eye movements to be recorded using the eye-tracking equipment. Interviews were also audio recorded. The interviews lasted between 45 minutes and 1 hour.

Analysis and reporting

Researchers listened to the audio recordings after each interview and summarised findings directly into a framework matrix (see Chapter 7). Researchers referred back to the gaze-replay videos whilst reviewing the audio recordings to see where participants were looking on the screen.

As well as the data from the audio recordings and gaze-replay videos we generated heat maps and gaze plots. Heat maps show you how long the participants(s) looked at a particular section of the screen for, ranging in colour from red (the areas they looked at for the longest amount of time), to yellow, to green (the areas they looked at for the least amount of time). Gaze plots show every point on the screen the respondent(s) looked at in one image; each point is sequentially numbered and joined up by a line (see Figure 2.3 in section 2.2.7 for examples). By observing the heat maps and gaze plots we were able to compare which elements of the screens were looked at and which parts were overlooked.

Key findings

All participants, regardless of their confidence using computers, were able to log on to the web questionnaire without assistance. However, the eye tracking revealed parts of the log-on screen were not looked at. For example, a box on the right-hand side showing 'top tips' on how to complete the questionnaire was never looked at.

Participants found navigating the questionnaire straightforward. The eye tracking revealed that although participants had to search for the navigation buttons on the first screen; at subsequent screens they knew where to find them. Participants found the majority of question formats straightforward in terms of finding information and entering data. Key information (both words and pictorial definitions) were consistently looked at. Different spacing

(Continued)

(Continued)

conventions for question text did not appear to impact on whether information was looked at or not.

The testing revealed that not all participants understood how to skip certain questions or how to suppress automated check messages. These findings were used to inform the visual design of these features for the subsequent wave of the survey (IP6).

12.4 Testing public health information

Cognitive interviewing methods are now being used outside of the survey sphere to test an array of different documents. For example, cognitive interviewing is increasingly being used to test public health messages and materials. Cognitive interviewing techniques have been used to test public health communications on flu vaccinations (Lapka et al., 2008), bioterrorism (Lapka et al., 2008), colorectal screening (Smith et al., 2013), detection of oral cancers (Scott et al., 2011) and leaflets on constipation (Lake et al., 2007).

As described in section 12.3 there is an overlap between the methods used in cognitive interviewing and usability testing. Techniques used in both methods have been used to test health-based interventions conducted online. For example, observation, think aloud and qualitative probing techniques have been used in the development and testing of a web intervention for the self-management of colds and flu (Yardley et al., 2010) and the testing of an online intervention designed to increase physical activity levels (Hinchliffe and Mummery, 2008).

In practice, using cognitive interviewing follows the same structure regardless of the type of materials being tested. The interview stages are as follows:

a) Provide participants with the test document and observe their reactions. This should be done in a realistic context (i.e. participants should be given the test document in a way that mimics how they would receive it in real life). If this is not possible the interviewer should spend some time describing how people will receive the test documents in real life prior to the presentation of the documents.

b) Collect 'think aloud' data from participants as they read through the test documents.

c) Ask 'general probes' to supplement the think aloud data (see Chapter 5). The purpose of these general probes is to collect additional verbal information from the participant whilst limiting interviewer reactivity.

d) Ask more specific 'theory-driven probes' to explore areas of interest that have not been covered by the think aloud and general probes. These probes can be pre-scripted or spontaneous, based on the prior observations and think aloud.

Using these steps, cognitive interviews move from first mapping the participant's thought processes and capturing respondent-driven information to then capturing researcher-driven information. Cognitive interviews to test public information leaflets differ from cognitive interviews to test survey questions in that the theory-driven probes chosen may not be based on the four-step question and answer model. Instead they are based on theories relevant to the type of material being tested. For example, when testing health promotional leaflets scripted probes could be based on health communication theories.

If you choose to use cognitive interviews to test public health information you should have a clear rationale for choosing this method. The aims of cognitive interviewing could be to:

a) establish whether the information is communicated in the intended way (e.g. do participants understand the information provided and does it increase their knowledge of the subject matter?); and

b) explore whether participants think they will act on the information provided in the intended way and, if not, why not.

It is worth noting that the second objective will rely on you asking *hypothetical probes* of your participant (see section 12.2). As described previously, participants' responses to hypothetical probes may not be an accurate reflection of how they would actually behave if they were given the information in context. Even if participants react positively to the information provided, there are a wide range of environmental and psychosocial factors that influence behaviours. Cognitive interviews can be used as a starting point to identify features of an information leaflet that people find disagreeable and to explore what ways of framing a message may be more appealing. Cognitive interviewing is insufficient to determine what impact, if any, public health information will have on changing behaviour.

Example 12.3 provides an example of how we used cognitive interviewing methods to test leaflets designed for the NHS Cervical Screening Programme.

Example 12.3   Testing Cervical Screening Programme leaflets

Background

The NHS Cervical Screening Programme is aimed at women between the ages of 25 and 64 and provides a free cervical screening test every three to five years. This is usually performed at family doctor practices. We were asked to test, using cognitive interviewing methods, the content of three leaflets designed for members of the public about cervical screening. The aims of the testing were to collect information on whether the leaflets were easy to understand, whether people felt comfortable reading them and whether they promoted informed choice.

(Continued)

253

(Continued)

Methodology

Protocol design

As with a standard cognitive interviewing, study protocols were designed to include the following three elements: observation, think aloud and probing.

Observations were collected on how participants read and reacted to the leaflet. For example, the observations collected information on whether the participant read the front page of the leaflet, whether they looked at the diagram of the cervix, whether any sections of the leaflets were re-read, whether there were any sections where participants appeared overly confused and whether participants asked questions at any stage. Participants were trained in think aloud and encouraged to articulate their thought process whilst reading the leaflets.

The majority of the probes were designed to explore *comprehension* of sections of text within the leaflets as opposed to specific words. To test whether the leaflet had successfully communicated key messages, probes were included that explored respondents' knowledge and understanding of the content. For example, in relation to a section about the Human Papilloma Virus (HPV), participants were asked *'Had you heard of the Human Papilloma Virus (HPV) before reading this leaflet?'* and *'What did HPV mean to you in this section?'*. In a section about the cervical screening test, respondents were asked *'After reading the section on cervical screening, would you be able to describe what happens in the test to someone else?'* Judgment probes related to comfort reading the information and the perceived helpfulness of the information were also included.

Additional interview features

One aim of testing the leaflets was to check whether they promoted informed choice. To provide evidence around this the research team designed a knowledge and attitudes questionnaire. This short questionnaire, based on an adapted model used by Marteau et al. (2001), was administered at the start of each cognitive interview, before the participant had been shown the leaflets, and at the end of the interview. This questionnaire aimed to collect supplementary information on whether there had been a shift in knowledge and attitudes as a result of exposure to the materials. The results from the questions were used in combination with data elicited through observation, think aloud and probing.

Sampling and recruitment

Fifteen women took part in cognitive interviews in three areas within Great Britain. Quotas were set to ensure the recruited women varied by age, education level and knowledge of cervical screening prior to interviewing.

Fieldwork

Face-to-face interviews were conducted by experienced cognitive interviewers. Interviewers were briefed to allow each respondent to read each leaflet as if they were not there, taking as much time as they needed to. Interviews were conducted in participants' own homes and were audio recorded.

Analysis and reporting

Interviewers made detailed notes after listening back to the recordings of the interviews and summaries of these were subsequently entered into a framework for analysis. Researchers then conducted a within-and-across case analysis, following the approach to analysis described in Chapters 7 and 8. The findings were used by the research sponsor to advance their thinking around the promotion of informed consent in relation to patient information for this cancer screening programme.

Key findings

On the whole, the leaflets were positively received, though some evidence was found to suggest that specific pieces of information could be made clearer. For example, the link between HPV and cervical cancer in the first leaflet was not understood by all participants. Equally, participants did not always understand the differentiation between the procedure used to explore the presence of abnormal cells (a colposcopy) and the treatment for abnormal cells (i.e. their removal). Specific words were found to be problematic. This was either because they were off-putting (for example using the word 'pain' was thought to be less appropriate than 'discomfort' in the context of cervical screening) or because they were too technical for the intended audience (for example 'dyskaryosis' a medical term that refers to changes in the appearance of cells).

In relation to informed choice, in this small sample 9 out of 15 respondents would have made an informed choice before exposure to the leaflets (as their knowledge was good and their attitudes and intention were positive). In contrast, 6 of the 15 respondents would only have made an informed choice *after* they had seen the leaflets (as previously their knowledge was poor, despite the fact that their attitudes were positive). The leaflets did appear to increase knowledge in some cases, but did not have a dramatic impact on attitudes, mainly because the attitudes of all people in the sample were positive in the first place. This raises an important issue regarding the sampling design for this study. Ideally a quota should have been included to ensure that women with varying pre-existing attitudes to cervical screening were recruited in addition to women who had varying knowledge.

12.5 Other uses of cognitive interviewing methods

We have used cognitive interviewing methods in a study that explored the relationship between gambling machines' characteristics and player behaviour, see Example 12.4. More details on this study can be found in Husain et al. (2013).

Example 12.4   Relationship between gambling machine characteristics and player behaviour

Background

Commissioned by the Responsible Gambling Trust, this study examined the relationship between gambling machines' characteristics and consumer behaviour. The main objective of the research was to explore how players interact with a range of machine features during 'real-time' play at selected gambling venues. The specific aims of the research were to:

- observe what happens within an individual machine play session;
- explore how different machine features affect what happens within play sessions and to what extent players are aware of them;
- assess to what extent different machine features may shape decisions made by players within sessions and how this may relate to the session outcome; and
- examine overall session outcome compared with what the player expected at the start of the session.

Methodology

The research was conducted in two stages.

- **Stage 1:** Observing the player playing a machine of their choice, (a) using an observation schedule and (b) video recording the play.
- **Stage 2:** In-depth interviews with each participant were conducted after the observation, using the video recording as an elicitation tool. Participants were asked to retrospectively think aloud about how they went about their play and probed on specific points.

Each stage was conducted by one of four NatCen qualitative research experts. The same researcher conducted stage 1 and 2 for each individual participant.

Protocol design

Given the complexity of collecting data on this topic a full methodological review was carried out prior to finalising the study design (see Gray and Wardle, 2013). This outlined key issues with different qualitative approaches, traced the benefits and limitations of each and made recommendations about the study approach. In particular, this review focused on the pros and cons of conducting concurrent or retrospective think aloud whilst participants were playing machines (see Figure 12.1), the ethics of asking participants to use their own money whilst participating in the research, and the ethics and practicalities of conducting research in real venues and also of video recording behaviour. In addition to reviewing current research literature on these issues, the review also included information from interviews with machine players outlining what they felt would be acceptable to participants and what the limitations may be. Recommendations from this report were built into the finalised study design.

Sampling and recruitment

To ensure research was conducted in naturalistic settings familiar to players, gambling venues were recruited first. Once this was done, participants who actively use these venues were then recruited. Two gambling venues were recruited: an adult gambling centre and a bingo club. Venues were recruited through our network of contacts with industry members

Participants were recruited using two separate recruitment methods.

- In the adult gaming centre, the research team worked closely with venue staff who acted as gatekeepers. The venue staff informed their customers about the opportunity to participate by handing out flyers and telling customers about the research.
- For the bingo club location, the venue provided the research team with a list of their members. The research team used this listing to select a sample of potential participants (based on age and sex). Those selected were sent a letter outlining the purpose of the study and inviting them to participate and giving them the opportunity to opt out. NatCen's telephone interviewers contacted those who had not opted out and ran through a short screening questionnaire that checked that they regularly played fruit machines and would be willing to take part.

Additional interview features

Observation: Players were asked to play as normal during the observation stage. Participants were asked to choose which machines they wanted to play on so as to better replicate naturalistic play

There were two elements to the observations: completion of an observation schedule by the interviewer during play; and video recording the play. The idea was to observe play, using the observation schedule, for around 10–15 minutes, and then, with the participant's consent, start to video record the machine session. In practice the observation time was limited by the length of time the participant wanted to play for. There were occasions when both observation stages happened concurrently because participants played for a short time and a sufficient length of video recording was needed to use during the interviews. However, the interviewer continued to note down observations while play was being recorded. There were no notable differences in participant responses as a result of the variation in technique at this stage.

The second element of the observation stage was video recording play. This allowed us to capture details of behaviour that might otherwise have been missed in fieldwork observation (Patton, 2002). As videos can be played back it is a useful elicitation tool to assist participants 'to recall and describe their thoughts, feelings and reactions at different points in time during a given event' (DuFon, 2002). It is this latter method that was used for this study as videos were deleted after the interview was completed.

(Continued)

(Continued)

A tripod and video recorder was used for this stage, positioned in a manner so as to record the screen of the fruit machine, and not the player specifically, to have a record of the play for the interview. The voice of the player and the sound of the machine were recorded on the video recorder.

Think-aloud techniques were used in some of the observations, if it came naturally to players, and were also used in the in-depth interviews. In this research both concurrent and retrospective think aloud were used. Concurrent methods were used during the observational stage and retrospective think aloud using video elicitation in interviews conducted immediately after the observational stage.

Interview: immediately after the observations, participants took part in an in-depth interview. All the interviews took place in designated areas in the gambling venue to ensure privacy and confidentiality at all times, for example in office spaces. At the start of the interview, the interviewer explained the structure and the purpose of the interview. The interviewer then played the video recording on a laptop and asked the participant to talk them through how they played using retrospective think aloud methods. To aid this process both the interviewer and participant could pause, rewind, forward and play the video as and when appropriate. The interviewer used a topic guide and observation notes to follow up on specific elements. Interviews varied in length, from 20 minutes to just over an hour depending on the length of play and time available for the interviews.

Once the interview was completed, the video recording was deleted in front of the participant.

Analysis

A mixture of interviewers' notes and transcripts were produced and summarised into a framework set up in Nvivo 9.2 (see Chapter 7). This analytical framework consisted of a number of descriptive and analytical categories. The framework included a summary of the characteristics of participants: such as their sex, age, the frequency they played on the machines, category of the machine they played on, highest educational qualification and interview location. The framework was organised by features. Under each feature, a summary was made of each interview's findings pertinent to that feature. Thus, data could be read horizontally as a complete case record for an individual, or vertically by question, looking across all cases.

Findings

The accounts from participants suggested that patterns of play are complex and driven by the interplay of three factors: personal, environmental and machine. Evidence from our research indicates that these factors play an important role in how players make decisions and judgements in relation to starting, progressing and ending a play session. Crucially, the potential impact of machine features upon play should be considered alongside these other issues.

Analysis of player behaviour supported the development of a player typology based on player interactions and play session outcomes. The typology emerged through identification of two individual attributes: a predetermined play strategy (play intentions) and maintenance or cognitive control (the extent to which players were able to keep to their intentions). Pre-play intentions and maintenance of these during play suggested a spectrum of player behaviour ranging from those who were very controlled and were able to maintain all intentions, to the other end of the spectrum where players had a poor or limited level of control and/or abandoned their pre-play intentions. Three types of machine player were identified:

- **More controlled.** These players had very specific pre-play intentions and maintained these intentions as play progressed and ended. They used a range of strategies to support this, from choosing particular types of machines to play (generally simpler machines with fewer features) to using certain personal strategies such as only coming to the venue with the money they were willing to spend.
- **Less controlled.** These players also had specific pre-play intentions but did not maintain these as play progressed and typically spent more money and/or time than originally intended. They appeared to be more influenced by some characteristics of machines and in some cases used them in a way that did not support their intention – for example, using auto-play or changing stake based on how they felt the machine was playing.
- **Not controlled.** These players had no pre-play intentions and their session of play seemed to be guided more by their interaction with the machine. This group typically chose more complex machines with a greater range of features to play and did not appear to have any personal strategies in place to help them limit their play.

Evidence from this study suggests that players do not remain static along the control spectrum because of the dynamic nature of gambling behaviour. Players' ability to maintain pre-play intentions are mediated by the interaction of personal, environmental and machine factors. It is likely that the level of cognitive control displayed by players varies from one session to another and fluctuates, often rapidly, in response to specific stimuli, within a single play session.

12.6 Chapter summary

This chapter has illustrated some of the wider applications of cognitive interviewing.

- Cognitive interviews have been used to test survey documents such as advance letters, leaflets and consent forms.
- Cognitive interviews can be combined with usability testing to investigate participants' reactions to visual and navigation aspects of a questionnaire. Eye-tracking methods can be included in a cognitive interviewing study to increase the specificity of observations and to help generate spontaneous probes.
- Cognitive interviews can be used to test public health information such as leaflets and websites. The theory-driven probes chosen may not be based on the four-step

Concurrent think aloud		Retrospective think aloud	
Concurrent think aloud requires the research participant to talk aloud, or think aloud, as they are completing a task.		*Retrospective think aloud requires the research participant to think aloud directly after a task has been completed. This method is usually used whilst the participant is reviewing a video recording of themselves completing the task.*	
Advantages	**Disadvantages**	**Advantages**	**Disadvantages**
Information in the short term memory is directly reported (Taylor and Dionne, 2000).	The act of thinking aloud affects the natural behaviour being observed, if it is not the usual practice (Griffiths, 1994).	Does not affect the behaviour being observed.	Participants have to recall the behaviour retrospectively creating a risk of editing and rationalisation behaviour. There is a risk of 'usual' behaviour being reported rather than that of a particular episode (Taylor and Dionne, 2000).
Direct reporting minimises the relative demand on the short-term memory (Taylor and Dionne, 2000).	Only the thought process that the participant is aware of is reported. Studies have shown that simple rules can be processed quickly and consequently not verbalised (Essens et al., 1991). Verbalisations elicited via concurrent think aloud are limited by the capacity of the short-term memory to concurrently think and report thinking. Difficult tasks may not be reported because of the high cognitive load (Ericsson and Simon, 1993: 91).	Participants who use retrospective think aloud can give more information compared with participants who used concurrent think aloud because they provide explanations and suggestions for their actions (Bowers and Snuder, cited in van den Haak et al. 2003).	Not a live account, so possibly detail could be lost through recall difficulties. Information is retrieved from the long-term memory. Not all the information noted in the short-term memory is fixed in the long-term memory (Hayes and Flower, cited in Taylor and Dionne, 2000) and not all is retrievable on demand (Ericsson and Simon, 1987, cited in Taylor and Dionne, 2000).

Figure 12.1 Advantages and disadvantages of think-aloud techniques

Reproduced from Gray and Wardle (2013),

question and answer model but rather on theories relevant to the type of material being tested, such as theories of health communication.

- Cognitive interviewing methods can also be combined with observation and traditional qualitative interviewing methods to explore behaviour.

If you are considering cognitive interviewing for a new application you will need a clear rationale for using the method and study aims that are suited to the method. The case studies provided in this chapter have provided examples of how cognitive interviewing can be used to test different materials.

References

Balarajan, M., d'Ardenne, J., Gray, M. and Blake, M. (2012) *Welsh Health Survey: Cognitive Testing of Data Linkage Consent Forms and Supporting Documents*. Welsh Government Report. Available at: http://wales.gov.uk/docs/statistics/2013/130424-health-survey-cognitive-testing-data-linkage-consent-forms-en.pdf

Buck, N. and McFall, S. (2012) 'Understanding society: design overview', *Longitudinal and Life Course Studies*, 3(1): 5–17.

Burton, J. (ed.) (2013) Understanding Society Innovation Panel Wave 5: *Results from Methodological Experiments, Understanding Society Working Paper 2013–06*. Available at: https://www.understandingsociety.ac.uk/research/publications/working-paper/understanding-society/2013–06.pdf

Chan, V., Murray, L., Sewel, K. and Treanor, S. (2013) *Testing the Young Voter Registration Form for the 2014 Referendum on Scottish Independence*. Available at: www.scotland.gov.uk/Resource/0042/00421718.pdf

d'Ardenne, J. and Collins, D. (2013) 'Horses for courses: why different question testing methods uncover different findings and implications for selecting methods'. Paper presented at 5th European Survey Research Association 2011 conference, Ljubljana, Slovenia.

DuFon, M. (2002) 'Video recording in ethnographic SLA research: some issues of validity in data collection', *Language Learning and Technology*, 6(1): 40–59.

Ericsson, K.A. and Simon, H.A. (1993) *Protocol Analysis: Verbal Reports as Data*. Cambridge, MA: MIT Press.

Essens, P., McCann, C. and Hartevelt, M. (1991) 'An experimental study of the interpretation of logical operators in database querying', *Acta Psychologica*, 78: 201–25.

Gray, M. and Wardle, H. (2013) *Observing Gambling Behaviour Using Think Aloud and Video Technology: A Methodological Review*. NatCen Social Research. Available at: www.natcen.ac.uk/media/205548/methods-review-final-for-publication.pdf

Gray, M., Constantine, R., d'Ardenne, J., Blake, M. and Uhrig, N. (2008) *Cognitive Testing of Understanding Society: The UK Household Longitudinal Study Questionnaire*. Understanding Society Working Paper Series, No. 2008 – 04 available at: www.understandingsociety.ac.uk/research/publications/working-paper/understanding-society/2008–04.pdf

Griffiths, M.D. (1994) 'The role of cognitive bias and skill in fruit machine gambling', *British Journal of Psychology*, 85: 351–69.

Hinchliffe, A. and Mummery, W.K. (2008) 'Applying usability testing techniques to improve a health promotion website', *Health Promotion Journal of Australia*, 19(1): 29–35. Available at: www.ncbi.nlm.nih.gov/pubmed/18481929

Husain, F., Wardle, H., Kenny, T., Balarajan, M. and Collins, D. (2013) *Examining Machine Player Behaviour: A Qualitative Exploration*. NatCen Social Research. Available at: www.natcen.ac.uk/our-research/research/exploring-machine-player-behaviour/

Lake, A.A., Speed, C., Brookes, A., Heaven, B., Adamson, A.J., Moynihan, P., Corbett, S. and McColl, E. (2007) 'Development of a series of patient information leaflets for constipation using a range of cognitive interview techniques: LIFELAX', *BMC Health Services Research*, 7(3). doi:10.1186/1472–6963-7-3

Lapka, C., Jupka, K., Wray, R. J. and Jacobsen, H. (2008) 'Applying cognitive response testing in message development and pre-testing', *Health Education Research*, 23(3): 467–76. doi:10.1093/her/cym089.

Marteau, T.M., Dormandy, E. and Michie, S. (2001) 'A measure of informed choice', *Health Expectations*, 4: 99–108.

Martin, Chris. Murray, Lorraine. Treanor, Steve. Chan, V. (2012) *Testing of the Ballot Paper for the 2012 Local Government Elections in Scotland*. Available at: www.scotland.gov.uk/Resource/Doc/345798/0115097.pdf

McGee, A. and d'Ardenne, J. (2009) *'Netting a Winner': Tackling Ways to Question Children Online. A Good Practice Guide to Asking Children and Young People about Sport and Physical Activity. Prepared for the Sports Council for Wales.* Available at: http://www.sportwales.org.uk/media/351853/netting_a_winner_-_english.pdf

Neuert, C. and Lenzner, T. (2013) 'Combining eye tracking and cognitive interviewing to pretest survey questions'. Paper presented at 5th European Survey Research Association 2011 conference, Ljubljana, Slovenia.

Pan, Y., Landreth, A., Park, H., Hinsdale-Shouse, M. and Schoua-Glusberg, A. (2010) 'Cognitive interviewing in non-English languages', in J.A. Harkness, M. Braun, B. Edwards, T.P. Johnson, L. Lyberg, P. Mohler, B.E. Pennel, T.W. Smith (eds), *Survey Methods in Multinational, Multiregional and Multicultural Contexts*. Hoboken, NJ: John Wiley. pp. 91–115.

Patton, M.Q. (2002) *Qualitative Research and Evaluation Methods* (3rd edition). Beverly Hills, CA: Sage Publications.

Romano Bergstrom, J., Childs, J., Olmsted-Hawala, E. and Jurgenson, N. (2013) 'The efficiency of conducting concurrent cognitive interviewing and usability testing on an interviewer-administered survey', *Survey Practice*, 6(4). Available at: www.surveypractice.org/index.php/SurveyPractice/article/view/79

Scott, S.E., Weinman, J. and Grunfeld, E.A. (2011) 'Developing ways to encourage early detection and presentation of oral cancer: what do high-risk individuals think?', *Psychology & Health*, 26(10): 1392–405.

Sheeran, P. (2002) 'Intention–behavior relations: a conceptual and empirical review', in W. Stroebe and M. Hewstone (eds), *European Review of Social Psychology*, 12: 1–36.

Smith, S.G., Vart, G., Wolf, M.S., Obichere, A., Baker, H.J., Raine, R., Wardle, J. and von Wagner, C. (2013) 'How do people interpret information about colorectal cancer screening: observations from a think-aloud study', *Health Expectations*, doi:10.1111/hex.12117.

Taylor, K. and Dionne, J-P. (2000) 'Assessing problem-solving strategy knowledge: the complementary use of concurrent verbal protocols and retrospective debriefings', *Journal of Educational Psychology*, 92(3): 413–25.

van den Haak M.J., Jong de, M.D.T. and Schellens, P.J. (2003) 'Retrospective vs. concurrent think aloud protocols: testing the usability of an online library catalogue', *Behaviour & Information Technology*, 22(5): 339–51.

Willis, G. (2006) 'Cognitive interviewing as a tool for improving the informed consent process', *Journal of Empirical Research on Human Research Ethics*, online ISSN 1556–2654, 9–24.

Yardley, L., Morrison, L.G., Andreou, P., Joseph, J., and Little, P. (2010) 'Understanding reactions to an internet-delivered health-care intervention: accommodating user preferences for information provision', *BMC Medical Informatics and Decision Making*, 10 (52), doi:10.1186/1472–6947–10–52.

INDEX

Numbers in **bold** indicate entries within tables and figures.